MW01137749

Annice Carter's Life of Quaker Service

Harmonizing practice with principle at home, in Palestine, and in Kenya

Betsy Alexander
Max L. Carter
Sarabeth Marcinko

Friends United Press
101 Quaker Hill Drive
Richmond, IN 47374
friendsunitedmeeting.org

ISBN 978-1-956149-22-7

CONTENTS

FOREWORD

v

INTRODUCTION

vii

ACKNOWLEDGMENTS

x

CHAPTER 1

An introduction to Ramallah and Annice Carter's life

1

CHAPTER 2

Annice Carter's first experience in Ramallah

20

CHAPTER 3

Annice at Pacific College and the decision to return to Ramallah

29

CHAPTER 4

Annice in Ramallah from 1935 to 1941

42

CHAPTER 5

Annice at home between 1941 and 1957

59

CHAPTER 6

Events in the Middle East while Annice was home

69

CONTENTS

CHAPTER 7
Ramallah 1957–59
73

CHAPTER 8
Annice in Kenya
99

CHAPTER 9
Annice in Ramallah 1963–1966
120

CHAPTER 10
Return to Ramallah in 1967
147

CHAPTER 11
Annice and USFW
160

CHAPTER 12
Annice in retirement
185

CHAPTER 13
Reflections on Annice Carter's life
193

CONCLUSION
218

APPENDICES
222

BIBLIOGRAPHY
251

FOREWORD

Annice Carter's Life of Service: Harmonizing Practice with Principle is a story told by members of Annice's family, Max Carter and Sarabeth Marcinko. In partnership with their cousin, Betsy Alexander, they collected family remembrances, letters, and archival records to tell the story about the life and service of Annice Carter, a lifelong member of the Religious Society of Friends and missionary to Palestine and Kenya. However, this biography is more than a family story. It provides an insightful look into the joys and challenges of missionary service; a helpful history of Ramallah Friends School; a first-hand account of Palestinian and Israeli conflicts between 1929 and 1967; and an inspiring account of a Friend who committed her life to Christian service.

At the age of twenty, Annice consecrated her life to the service of Christ. In May, 1935, Annice applied through the American Friends Board of Missions for a "long-term" assignment at Ramallah Friends School. When asked, "What have you in your Christian experience to share with non-Christians?" she answered, "A love for and desire to be of service to our fellow men instilled through a love of God, our common Father." Whether sewing costumes for Christmas pageants, providing hospitality for guests, delivering relief to villagers, preparing home economics courses, overseeing construction projects, or balancing school finance, providing practical service is the legacy of Annice's life. She spoke little on matters of doctrine or theology, but her Christian witness was evident from the patterns of her life.

Aside from one term of service in Kenya, Annice served five terms at Ramallah Friends School. Each term was marked by the dynamic political tensions on the ground. She arrived in Palestine following the 1929 Arab Revolt, when Palestine was still under British control, served at the school during the Second Arab Revolt, and witnessed the rise of Zionism. She returned to the region following World War II and the establishment of the state of Israel. She served in Ramallah while the West Bank was governed by Jordan. She returned again in 1967, a month after the Six-Day War and the Israeli occupation of Ramallah. She observed Ramallah growing from a small town to a bustling city full of refugees displaced from ancestral lands because of Israel's expansionist agenda. Annice offers a first-hand account of these global events and was not shy about her criticisms. Annice was disappointed to encounter fellow Friends and Christians in the United States who supported Zionist policies. In one letter she wrote: "I do not wish to give the idea of being anti-Jewish, although I am definitely anti-Zionist. I believe that Jews are a part of God's creation and have the same opportunity to become God's children through faith and works as have all other people. I believe that a political movement such as Zionism has no place in religious activities."

During her terms of service at Ramallah Friends School, Annice served as the home economics teacher and as head of the girls' dormitory, and was eventually appointed principal of the Friends Girls School. She was forthright with her opinions and often critical of her co-workers, and freely voiced her frustrations with the leadership of Five Years Meeting. She wouldn't have been the easiest person to work with, yet she was respected. Concerning one of her colleagues she wrote, "He admitted that I sometimes make him mad, but he knows where I stand, and that I keep my word, and when I am most firm it is for the good of the School." Annice also confessed, "I could live a much easier life if I would only close my eyes to lots of things that are wrong." Thankfully, she didn't.

While Annice may have been hard on others, she was also critical of herself. When she was appointed as principal, she outlined the reasons why she wasn't suited for the job. Yet, she accepted the role, and over the years improved campus facilities, raised educational standards, collected school fees, and balanced budgets. She was invited to return as principal for several terms.

All readers, not only Friends, can be inspired by Annice's legacy of practical service.

Kelly R. Kellum
August, 2023

INTRODUCTION

Annice Carter (1902–1988) is not one of the names recorded in the basic texts of Quaker history, but to those who knew her, she was no less significant and inspiring than the more familiar names in the annals of the Religious Society of Friends. Born on a farm in Indiana, her life came to encompass the breadth of the United States as well as service in Palestine and Africa. She came of age during World War I. She was a direct witness to conflict in the Middle East, dodged German U-boats during World War II, and encountered the anti-colonial movement in Kenya. Although spiritually rooted in Christian revivalism of the early 1900s, she grew to have an expansive, non-doctrinal understanding of her faith. Born in horse-and-buggy days, she made her first trips to Palestine on a steamer and her last one on a jet plane.

Annice had wished to become a nurse, but those hopes were frustrated, so she trained in home economics. She had a successful teaching career at the high school and college level in the 1920s before helping start a home economics department at the Friends Girls School in Ramallah, British Mandate Palestine. That first encounter with the Middle East led to several more terms of service as a teacher and principal at the School. Her first two appointments there came during the dramatic events that led to the creation of the modern state of Israel and the displacement of hundreds of thousands of Palestinian Arabs. Her later appointments in Ramallah came during Cold War intrigue, Jordanian occupation, and finally the Israeli occupation following the 1967 war.

In Africa Annice taught in another Friends school for girls and did extension work in rural areas of Kenya. Although her experience there was brief, it coincided with Kenya's growing independence movement and the rise to prominence of Jomo Kenyatta.

When "back home" in Indiana between assignments through the American Friends Board of Missions, Annice spoke widely among Friends, served in leadership with the United Society of Friends Women (USFW), edited a missionary magazine, and worked in her county's welfare office.

All of these events and activities were chronicled in thousands of letters that Annice wrote to family, friends, colleagues, and the Board of Missions in Richmond, Indiana. It was her practice while abroad to roll several sheets of paper and carbon paper into her typewriter each Sunday morning and cover every square inch with details of her life and work. Fortunately, most of those letters survive, except for the ones sent from Ramallah from 1929 to 1932. Her letters to the Board in Indiana detail important matters concerning Quaker mission work and the challenges to carrying out Friends education and witness in difficult political, religious, and cultural situations. In letters to friends and family Annice revealed her personality, her private thoughts and attitudes, and the ways in which she grappled sometimes with being "born too soon," as she put it, or having ideas that were ahead of their time.

In this biography of Annice Carter's life, we—three grandchildren of Annice's siblings Walter, Nora, and Achsa—have tried to be faithful to her self-revelation in those letters while also attempting to put their content in historical context. On occasion we try to understand some of the complexities of her life by analyzing the home environment she came out of and its influences on her later life. It is our hope that Annice's life can serve both as an inspiring example of service, faith, fortitude, and risk as well as a cautionary tale about trying to understand a person's life and attitudes formed in one era, influenced by a variety of settings, and reflected on in a later time.

On a personal note, each of us has had to re-evaluate our memories of Annice in light of what we have learned from these letters. We had varying degrees and types of contact with her, and we had formed impressions that reflected those various experiences. We all, however, regarded Annice with a kind of awe. She was a woman of imposing presence, definite opinions, and sometimes sharp tongue. Nearly six feet tall and ramrod straight, she was physically as well as personally impressive—and could be intimidating. Among us, Max had perhaps the most contact, since he grew up near Annice's home in Russiaville, Indiana, and himself served in Ramallah as a teacher at the Friends Boys School. He jokingly describes Annice as "eating raw nephews for lunch!"

Reading her letters, however, has softened the edges of the "sharp" Annice we remember. She may have been somewhat gruff on the exterior and apparently certain of opinion, but we have discovered a more gentle, self-reflective, often self-denigrating and doubtful woman with a heart of gold, a passion for service, and a personal faith that cared more for "seeing a sermon" about Christian witness than for hearing one.

As for the writing of this biography, we have shared tasks of reading and interpreting Annice's letters, editing the manuscript, and providing historical background. Max took primary responsibility for the chapters on Annice's life before her missionary service, her time in Ramallah, Kenya, and at Pacific College. Sarabeth—current editor of *The Advocate*, a publication of the United Society of Friends Women International (USFWI)—did the heavy lifting on providing the chapter on Annice's relationship to USFWI and its magazine. Betsy's professional editing expertise added greatly to the content.

John Woolman, an 18th-century Quaker known for his life of service, once defined the "substance of true religion" as "harmonizing practice with principle." Annice, grounded in the principles of her Quaker Christian faith, certainly lived out that understanding. It is our hope that in these pages you, too, will discover the complex, nuanced, inspiring, and impressive woman that Annice Carter was. And if you come away with a sense that she might well deserve some mention among other "worthies" of Quakerdom, we are sure that Annice would respond, "Oh, pshaw! I was only doing what anyone ought to do who takes the example of Jesus seriously. Besides, I'm not so sure about how these grand-nieces and grand-nephew have presented me. I may have to have a word with them."

Betsy Alexander
Max L. Carter
Sarabeth Marcinko
DECEMBER, 2022

ACKNOWLEDGMENTS

Putting together the biography of a person with such far-reaching life experience would not be possible without the assistance of many people, not the least of whom is Annice Carter herself. Reading the more than 2,000 letters she sent home was something of a task, but this book would be far poorer without them.

Many of those letters are held privately by Sarabeth Marcinko, who scanned the ones saved by Annice's family. Others are in microfilm and digitized collections in the Archives of George Fox University and Earlham College. We are grateful to Rachel Thomas at George Fox and to Tom Hamm, Jenny Freed, and Lydia Allen at Earlham for their invaluable assistance in locating materials that have contributed substantially to this work. Gwen Gosney Erickson, director of the Quaker Archives at Guilford College, shared letters of Guilford alumnae who served in Ramallah with Annice.

Kelly Kellum, General Secretary of Friends United Meeting (FUM), not only wrote the preface for the book but also gave us access to the files at FUM's Central Office in Richmond, Indiana, that contain letters and photographs from the time Annice was in missionary service for Five Years Meeting (FYM), which later became FUM.

Jordan Landes at Swarthmore College's Friends Historical Library helped solve a mystery about Annice's 1935 summer term at Pendle Hill, and Don Miller, archivist for the American Friends Service Committee (AFSC), helped as well. Mary Crauderueff, archivist in the Quaker and Special Collections at Haverford College, answered questions regarding one of Annice's letters of recommendation.

Annice's niece Mary Frances Taylor offered important details about the work Annice did in Howard County, Indiana, during one of her extended times at home, and Peggy Hollingsworth, a member of Russiaville Friends Church, provided materials from the local newspaper about Annice and her family.

In the "Reflections" section of the book, many people who knew Annice have shared their personal memories of her, and these make a rich addition to the book. We are grateful.

We would also like to acknowledge the work of Dan Kasztelan of Friends United Press and his team of Shari Veach, Sabrina Darnowsky, and David Botwinik in bringing this book to the public.

Finally, we would like to express our love and gratitude to spouses and family members who had to endure the many hours we spent reading and scanning letters, editing, e-mailing, and otherwise submerging ourselves in this multi-year task.

To all, "shukran/thank you!"

Betsy, Max, and Sarabeth

CHAPTER 1

An introduction to Ramallah and Annice Carter's life

Quaker sociologist Elise Boulding has written that most of us live in "the 200 year present." At our birth, our grandparents and great-grandparents are often still alive, connecting us to a near century in the past. If we're lucky, we live long enough to overlap with generations that will live past another century.

At Annice Carter's birth in 1902, three of her grandparents were living—Rachel Johnson (1834–1904), Levi Carter (1838–1905), and Fleming Johnson (1833–1910). Prior to her death in 1988, Annice interacted with nieces and nephews, grand-nieces and -nephews, and even 2x grand-nieces and -nephews whose lives not only overlapped with hers but were influenced by hers.

ORIGINS OF RAM ALLAH/RAMALLAH

The village—later a city—and region to which Annice dedicated a good portion of her life, and which so shaped her, had a much longer "present," and events that dramatically shaped the region occurred during her lifetime.

The first known mention of Ramallah occurred in an 1186 Crusader document. It was described as the settlement of Ramalie, ten miles north of Jerusalem. Crusaders built a small church there and a larger one dedicated to the Holy Family in nearby El-Bireh. According to Ramallah historian Naseeb Shaheen in his *A Pictorial History of Ramallah*, the place was probably settled long before the Crusaders came. *Ram* is an Aramaic word for "hill," and *Allah* is the Arabic name for God. There could be an association with biblical *Rama*, a village on the road from Jerusalem to Bethel, just north of present-day Ramallah. There is still a village of Er-Ram, four miles south of Ramallah.

Allah would not have been added to the name until Arabs arrived after the Byzantine period, and settlement of the site would have been temporary until a permanent population was noted in a Turkish census of 1563.

Present-day Ramallah (spelled Ram Allah when Annice first visited in 1929) was founded between 1553 and 1562 when a Christian family, in a dispute with a Muslim family, fled from east of the Jordan River. The Christian family's daughter was desired as a bride for the son of the *emir* of the Muslim family. Ottoman Turks had conquered the area in 1516–17, and their 1563 census noted 63 Christian families, 8 single men, and 10 Muslim families living in Ram Allah. No Jewish residents were listed.

QUAKER WORK IN PALESTINE

Quakers first arrived in Ramallah in 1869, when New England Quakers Eli and Sybil Jones visited the village while attending a conference of international Christian educators in Jerusalem. Accompanied by translator Jacob Hishmeh, they held a meeting for worship at which Sybil preached. Later, Eli was stopped on the street by a 15-year old girl, Miriam Karam, who had been in the meeting. Having benefited from education at a mission school in Jerusalem, she asked the Quaker to start a school for girls. When Eli asked her who would be the teacher, Miriam replied, "I will."

The Joneses left money with Jacob Hishmeh to start the school, and the Hope School opened that fall with 20 students and Miriam Karam as the teacher. Within four years there were four schools for girls under the care of English Friends.

Following an 1887 conference of Orthodox/Evangelical Friends in Richmond, Indiana, enthusiasm for missions led New England Yearly Meeting to assume responsibility for the Ramallah mission, and in 1889 a private home was converted into a boarding school. Timothy and Anna Hussey of Maine, along with Timothy's sister Sarah, took on the task of getting all things prepared for the opening of the boarding section. Initially there were 15 girls, recruited with some difficulty from families all over the region. Katie Gabriel from Lebanon served as the first principal of the school and remained until 1929, the year Annice arrived.

In 1901, at the insistence of local residents, a boys school was established. For the first several years the Friends Boys School occupied a number of temporary quarters, including a house across the street from the Girls School. In 1914 a permanent building was finally erected in the village of El-Bireh, but the outbreak of World War I intervened before the first student could take up residence, and the building was commandeered by the Turkish army for use as a hospital. Later, the British army occupied it—along with the 1910 Quaker meetinghouse, which they used as a saloon! Ramallah lore has it that after the war, Friends swept 1,000 gin bottles out of the meetinghouse.

By 1919 "normal" had returned to Ramallah, and the Boys School was refurbished and finally opened. Soon a third floor was added to the Girls School, and Whittier and Swift Halls were added for a kindergarten and auditorium. In 1922, a "new normal" came into being: the League of Nations gave Great Britain the Mandate for Palestine, and British culture and educational standards came to Ramallah.

Also in 1922, another Hoosier Quaker, Mildred White, arrived for her first work at the Friends Girls School. She would become not only a colleague of Annice's but also a lifelong friend. A 1918 graduate of Earlham College, Mildred had been a friend and Earlham classmate of Annice's sister Achsa. After graduation, the two Earlhamites taught at Southland Institute in Arkansas, a school established for Blacks by Indiana Quakers after the Civil War. Following further education at Columbia Teachers College, Mildred accepted an assignment from the Friends Board of Missions in Richmond, Indiana, to teach in Ramallah.

Mildred's experience in Ramallah is described in her niece Lois Harned Jordan's *Ramallah Teacher: The Life of Mildred White, Quaker Missionary*. Lois writes that, when Mildred arrived in Palestine in 1922, she found the Palestinians disappointed by the Mandate. Both Palestinian Arabs and Jews had been promised their independent states by Britain and France, if they helped in the war effort against Turkey and Germany. Both were angry at the betrayal when, instead of fulfilling the promise of independence, the British took over with the 1922 Mandate. Palestinians still hoped for independence and self-government, while recognizing that the rise of Zionism might set Jews and Palestinian Arabs on a collision course.

Ramallah Teacher offers a good understanding of the Friends schools in the 1920s. The Girls School was very much in the pattern of American mission schools: an active Christian Endeavor club, evening prayers, daily chapel, and required attendance at Friends worship on Sundays. Mildred wrote home that the Schools were very attractive, with evergreen trees and building entrances covered in ivy. After the rainy season, the land was covered in wildflowers. In many ways Mildred found life in Ramallah a continuation of life back home in rural Henry County, Indiana: both had agricultural, close-knit families and community, and rich traditions of hospitality. There were certainly differences, however. The cold, rainy season and unheated stone buildings caused her to suffer from chilblains. The stone floors and rocky terrain wore out her shoes; travel of any distance was typically by mule. Diseases such as malaria and eye problems were commonplace. All water came from cisterns, necessitating careful usage; Mildred would write home, "Please take a shower in memory of me."

The curriculum at the Girls School included Arabic and English literature and language. Home economics was a popular subject, and a cottage was built for that department in 1929. What Mildred doesn't describe are the cultural assumptions that American Quakers of the era brought with them and inculcated in the girls, some of which caused tensions back in their homes and in their later marriages.

THE 1929 ARAB REVOLT

In 1929, Mildred became the principal of the Girls School. It was a year of growing political upheaval and turmoil as fighting broke out among Arabs, Jews, and the British Mandatory Administration. The issue, for Palestinians, was fear that increased numbers of Jewish immigrants from Europe, and large land purchases by the Jewish National Fund, would threaten Arab self-determination. The population of Jews had doubled between 1919 and 1929. Although Jewish residents in Palestine were still outnumbered 600,000 to 80,000, Palestinian Arabs were deeply concerned about the rise of Zionism, the Balfour Declaration, strategic colonization, and continued immigration.

Joseph Abileah, an Israeli pacifist and early European Jewish settler in Palestine, became a regular attender at the Ramallah Friends Meeting after

4

borders opened following the 1967 war. He described his own experience during the unrest of 1929.[1] As was typical of many of the early Zionist communal settlements, *kibbutzim*, Abileah's commune was secular and enjoyed friendly relations with its neighboring Arab village. In fact, the largely urban European *kibbutzniks* learned their agricultural skills from the local Palestinian farmers. But relations changed in 1929.

One Friday after the local prayers in the mosque, a group of villagers surrounded Abileah as he worked in the kibbutz fields. The leader of the group told him that, although they liked him and hated to do it, they had to kill him. When Abileah asked them why, he was told that the imam of the mosque had preached that the Jews intended to take over the land and expel the Arabs, and they must rise up and kill them.

Abileah, a pacifist, said that he would not fight but that he also didn't want to be killed. The Arab villagers repeated that they also didn't want to kill him. "Well, then. What can we do?" Abileah asked.

"If you convert to Islam, we wouldn't have to kill you," he was told.

"Okay, how do I do that?" Abileah asked.

"If you repeat the *Shehadah* (the Muslim statement of faith), you would become Muslim," he was told.

When Abileah asked what it was, he was instructed, "There is no God but Allah, and Mohammed is the messenger of God."

"I have no problem with that," he replied. Abileah repeated the Shehadah; the villagers expressed their relief—as did he!—and they left him in peace in the field.

Meanwhile during riots in Jerusalem and Hebron, things did not end so well.

In August of 1929, Arab rioters from Jerusalem attacked Jewish residents of the primarily Muslim Arab city of Hebron, where Jews and Arabs had lived peacefully side-by-side for centuries. Sixty-seven Jews were massacred, but hundreds of others were saved by their Muslim neighbors. In one famous incident, an Arab family was harboring Jews when rioters beat on the door, demanding that the Jews be sent out. The crowd dispersed only when the mother of the family climbed onto the flat roof of the house, and in full view of the crowd bared her breasts! In that

---

[1] Conversation with Max Carter in 1971.

culture, to view such a scene was an embarrassment to the onlookers, and they left the family and their Jewish guests alone.

Mildred further described the year, "Here in Ram Allah we were quite safe and quiet, but we felt great distress and fear for our friends in Jerusalem and various places in the land where the riots occurred. . . ."[2] In her estimation, the problem originated with the Balfour Declaration and the Mandatory Administration's encouragement of Jewish immigration.

THE ORIGINS AND RISE OF ZIONISM

Ari Shavit, an Israeli journalist, wrote *My Promised Land: The Triumph and Tragedy of Israel*, in which he relates the Zionist narrative of the events leading up to 1929 and the later establishment of the modern state of Israel. His description begins in the 1890s with Theodor Herzl (the founder of political Zionism and organizer of the 1897 World Zionist Congress) expressing interest in the prospect of colonizing Palestine. Waves of pogroms and antisemitism in Eastern Europe had convinced Herzl and other secular Jews that the only hope for preserving non-Orthodox Judaism and Jewish identity was the establishment of Jewish sovereignty somewhere in the world.

Shavit writes about his own British great-grandfather's 1897 visit to Palestine to see whether it might be the right place for colonizing. Even though there were already 500,000 Palestinian Arabs in the land at the time, Shavit's ancestor described it as "quiet, empty, a promised land for Jews."[3] He was unable to "see" the Arab inhabitants, Shavit explains, because his Victorian attitude was that non-whites were inferior, Arab culture was inferior, and thus the native population was "invisible."

Shavit goes on to explain, however, that others realized that the existence of half a million Palestinian Arabs posed a problem, and force would be needed to drive out ". . . the tribes in possession, as our forefathers did."[4] With an eye to colonizing by any means necessary, Jews

2 Lois Jordan, *Ramallah Teacher: The Life of Mildred White, Quaker Missionary* (self-published, 1995), p. 121.

3 Ari Shavit, *My Promised Land: The Triumph and Tragedy of Israel* (New York: Random House, 2013), p. 12.

4 Shavit, p. 16.

were encouraged to immigrate to Palestine. The first Zionist communal settlement, Degania, was established in 1909. More would follow.

Then came the famous Balfour Declaration. On November 2, 1917, Arthur James Balfour of the British Foreign Office wrote in a letter to Lord Rothschild, "His Majesty's Government views with favor the establishment in Palestine of a national home for the Jewish people . . . it being clearly understood that nothing shall be done which may prejudice the civil and religious rights of existing non-Jewish communities in Palestine. . . ."

While that declaration was being made to the Jewish community, Arab leaders were being promised independence in return for cooperation in the war effort. But in secret, in 1916 the British and French had already formed the Sykes-Picot Agreement, in which they determined how they would carve up a defeated Ottoman Empire among themselves.

In 1920, the militant Jewish Labor Brigade was formed, and in 1921 Kibbutz Ein Harod was established in the Jezreel Valley with the stated purpose of "conquering" the area inhabited by several Arab villages. Shavit writes, ". . . only the Labor Brigade ethos of kibbutz socialism will enable Zionism to take the valley and to take the Land."[5]

Still, in 1921 Jews were outnumbered 600,000 to 80,000. But by 1948, Kibbutz Ein Harod had developed real military might and drove all Palestinians out of the valley.[6]

ANNICE CARTER'S CHILDHOOD

Annice Carter was born in 1902 to Charles and Milley Carter on a farm on the outskirts of Russiaville, Indiana, 6,000 miles away from where all of this history was unfolding. Russiaville was named for a French/Indian chief of the Miami nation living in Indiana into the early 1800s. Chief Jean Baptiste de Richardville's name was pronounced in French, and in the early Hoosiers' pronunciation, it came out "Rooshaville"

Annice, age 5 in 1907.

5 Shavit, p. 31.
6 Shavit, p. 47.

7

Parents Charles and Milley in the late 1800s.

and was spelled "Russiaville." Somehow, the Russiaville High School's teams were called the Cossacks, even though there was no connection with Russia. Little would Annice know while attending Russiaville High School and playing on the girls' basketball team that the actions of the antisemitic Cossack brigades would play a role in encouraging Jewish migration to Palestine.

Annice was descended from long lines of Quakers on both sides of her family. Her mother, Milley, was the daughter of Fleming and Rachel (Bundy) Johnson. Fleming was born in a Quaker community in southeast Virginia, but departed in the 1840s with his family in the great Quaker anti-slavery and economic migrations to the Midwest. Rachel was born to prominent Quaker families in eastern Indiana that had also migrated out of the South to "free states" and rich Midwestern soil.

Charles, Annice's father, was the son of Levi and Emily (Newlin) Carter. The Newlins were another prominent Quaker family that had migrated out of North Carolina. Levi was born out of wedlock, keeping his mother's surname of Carter. The acknowledged father was later known to be Josiah Trueblood, already married with children when Mary Carter worked in the Trueblood home.

Levi and Emily were married in a civil ceremony, contrary to Quaker discipline at the time, a fact that implies that Emily may have been pregnant

The newly built homeplace in Russiaville in 1913. Annice is on the porch between her parents.

at marriage. Although the Carters became a prominent and respected family in Russiaville, it was widely rumored that they were descended from an "illegitimate" birth and a "hurried" wedding. This may have contributed to a Carter propensity, that Annice inherited, to work hard and not bring shame to the family name. Her brother Walter was once queried by a grandson about the rumors and responded only with, "There are some things you're better off not knowing. Just this: Mary wasn't trash."

The Carters did work hard and were quite accomplished. Charles and Milley's farm prospered, and after its mortgage was paid they bought another farm closer to Russiaville where Charles built a large, two-story frame house in which the couple lived until Charles's death in 1943 and Milley's in 1955. Their children, too, prospered. Annice was the youngest of five siblings. Walter and Oakley both finished high school in Russiaville and took up farming. Nora attended a teacher training institute after high school and taught at the Russiaville school until she married a Quaker pastor. Achsa, unlike most farm women of that time, finished four years at Earlham College—an Indiana Quaker institution founded in 1847—and then taught for two years at Southland Institute before marrying a farmer herself.

And then there was Annice.

Parents Charles and Milley in the 1930s.

Annice's early years were spent on a farm whose operation had changed little over the generations. Born before widespread use of the automobile and before the invention of the airplane, Annice was familiar with horse power on the farm and in transportation. Her childhood home had no electricity, and heating and cooking depended on a wood fire. Her father and brothers typically worked in the barn and fields while the girls and their mother kept the house, cooked three meals a day, tended to a large garden in the summer, preserved the fruits and vegetables, and made and mended the family's clothing.

The Kokomo, Indiana, paper carrying a notice of her parents' golden wedding anniversary in 1936—while Annice was on her second "tour of duty" in Ramallah—described the evolution of farm work during her lifetime: "Fifty years ago . . . a farmer had a few acres of land, a team of horses, one or two cows, and some chickens. . . . The farm work then was done by horses and manual labor. During the 50 years more land has been acquired and the family has moved to a new modern home. . . . The most outstanding piece of machinery is the rubber-tired tractor with which most of the farm work is done."

The Carter family in 1907. Annice is in the first row second from the right.

As Mildred White commented, Annice would have found the "primitive" life of Palestine in 1929 not unlike her childhood on the farm. Plowing was still done walking behind a horse or mule. Grain was threshed by animals treading on the stalks to separate grain from chaff. No olives on her childhood farm, but in Palestine those, too, were pressed using animal labor to run a grindstone.

Annice had the opportunity to watch life and technology evolve in Ramallah just as she did in Indiana. Like her parents' Indiana farm, Palestine in 1979, when she arrived for her last visit, was vastly different than it had been 50 years before. How did Annice deal with such enormous change? It would have been in the same way that her older brother Walter did, who lived until 1975. When asked about how he had coped with the changes, from the invention of the first airplane when he was a teenager to men walking on the moon in his later years, his response was simply, "What did you expect me to do?"

The Carters' home life was deeply influenced by the family's adherence to the strict tenets of the Religious Society of Friends at the time. That meant morning devotions at the breakfast table, Bible reading at night, and family hymn singing. There would be no card playing with "face cards," as that was too closely associated with gambling. No going off to dances or other "worldly" amusements, either. And on Sundays, the "Sabbath" was strictly observed. It was necessary to care for the animals, as on any day, but no other work was to be undertaken on the Lord's Day. The family attended

Annice's family in the early 1900s. Counter-clockwise from bottom left: Charles, Milley, Achsa, Annice, Oakley, Walter, and Nora.

Sunday School and church in the morning and a worship service at night. Between the big noon meal and evening chores, there were quiet parlor games, reading, outside games in warm weather, and lots of family visiting.

Life was very much influenced by the traditions of Friends, and Annice's grandparents were "plain," wearing the simple clothes of early Quakers and using the "plain speech" of thee and thou. However, her parents did not dress plainly, nor did the children, and the plain speech was used only with the older generations, not among Annice and her siblings. But Annice intersected with the "old ways" enough to be able to remember the "sing song" of the elders' ministry out of the silence of meeting for worship and to have an understanding of Quakerism as distinct from mainstream Protestantism.

What passed for a social life for young Annice consisted largely of school and church—both in Russiaville, a mere half mile from the farm. And there wasn't a great deal of difference between the two! Many of her teachers and her classmates were also Quakers. Religious activities in the public school were common, and although there were Quaker, Baptist, Christian Church, and Methodist congregations in town, they all shared a basic Protestant culture that was seamless between home and school.

Church made up the third "leg" of Annice's childhood experience. Russiaville Friends Church, where her family were members, was established in 1877. Prior to that, her immediate ancestors had attended scattered rural Friends meetings that made up Honey Creek Monthly Meeting, whose main meetinghouse was in New London, a mile and a half away. Russiaville Friends began as a Quaker meeting that was the product of the enormous changes that had occurred among Midwestern Friends after the Civil War. Unlike the "silent," unprogrammed meetings for worship of previous generations (the type Annice's grandparents attended), Russiaville Friends bore elements of the new "pastoral" movement—music, a prepared message by a paid pastor, vocal prayer, and an evangelical tenor—and the "silent waiting worship" was reduced to a short "testimony time."

In fact, in the very year that Russiaville Friends was "set off," its parent organization Western Yearly Meeting (headquartered in Plainfield, Indiana) experienced a separation at its annual sessions. Following years of turmoil about the "great changes" being introduced through the revival and holiness movements, the last of the "Conservative" Friends were literally driven out of the annual sessions, and the congregation sang a hymn for good measure as the last two "plain" Friends exited the meetinghouse. Russiaville Friends remained with the larger body of the Yearly Meeting, which approved of programmed worship, paid pastors, singing, and revivals.

Annice's Quaker faith was deeply Christian of an evangelical sort, distinctive in its Quaker opposition to the "outward sacraments" of physical baptism and communion, but generally Protestant in most other expressions and deeply influenced by Wesleyan theology. The Religious Society of Friends had no seminary at the time, so pastoral leadership at Russiaville was only minimally educated in formal theology and pastoral counseling. If there was any post-secondary education at all in preparation for pastoral ministry, it was at a Bible college or in the Bible department of a college, quite often a non-Friends institution. And many of those departments had been purged of "liberal" theology and biblical interpretation by a growing fundamentalist element among pastoral Friends.

Sermons at Russiaville Friends reflected a Wesleyan understanding of justification and sanctification, with a good seasoning of the emotional style of revivalistic preaching. Sam Turner, a pillar of Russiaville Friends and husband of one of Annice's close relatives, was known to express how he had been "saved and sanctified and could do no sin." In his testimony out of the period of "open worship," he would fall to his knees and share an emotional message about salvation by the blood of Christ.

Annice would have attended the annual spring and fall revivals and the regular weekly activities of the church. There were Sunday morning and evening worship, midweek prayer meeting, youth activities, and further meetings sponsored by groups such as the Women's Christian Temperance Union. She accepted the church's teaching—a result of both Quaker testimony and holiness morality—that she should forever avoid the use of alcohol and tobacco. As a condition of full membership in Russiaville Friends, she understood that she had to give evidence of having committed her life to Christ. The annual revivals and altar calls at meetings for worship gave ample opportunity for that.

In her 1929 application for short-term service as a missionary in Ramallah through the American Friends Board of Missions—a program of Five Years Meeting of Friends (FYM) in Richmond, Indiana—she wrote in an essay titled "My Christian Experience":

> I have been reared in a Christian home. My father and mother are active members of the Russiaville Friends Church. Since they first established a home more than 40 years ago, they have had family worship at the breakfast hour. In coming from a home of that type, I think it is very difficult to describe my personal Christian experience. I was converted when about 11 or 12 years old. I took active part in Junior and Intermediate Endeavors in our church.[7] When I was old enough to work in Senior Endeavor, we no longer had that organization in our church, but I have helped in organizing the Young Friends Society at home.... When about 20, I attended a consecration service and consecrated my life to the service of Christ....[8]

It was a happy and consistent, if somewhat constrained, youth. Home, school, and church provided a safe, extended, and emotionally comfortable life. Family and community members supported each other, assuring both financial and personal security.

But something seemed to tug at Annice. While her sister Achsa attended Earlham College—which would seem the natural destination for

---

[7] Christian Endeavor was an international young people's organization established in 1881 by Francis Edward Clark (1851-1927), a Congregational clergyman. There were Christian Endeavor programs at the Friends Girls School in Ramallah from its beginning into the early 1900s.

[8] From materials sent to the American Friends Board of Missions, Annice Carter Microfilm, MR-157, Earlham Friends Collection and College Archives, Richmond, Indiana.

a young Quaker woman who wanted further education after high school—Annice went to Michigan to attend a Seventh Day Adventist school, the Battle Creek Sanitarium in Battle Creek, to study home economics and science. But she had always wanted to be a nurse, and without telling her family (her mother opposed Annice's interest in nursing), she also took nursing classes. That plan was terminated, however, when her report card of classes reached home! Annice had to return home.

Back in Russiaville, Annice taught second and third grades at the local school for a short time, then enrolled at Ball Teachers College in Muncie, Indiana—today's Ball State University. In 1917 the Ball brothers of canning jar fame had purchased college buildings from a foreclosed

Annice with her baby niece Madeline, daughter of Annice's sister Achsa, in 1923.

school, and in 1918 the institution reopened as a "normal school," or teacher training college. Annice majored in home economics and for three years worked as a laboratory assistant in the Department of Geography and Geology. Following graduation in 1927, she spent two years teaching high school in Bloomingdale, Indiana, while living with her sister Nora and her brother-in-law, Lyman Cosand, the pastoral minister of Bloomingdale Friends. For three summers, in 1927, '28, and '29, Annice returned to Muncie as an assistant instructor in Ball State's Geography and Geology Department.

Annice in the 1920s.

On June 9, 1929, Annice traveled to the Central Office of FYM in Richmond, Indiana, to meet with Richard Ricks Newby, superintendent of Western Yearly Meeting and a member of the Candidates Committee of the American Friends Board of Missions. She had learned through a friend, Clara Mary Newsome, about the prospective opening in Ramallah for a teacher of home economics, and filled out an application that day. In a letter to references for Annice, Newby described the visit:

Bloomingdale, Indiana, High School teachers in 1927. Annice is on the far left.

> Miss Carter is very much interested in missionary work and particularly
> interested in Palestine....This has come up so unexpectedly that she has
> not had opportunity to talk with her family....Do not mention this outside
> of your house....She is confident her parents will not object to her going
> out for a short term....[9]

Lenora N. Hobbs (a teacher at Bloomingdale High School and
daughter-in-law of Barnabas C. Hobbs, Earlham College's first president
and a Superintendent of Public Instruction in Indiana) wrote to the Board
of Missions about Annice, expressing that she had taught with "entire
satisfaction" and that "the pupils adore her." She went on to say that Annice
was not only a leader in home economics but also in all activities of the
school, especially plays and support of athletics. "Annice attends the boys'
and girls' basketball games away, chaperoning with her own car. I shall be
sorry for her not to return....As to Miss Carter's health, although she does

[9] June 10 letter sent to Lyman Cosand (brother-in-law), Clyde Wilson (principal of
Bloomingdale H.S.), and Professor Fred Breeze (Chair of the Geography and Geology
Department at Ball State Teachers College), Annice Carter Microfilm, MR-157, Earlham
Friends Collection and College Archives.

Bloomingdale Friends Meeting Sunday School picnic in the late 1920s. Annice is second from the right.

not look very rugged, I never knew of her being ill even a day in the two years work in this place. She is one of the best we had here, in a long line of really good instructors."[10]

Flora Sayers, a Sunday School teacher at Friends Memorial Church in Muncie, wrote that Annice had attended her classes for the parts of three years she had taught at Ball State and that Annice had impressed her with her desire to be of Christian service over any prospects of a line of work that might earn more money.

Waldo Woody, a Friends minister living in High Point, North Carolina, also wrote to the Board with his approval of Annice as a prospective missionary, adding a note of encouragement to Annice to let her teaching be a reflection of her Christian life.

Evidently, the people that Annice suggested to the Board as references also responded favorably. Following a satisfactory physical examination report to the Richmond Office, Annice received this word on June 28:

[10] June 11 letter to the American Friends Board of Missions, MR-157, Earlham Friends Collection and College Archive.

"This is to certify that Miss Annice Carter has been appointed by this Board to serve as a Missionary in Ram Allah, Palestine, and to teach for the coming year in the Friends Girls School."[11]

Subsequent letters from the Board to Annice detailed how she should prepare for her assignment. She needed to get a passport, a clergy certificate, typhoid and smallpox vaccinations, a dental visit to make sure her teeth were in good condition, and even a recommendation to build up her weight with a careful diet.

On July 24, Annice received her steamship ticket and baggage tags, and wrote to the Board that it was beginning to seem more real that she was going to Palestine. She asked for additional information about what equipment and personal belongings she should plan to take with her, suggesting a sewing machine, kerosene heater, scissors, tape measure, and thimbles. She concluded her letter by saying, "I would appreciate heaps of information."

In response, Annice was told that she should pack towels, a dresser scarf, a rug, warm woolens, and low-heeled shoes for hiking over the rocky hillsides in Palestine. No particular "costume" was recommended for teaching, but she was encouraged to wear "hose instead of silk" as a good influence on the girls at the School.

On August 12, Annice reported to the Board that Russiaville Friends and Honey Creek Quarterly Meeting had given her money to purchase a Singer sewing machine and an oil stove.

Thus equipped, and with between $50 and $75 over and above the cost of her train ticket to New York and steamship passage, Annice began her journey to Palestine.

---

[11] Letter from the American Friends Board of Missions, MR-157, Earlham Friends Collection and College Archives.

CHAPTER 2

Annice Carter's first experience in Ramallah

In August 1929 Annice set sail for Palestine, where she had been asked to establish a home economics department and act as head of the dormitory at the Friends Girls School. When asked by a Russiaville woman why she wanted to "go over there and work" when there was so much to be done locally, Annice replied, "Why, I expect someone here to do this work."

Was the attraction to the mission field the result of her evangelical Christian upbringing? Was it influenced by hearing reports of other missionaries who had spoken at Quaker gatherings? Was it because of a sense of adventure? Might it have been a response to the control she felt from her family? We'll never know the particular reason, other than Annice's own acknowledgment that she wanted to be of service and that she felt a call to serve in Palestine. Annice was as tight-lipped about this as her brother Walter was about "great changes" and family history. But off she went to the adventure and challenge of teaching in Ram Allah.

ANNICE ARRIVES IN PALESTINE FOR THE FIRST TIME

Beatrice Kimball, in her 1988 book *Good News Goes a Long Way*, includes a description of Annice's first trip to Palestine:

> In July 1929 Annice Carter and her friend, Clara Mary Newsom, traveled by train from Indiana to board a ship in New York. For a whole month they traveled across the Atlantic, past the Straits of Gibraltar, and across the length of the Mediterranean Sea.
>
> Their port was Joppa, but a mile from the shore the ship stopped. It could not land, because the sea bottom was too rocky. Small flat boats sailed out to the ship to take the passengers to the shore.
>
> Climbing down the roped stairway on the outside of the ship to get to the small boats was a challenge. When they reached the last rung, 30

passengers, one by one, leaped from the rope ladder into the arms of the waiting boatman on the flat boat.

As the flat boat brought them closer to the shore of the Holy Land, Annice looked at the coastline and the mountains in the distance. She remembered that Jesus' disciple, Peter, had stayed with Simon, the tanner, at his house by the seaside in Joppa. Here Peter struggled with the call of God to bring the message of Jesus to other people besides those in his own country. Cornelius, a Roman soldier, had asked Peter to come a day's journey north along the coast to Caesarea. Peter had said, "I now realize that it is true that God treats everyone on the same basis. Whoever fears him and does what is right is acceptable to him, no matter what race...."

Annice prayed, "Lord, make me ready."

It wasn't just the unusual disembarking that would be remarkable for Annice upon arriving in Palestine. The travel by train from "Joppa"—actually Jaffa—would be exotic. As she first crossed the coastal plain dotted by palm trees, citrus and olive groves, the stone huts of Palestinian villages, and the occasional minaret, it would have been clear she wasn't in Indiana anymore! Then on the gradual climb from sea level to Jerusalem, 2,400 feet above sea level, she would have marveled at the Palestinian highlands and their terraced limestone hillsides—some caused by natural erosion, others by the work of farmers for millennia as they claimed arable land from the bare topography. Raised in the verdant flatlands of the Hoosier state, it would take Annice a while to grow to love the more austere folds of this landscape and the deep valleys that cut through the hills.

At the train station in Jerusalem, she would be picked up by School conveyance and driven to Ramallah. On the way, Annice would pass by the towering wall surrounding the Old City, built in the 16th century by Sultan Suleiman the Magnificent. She would see Jaffa Gate, New Gate, and Damascus Gate before turning north along the ancient highway that traverses the highlands. To the east she would see the Hills of Moab across the Jordan Valley. To the west, she would see Nabi Samwil, the hilltop tomb of the prophet Samuel. Passing through Arab villages, and across the runway of the Jerusalem airport, she would finally arrive in Ramallah, nine miles north of Jerusalem and 40 miles from Jaffa.

While there are more than 1,000 letters available that Annice wrote from Palestine and Africa in the 1950s and 1960s, only a very few exist from her first assignment in Ramallah. What we can conjecture about her introduction to the Quaker work there depends largely on accounts left by some of her co-workers. One of those was Ruth E. Outland (later Maris), a member of the Friends Meeting in Woodland, part of North Carolina Yearly Meeting (Conservative), who taught at the Friends Girls School for two years, 1930 to 1932. Her letters are in the Quaker Archives at Guilford College in Greensboro, North Carolina. Another was Mildred White, a classmate of Annice's sister Achsa at Earlham who was from Richsquare Friends Meeting in Indiana Yearly Meeting. In 1929 Mildred became the principal of the Friends Girls School after the retirement of Katie Gabriel and Alice Jones, long-time workers at the School.

RAMALLAH AND ANNICE'S WORK AT THE SCHOOL

Ramallah was a Christian village of about 5,000 residents, most of them *felaheen* (peasants) who lived a simple life dependent on the land. A Muslim village, El-Bireh, was nearby. Dress was traditional, the women wearing long, embroidered *thobes* and head scarves; the men wearing long *dish dashes* and either the Turkish *fez* or peasant *hatta* headcovering. Transportation was mostly by donkey or the occasional camel, although there were a few cars among the more well-to-do, who also dressed more "Western" under the influence of the British. Women typically performed all the household chores and carried water from the village well, as well as vegetable market purchases, balanced on their heads. The men worked the fields, operated small shops, sold produce, or served in the British ministries.

The Friends Girls School was on the outskirts of the village, surrounded by small fields. In 1929 there were 144 students at the School, about half of whom were boarders. Thirty of those students were enrolled in the new home economics program that Annice was to develop. While most of the students were Christian, there were also Muslim students and even a few Jews. Attendance at the Friends Schools was highly valued, but even their low tuition and room and board rates were out of the reach of many. Much of the population was illiterate, and an education at the Friends Schools offered a way for personal advancement.

Annice's responsibilities at the School included heading a "family" of girls whom she met every school morning to see that they were ready

The staff of the two schools – Boys & girls.

1st row.
Khouri (Arabic)
Sutton ; science
mrs ") english
miss white
mrs. goddard (Bible miss
mrs. odeh
Dr "
miss Malouf
B. Haramy
Chile - Boy sec.
Taleri (arabic
Khaddis (agri.)
Terogi . (math
Karkoubian (ath
Haddad (hist)
Jamul (young boys)
Helani (girls #K)
K. Halaly.

3rd row.
K. Haviland
R. O uthand
C. Newsome
a. Carter
k. Nassi
J. Lulabat
nursia
miss olga (Boys
H. Hafey
Ellen andi
Victoria Hammuda
miss Wadia
miss David

The staff of the Boys and Girls Schools together during Annice's first years in Ramallah. Annice is fourth from the left in the third row.

for the day with nails clean, hair brushed, clothes neat and tidy, and in their proper school uniform. Each Monday, the girls' heads had to be checked for "inhabitants." By rotation, the teachers also had a "duty day" on which they saw that the girls were up at 6:00 A.M. and in bed by 9:00 P.M. They lined the students up to march to the dining room and to worship at the Friends meetinghouse on Sundays. Although she had dorm responsibilities, Annice's room was in the Home Economics cottage, one of the village's newest buildings.

Unlike Annice's home back in Indiana, the School enjoyed electricity, but it was generated by a Westinghouse engine that didn't always function, or whose use had to be limited by the scarcity or cost of fuel. Water, collected in cisterns during the seasonal rainfall, was always a concern. It rained only from late fall through early spring, so water had to be used judiciously, and whenever the usual rains didn't come, there was worry about whether crops would provide enough food in the markets, and whether the water supply would last.

Boarding students did most of the work at the School, except for the cooking and washing, which was done by local staff. Each Saturday the girls mopped the floors and aired the bedding on the balcony railings.

In addition to "duty," supervising her "family," and teaching her home economics classes, Annice assisted in extracurricular activities. Her sewing skills were often needed in preparing costumes for school plays. She assisted in the collection and distribution of the "White Gifts" that were shared with the poor in the village. Rice, tea, beans, sugar, and garments were shared, and carrying them to the recipients introduced Annice to the conditions in which so many lived: one-room hovels with no utilities, no windows, and large families in a tiny space. On other excursions, Annice accompanied students on hikes through the valleys to collect wildflowers or to have a picnic under the trees, building a fire and roasting nuts. She also taught extension classes for adults, riding the School's donkey to reach them in outlying areas.

In a January 1931 article in the *Friends Missionary Advocate*, Annice wrote, "The second year of work in the Home Economics Department of the Girls School is progressing nicely, and I like my work."[12] Khalil Totah and Alice Jones, principals at the Boys and Girls Schools respectively, had initiated the home economics program and had the Home Economics Cottage built in 1929 as part of a demonstration of the importance of homemaking skills. Donations Annice had received before traveling to Ramallah included an oil stove, a sewing machine, and furnishings for the cottage. One of the newest buildings in Ramallah, it was becoming something of an attraction. Annice noted that the local people were surprised by its large and light-filled kitchen. Kitchens in native houses, she observed, were small, dark rooms that couldn't be used for anything else.

Annice worked to counter the impression, prevalent in the local society, that it was beneath an educated girl's dignity to learn how to cook and sew. Even at the School, girls who were "irregular" in classes were enrolled in home economics. As Annice developed her classes, though, and demonstrated the value of the skills taught, some girls were even

12 *Friends Missionary Advocate*, January 1931, pp. 28–29.

The "Home Economics cottage," presently the home of the Pre-Kindergarten program of the Ramallah Friends School. Completed in 1929, Annice Carter's first year in Ramallah, it was her home and classroom the first several years of her time at the Girls School. Later it served as the Girls School principal's cottage, and Annice lived there while principal in the 1950s and '60s

encouraged by their families to switch from a math and science curriculum to home economics.

A few girls came to the School for a year or two specifically to learn skills before marriage, and Annice reached out to young married women in the villages to teach them how to cook and sew. For some girls, Annice assisted in making the clothing for their trousseaus, in defiance of the tradition of purchasing these items at great expense. One girl she assisted purchased only items for her trousseau that were simple and practical, explaining to others that she was a Quaker.

Annice concluded her report by saying, "The men urge us to do anything we can to train the girls to be economical in the home. The longer I stay, the more I realize the need of simple Christian living."

In the Girls School's report to the *Advocate* in 1931, it was reported that the Home Economics Department continued to grow in popularity and usefulness. Annice's "babycraft" class with its full-sized celluloid baby doll had become popular among the girls. The article went on to say, "The rightness of living within one's means is constantly put before them, as well as the honorableness of thrift and of work with the hands."[13]

Annice's work was understood not only as providing an education in managing a home and family. The country was adopting Western ways, the *Advocate* article said, and that was causing difficulties. The Home Economics Department was seen as the greatest hope in addressing the problem, since the girls were being taught very practical things.[14]

THE POLITICAL SITUATION

In her first report as the new principal of the Girls School, Mildred White wrote in the December 1929 issue of the *Friends Missionary Advocate* about the trouble that had erupted in the region that fall—just as Annice arrived. After noting that the School had a new tennis court, she went on to write:

> You doubtless have read in the papers about our recent riots in this country. Here in Ram Allah we were safe and quiet, but we felt the great distress and fear for our friends in Jerusalem and various places in the land where the riots occurred. . . . There were many Moslems in the fighting who considered themselves heroes for their country, and those who were killed by the Jews as martyrs. The Jews, of course, considered themselves as fighting a war of defense. To tell the truth, to judge by the methods used on both sides, it was more like rioting and mobbing than warfare. . . . These things all make one feel that our peaceful fight in this land must not cease.[15]

Mildred went on to express the belief that the trouble stemmed from the Balfour Declaration, and that the future was hard to foresee, but the

[13] *Friends Missionary Advocate*, July/August 1931, pp. 230–231.

[14] The article in the *Advocate* does not describe what the "difficulties" were, but Annice's earlier observations suggest that they may have been related to the feeling, on the part of some, that education in traditional homemaking skills was "beneath the dignity" of modern girls. While this was probably the case, it must also be admitted that some of the early workers at the Friends Schools insisted that the "traditional ways" of Palestinian society must be set aside in preference for Western ways—and in some cases for observance of the restrictions on personal habits preferred by the Quaker missionaries. That caused conflict in some families as students, in admiration for their teachers, rebelled against traditional ways.

[15] *Friends Missionary Advocate*, December 1929, pp. 429–430.

effect was already apparent in the loss of business and tourism. She noted that the big hotel that had just opened in Ramallah in the summer of 1929 had to close for want of anyone to stay in it. The manager and the hotel's orchestra were all Jewish, and they had left the area to find a safer place.

In an issue of the *Advocate* a few months later in the summer of 1930, Mildred wrote that the events of the previous August and September shouldn't be allowed to conceal the fact that the greater part of the year had been normal.[16]

While Ramallah was somewhat isolated from the events of the 1929 Arab uprising and remained fairly quiet throughout the disturbances, the difficulties were never too far away from people's consciousness. In 1931, there was an extended Arab car strike in protest against the increasing immigration of Zionists. This was one of dozens of actions used in popular resistance against British policies. In conversations with students, Annice heard their opposition to the idea of Jews' returning to Palestine to establish a national home. The Zionist movement received very little sympathy in Ramallah. There was worry about how it would affect, especially, the peasants living on the land.

TRAVEL AND CULTURAL EXPERIENCES

For Annice, it wasn't all work and concern for the situation. With her colleagues, she traveled extensively, taking advantage of being in the "Holy Land" she had grown up hearing about through reading the Bible and attending Sunday School. On frequent trips to Jerusalem, she became acquainted with the various holy sites and witnessed the rituals of the different religious communities in the Old City—along with occasional cultural events. She attended Christmas Eve services in Bethlehem and the nearby Shepherds' Field. On trips farther afield, she explored the Jordan Valley and toured the sites associated with Jesus' life around the Sea of Galilee.

She also had opportunities to share in the local culture. There were traditional engagement and wedding parties; the Greek Orthodox "Holy Fire" of Easter that started with one flame in the Church of the Holy Sepulchre in Jerusalem and was rapidly spread by thousands of the faithful

---

16 *Friends Missionary Advocate*, July/August 1930.

carrying the fire in torches to all the Christian villages; and picnics with graduating students featuring roast sheep, tomatoes, cucumbers, olives, flat bread, and bananas. The Friends Boys School faculty also hosted a sheep roast for the teachers and staff at the Girls School, but as the home economics teacher, Annice wound up helping manage the stuffing of the sheep!

ANNICE LEAVES RAMALLAH

In the September 1932 issue of the *Friends Missionary Advocate*, Mildred White wrote, "Annice Carter, Margaret Grant, and Ruth Outland all had to go home this year and oh, how we shall miss them! Their influence and service have been so fine and helpful, and we have all grown so fond of them."[17] She went on to say that Annice and Margaret had traveled through Turkey and Europe together on their way back home. Mildred also noted that the Home Economics Department had done "splendid" work the previous year.

During Annice's time at the Girls School, enrollment had grown to 166 students, with 84 boarders. In her last year at the School there were only five graduates, the low number being the result of many dropping out before graduation—in order to marry, or for financial reasons, or owing to an inability to successfully do a high school curriculum.

Without access to Annice's own letters, it is hard to know how she felt about leaving Ramallah after her three years there. Was it simply a matter of the end of her term of service through the Board of Missions? Was she ready for another adventure? Whatever the reason, she departed Palestine for the United States and her next assignment as a teacher at Pacific College in Newberg, Oregon.

17 *Friends Missionary Advocate*, September 1932.

CHAPTER 3

Annice at Pacific College and the decision to return to Ramallah

Following Annice's first assignment in Ramallah, she accepted a position on the faculty of Pacific College in Newberg, Oregon. A Friends college under the care of Oregon Yearly Meeting, it was founded in 1885 as Friends Pacific Academy by the Quakers who followed the Oregon Trail from the Midwest to the Pacific Northwest. In 1891, the Academy became a college and was named Pacific College. In 1949, the name was changed again to George Fox College, now University.

Among the school's most noted alumni are U.S. president Herbert Hoover, who attended the Academy in its early years when his uncle, H. L. Minthorn, was the college president; Quaker theologian, historian, and poet Arthur Roberts; and Richard Foster, a theologian and author in the Quaker tradition.

It remains something of a mystery how Annice came to join the faculty of Pacific College. There are no obvious connections with that community of Friends; no friends or relatives who attended the college or lived in the area; no known connections through the three years she had been in Ramallah. There is also the fact that Oregon Yearly Meeting in 1926 withdrew from FYM, the Quaker body whose Board of Missions sent Annice to Ramallah and to which her home Yearly Meeting, Western Yearly Meeting, belonged.

Oregon's dispute with FYM focused on a difference of opinion over what Friends workers in the mission field should be required to believe. Established by Quakers deeply influenced by the revival and holiness movements in the late 1800s, Oregon Yearly Meeting wanted mission workers to sign a statement affirming their evangelical beliefs. FYM was hesitant to require such an action, viewing it as requiring a creedal statement—something Friends had traditionally opposed. Annice's own responses to the Board of Missions' questionnaire in 1929 give evidence

Annice in the 1930s.

that her own beliefs were not fully in alignment with those of Oregon Yearly Meeting.

Evidently, Annice's identification with FYM was not a hindrance to her appointment. Perhaps it was her experience as a missionary. Maybe it was the fact that her home congregation, Russiaville Friends Church, had also been formed under the influence of the revival and holiness period, and she was comfortable with Wesleyan theology. Annice was certainly comfortable enough with that theology that she accompanied young college women under her care to the revival meetings held at nearby Newberg Friends Church.

Another factor in her acceptance may have been Levi Pennington's presidency at Pacific. Pennington headed the college from 1911 to 1941, in spite of sometimes running afoul of the more conservative members of Oregon Yearly Meeting—some viewed with concern his more inclusive attitude towards Friends of a "different stripe." It is certainly true that Annice and Levi remained lifelong friends.

Whatever the case, Annice packed her bags for Newberg and became Pacific College's instructor in Dramatics, Public Speaking, and Home Economics, and Director of Women's Physical Education. In addition to her teaching duties, she was matron of the women's dormitory and served as advisor to the Trefian Literary Society for faculty women and women students, to the campus YWCA, and to the Women's Athletic Association. She also supervised the formation of the Gold Q Club for the women who had earned athletic letters.

Her teaching load in Public Speaking included courses in public speaking, extemporaneous speaking, oratorical analysis, and forensics. In Home Economics she taught courses in foods and clothing. Her Dramatics curriculum included principles of acting and a practicum.

Supervising the women's physical education program required her to oversee the students' requirement to spend at least two hours each week in some form of active recreation. Annice also coordinated all women's sports, including coaching the women's volleyball and basketball teams. The college's 1935 *L'Ami* yearbook notes the volleyball team's successful season with a 4–1 record, the lone loss having been avenged later in the season. Basketball, however, seemed a different story. The opening game was a loss, 9–30.

The yearbook goes on to say this:

> The increased improvement shown by various Pacific College athletic teams during the 1934-35 year can be traced to the work done by three people who shaped the destinies of Quaker teams throughout that time. . . . Women's athletics were guided by Miss Annice Carter. . . . The director of physical education for women, Miss Annice Carter, took up her duties at Pacific College in 1932 after having taught for more than three years

in Palestine. Since Miss Carter has become affiliated with Pacific, women's athletics have taken a prominent place on the school's athletic calendar.

As if such a schedule of responsibilities weren't daunting enough, Annice was also tasked with directing the student plays at Pacific. *L'Ami* commented on her work as a director: "During the past three years the dramatics and public speaking department of Pacific College has been very efficiently directed by Miss Annice Carter of Russiaville, Indiana. Miss Carter has coached twelve three-act plays while at Pacific and numerous lesser plays and dramatic presentations."

These plays included an annual Freshman Play as well as a Student Body Play. Among the dramas presented were *The McMurray Chin, The Man from Nowhere, and Wild Ginger.* It was noted that *Wild Ginger* drew an audience of 250, the largest crowd in three years.

Along with her other responsibilities, Annice spoke in required chapels and convocations. The March 13, 1934, edition of the student newspaper, *The Crescent,* includes this description of one of her presentations:

Illustrated Lecture by Miss Annice Carter Is Third Lyceum Number—Gave a Lecture on The Holy Land

Miss Carter quoted Henry Van Dyke in saying, "Christianity is an out-of-doors religion. From the birth in a grotto in Bethlehem to the crowning death on the Hill of Calvary, all the important events took place out-of-doors. . . .

Palestine is a tiny land, about 150 miles long and 60 miles wide, a strip of fertile plain beside the sea, a blue strip of lofty and broken highlands, and a gray and yellow strip of sunken river valley. Palestine has seen many nations, tribes, and civilizations. "Crust after crust of pious legend has formed over the deep valleys and tradition has set up altars on every high hill and under every green tree."

After a brief description of the traveling facilities of Palestine, Miss Carter, with the aid of slides, took her audience on an interesting tour of the Holy Land.

The pictures shown centered about the countryside and towns where Jesus walked when he was on earth. They portrayed some of the places where important events in his life took place. They also made real to the audience many of the customs, home conditions and habits of the nomad people who claim the Holy Land as their home. Of special interest also were the pictures of scenery. The cities and people have changed since the time when Jesus carried on his work in that land, but the mountains and valleys—the landscape scenes—are the same, and Miss Carter feels that it is through these things, and through Him who gave them new meaning, that we can truly find the Holy Land.

Along with her duties at Pacific, Annice had opportunities to speak around the Yearly Meeting about her experience in Ramallah. She found it frustrating, however, that people were more interested in the native life and customs of Arabs than in the Friends Mission. She ascribed this to Oregon Friends' perception that the Mission lacked a proper focus on evangelism. She was further distressed by how many Friends she encountered who were sympathetic with the Zionist movement. It prompted her to submit an article to *The American Friend*, edited by Errol Elliott.

In her submission, responding to the critique that the work of the Friends Mission in Ramallah did not lead to conversions, Annice commented on the exploitative nature of colonial enterprises and remarked on the religious nature of all Arabs. She noted that Muslims believe in God and in the work of Jesus. Muslims' respect for Christians would increase, she asserted, if Christians actually lived a Christian life. She noted that the Mission sought to encourage better behavior. Consistent with her feelings throughout her life, Annice expressed that Christians' use of alcohol was one such behavior that needed to be addressed![18]

Annice also commented in her article on people's response to her disapproval of Zionism. She would be asked whether she believed in prophecy, and answered that if, indeed, prophecy about the Jews' return to Palestine were correct, she didn't think the time had yet come for its fulfillment. The editor, Elliott, responded approvingly and agreed with her concern about prophecy.

For all the work that Annice shouldered at Pacific, she was paid on the lower end of a $1,200–1,750 annual salary scale. And in 1933, citing financial exigency, the Board guaranteed only 60% of that pay. Indeed, for the next ten years, faculty at Pacific received no more than 60% of their contracted compensation.

[18] The text of the article, with Errol Elliott's edits on Annice's original submission on October 9, 1932, is in the collection of Annice's materials on microfilm, MR-157, Earlham Friends Collection and College Archives.

In February of 1935, Annice announced her resignation, effective at the end of the academic year. The February 19 issue of *The Crescent* shared the news:

> Miss Annice Carter, who has been instructor of Dramatics, Public Speaking, Home Economics, and Physical Education at Pacific for the past three years, and who has also acted as matron of the girls' dormitory, has resigned her position, her resignation to take effect at the close of this college year. It was with expressions of appreciation of her work done here at the college that the Board accepted her resignation.

There was obvious affection for Annice at Pacific College, and in spite of the low pay and heavy workload, she appeared to enjoy the community of the college and Newberg. A bit of her lighter side seems also to have come out at Pacific. In the 1935 *L'Ami* yearbook, the "theme songs" of the faculty and administration are listed. It's not clear whether the titles were chosen for them or selected by the faculty and staff themselves, but Annice's was "'Leven-Thirty Saturday Night," a popular song in 1930 whose lyrics follow:

> All events of consequence in history
> Are mysteries as to the time they happened
> My event was Heaven sent and you can bet
> I can't forget the time
>
> For it was at the dance, I was in a trance
> 'Leven-thirty Saturday night
> And in my arms I held a world of charms
> 'Leven-thirty Saturday night
>
> At eight my fate had just begun
> It grew quite late before love had won
> Ooh, can't you see, she accepted me
> 'Leven-thirty Saturday night
> Ooh, baby, 'leven-thirty Saturday night
>
> Now, when I met my pet, my little sugar pet
> 'Leven-thirty Saturday night
> I felt so weak, I could hardly speak
> But finally I got over my fright

And through my fear, she looked so dear
I had a whisper right in her ear
Can't you guess, golly gee, she accepted me
'Leven-thirty Saturday night

Now, I met a maid through an escapade
'Leven-thirty Saturday night
And pretty soon we were in her room
'Leven-thirty Saturday night

Well, we sat and talked, then suddenly
Yes, her husband, he came unexpectedly
Well, I got there looking debonair
When he got through I looked like a sight
Exactly 'leven-thirty Saturday night

ANNICE CONSIDERS HER RETURN TO RAMALLAH

There was no indication in the announcement that Annice was resigning in order to go to Ramallah again. In fact, at the time Annice was still in negotiations with the Friends School and with the Board of Missions about returning there. Another term of service in Palestine had been on her mind, and as early as May of 1933 the Board had asked her if she might be ready to accept another assignment at the Girls School. She responded that the offer was quite a temptation and that she had considered it carefully but decided against it. Had she simply stayed home in Russiaville rather than going to Pacific College, she claimed, she would have gone back to Ramallah.

The pressure to return to Ramallah continued throughout Annice's time at Pacific. In May of 1934 Khalil Totah, director of the Friends work in Ramallah, said he wanted Annice to be the matron of the Friends Boys School. Annice sent a cable to Totah refusing his offer, and wrote to the Board of Missions, "I was sorry to do it, but feel I am not capable of filling the position he wants filled. I would rather return to the Girls School sometime."[19]

---

[19] June 2, 1934, letter to the Board of Missions, Annice Carter Microfilm, MR-157, Earlham Friends Collection and College Archives.

Annice's family in the 1930s. Front row l-r: Nora, Charles, Milley, and Walter. Back row l-r: Achsa, Oakley, and Annice.

In November of 1934 Merle Davis, Administrative Secretary of the Board of Missions, wrote to Annice that Khalil Totah wanted her to head up the Home Economics Department at the Girls School. In January of 1935 he wrote again, saying that Totah wanted her back: "He states that after the three years that you were in the School, your work was very satisfactory and that they would like to have you return this next year."[20]

Annice wrote directly to Totah with questions about the prospective work at the Girls School. He responded that she would be fully employed at the Girls School in building up the Domestic Science Department, and that she would have support in doing home economics extension work in the villages. If she were agreeable to a five-year term, she would be hired by the School at a salary of $540 annually, with a little more if she covered her own travel expenses.

The offer concerned Annice. She would rather be hired by the Board of Missions and not by Khalil Totah. Furthermore, Annice felt that a five-year term wouldn't meet the approval of her parents.

Still, in a February letter to the Board, Annice said she had always wanted to return to Ramallah, but finances were an issue, and she

[20] January 24, 1935, letter from Merle Davis, Annice Carter Microfilm, MR-157, Earlham Friends Collection and College Archives.

Three generations of cousins, descendants of Charles and Milley carter (opposite ends of the second row). Annice is in the second row, third from the right, between siblings Achsa and Walter. 1930s.

wondered if she were the right person. Yet if all else seemed right, she would try to manage the finances. Merle Davis responded that she could be sent out by the Board, but a long-term assignment would require her to fill out a lengthy questionnaire in order to assure the Board that she was an appropriate person to represent them.

By April, Annice was considering going home to Russiaville, doing odd jobs, and returning to Ramallah in 1936. She was open to going in 1935 if everyone involved thought it to be the right thing, but she was also contemplating applying for work with the American Friends Service Committee (AFSC). Then in May, Annice received a letter from Merle Davis saying that Khalil Totah had cabled, "Carter this year."[21]

Annice relented and asked for the application for long-term service in Ramallah, writing in May to the Board of Missions, "I have fully and prayerfully considered the challenge and privilege of Christian service abroad and desire to share with my fellow-men the inestimable values of the Gospel of Jesus...."[22]

21 May 2, 1935, letter from Merle Davis, Annice Carter Microfilm, MR-157, Earlham Friends Collection and College Archives.

22 May 11, 1935, letter to the American Friends Board of Missions, Annice Carter Microfilm, MR-157, Earlham Friends Collection and College Archives.

RESPONSES TO THE BOARD OF MISSIONS
QUESTIONNAIRE FOR CHRISTIAN SERVICE

After agreeing to apply for a long-term assignment to Ramallah, Annice was sent the "blanks" (as the Board described them) to fill out to show that she was suitable for missionary service. Her responses to some of the more than 30 questions are found in Appendix B. She was also asked to write an essay about "the content of your Christian message." Annice wrote that it was nearly impossible to capture this content in words, and then summarized as follows:

Citing John 4:24 and I John 4:8, Annice emphasized worship in spirit and truth and the importance of love. God is a creative force in the universe that manifests Himself as energy, life, order, beauty, conscience, and love—self-revealed supremely in Jesus of Nazareth. "The Christian way of life seems so logical and so desirable that I have spent little time in thinking about or discussing doctrinal belief or church principles, but have tried to uphold in my daily living the commandments found in Mark 12:20, 21: love God and your neighbor as yourself."[23] Annice went on to comment that true religion is what one practices in daily life and that she would rather see a sermon than hear one, preferring that a person would walk with her rather than merely tell her the way.

In further questions from the Board, she was asked if she had accepted the Lord Jesus Christ as her personal Savior. She answered, "Yes." Asked if she would make her chief purpose leading souls to Christ, her answer was, "I think daily living will accomplish more than special effort." The questions continued with, "Have you had success in winning souls for Christ?" And Annice responded, "Very difficult to determine."

Finally, "Why do you want to be a missionary? Do you wish to be one for life?" Annice answered, "Opportunity for service" and "Yes."

In submitting her application and answers, Annice remarked that the questions were often a puzzle and that words were inadequate fully to express her beliefs. She didn't want to give the impression that she measured up to her own yardstick, but "neither do I want the Board to think I am radical on the side of living Christianity to the exclusion of

[23] May 11, 1935, responses to the Board of Missions, Annice Carter Microfilm, MR-157, Earlham Friends Collection and College Archives.

preaching it. I hope you can judge some of the answers in the light of the work I did when I was in Ramallah and not be too critical."[24]

Merle Davis later responded, for the Board, that her answers were satisfactory.

DRAMA IN THE MONTHS PRECEDING ANNICE'S DEPARTURE FOR RAMALLAH

However, that wasn't the end of the matter. On June 14, Merle Davis wrote to Annice that the Executive Committee of the Board of Missions could not approve her appointment, as Elizabeth Masters, the current Home Economics teacher at the Girls School, had not yet decided to leave as anticipated, and the Board could not support two teachers. It was hoped that Annice would go if needed, but she would have to hold up for the time being.

While awaiting resolution of the Board's uncertainty, Annice traveled to Pendle Hill, the Quaker conference center outside of Philadelphia. The Board's next correspondence to her was sent there. Having learned of Khalil Totah's request for her to return to Ramallah, Annice had decided against applying to AFSC to volunteer at one of their summer work camps, and had applied instead for the summer term at Pendle Hill. In her application to Pendle Hill, she wrote, "I would very much like to have a taste of the inspirational atmosphere that seems so prevalent there."[25] Not only was Annice admitted to the summer term, she received a scholarship for full tuition, room, and board.

In a July 5 letter, Merle Davis told Annice that Elizabeth Masters had, indeed, decided to leave, and the Board wanted Annice to be in Ramallah by October. In her response, Annice asked questions about the finances at the Mission and went on to suggest that another person at Pendle Hill at the time, Grace Schoonover, might be a suitable person to teach in her place, as her husband, Kermit, was already assigned to teach at the Boys School in Ramallah, and Grace was trained in home economics.

[24] May 12, 1935, letter to Merle Davis, Annice Carter Microfilm, MR-157, Earlham Friends Collection and College Archives.

[25] Carter, Annice, Pendle Hill Records, RG4 066, Ser. 2, Swarthmore College Friends Historical Library.

Merle Davis answered with a list of possible sailing times for Annice's departure, but also acknowledged that the Board had incurred an unexpected expense of $1,000 in its work in Africa and that perhaps she could talk over the matter with Grace Schoonover. This led to a series of letters back and forth, as Annice's appointment seemed to remain in question. Grace Schoonover was hesitant about taking on the teaching position, as her husband would be full-time at the Boys School, and they would be living at Swift House—the Mission house next to the Boys School campus, a mile away from the Girls School. The Schoonovers would talk it over with their friend Moses Bailey, however. Bailey had been the principal at the Boys School in the early 1900s and was a friend of theirs from New England Yearly Meeting. For her part, Annice said, "I want to do what is best for the Mission and will be quite happy to do whatever is best."[26]

Meanwhile, letters of support for Annice's appointment were arriving at the Board of Missions from a number of notable Friends, including Herschel Folger, Charles Woodman, Sylvester Jones, and Ward Applegate. One was from Margaret Grant (later Beidler), a 1930 Earlham graduate who had taught with Annice in Ramallah and was at Pendle Hill when Annice was. In her hometown of Richmond, Indiana, Margaret had lived next door to Merle Davis, the Administrative Secretary of the Board on Missions. In her letter to Davis, Grant urged the Board of Missions to send Annice, noting that she was sending her letter without Annice's knowledge.

"I need not speak for Annice's work and character," Grant wrote. "They have already spoken for themselves. All of us who know her and know Palestine are aware of the strong and vitally important contribution she has to give to those girls—not only in class work but in all her relations with them. Also she knows and understands the situation and will go back ready to give of her best.... Palestine may need the Schoonovers but, (oh my goodness, say I) it certainly does need Annice Carter in a hundred ways.... Believe me."[27]

26 July 16, 1935, letter to Merle Davis, Annice Carter Microfilm, MR-157, Earlham Friends Collection and College Archives.
27 July 17, 1935, letter to Merle Davis, Annice Carter Microfilm, MR-157, Earlham Friends Collection and College Archives.

Merle Davis responded with appreciation but reiterated the problem with funds. The Schoonovers wrote again that they were hesitant about having two full-time positions. Moses Bailey suggested that more financial support for the Girls School would be the solution. While supporting Annice's appointment and noting her fine work previously, Ward Applegate wrote with other questions. He worried that the Board was thinking of drawing funds to support the appointment from a budget dedicated to Mildred White. He was further concerned that Khalil Totah, who seemed so insistent on Annice's return, may have pressured Elizabeth Masters to leave.

Finally, Merle Davis wrote to Annice on July 22 while she was still at Pendle Hill, "After considerable debate, as you know . . . not because of you but because of the financial situation which has arisen, the Executive Committee . . . have definitely approved your appointment."[28]

Without any indication of frustration with the Board's indecision or the impact it had on her own plans, Annice responded to Merle Davis that, given the delay in reaching a definite decision, she would like to sail on September 14 rather than an earlier date. She felt that the later departure would still allow enough time for her to settle into her work, since the school year didn't start until mid-October. Indeed, she did set sail on September 14 on the S.S. Conte Grande—ticket price $129.50 plus $5.00 tax. It was ironically fitting that, given the Board's lack of decisiveness for so long, their cheque for $60.00 to cover Annice's incidental expenses during the trip didn't arrive at her home in Russiaville until after her departure.

In a letter to Merle Davis from Ramallah dated October 24, Annice reported that her ship had arrived in Haifa on October 3 and that school had already started. She was settled in at the Home Economics cottage with music teacher Mary Minnick.

[28] July 22, 1935, letter from Merle Davis, Annice Carter Microfilm, MR-157, Earlham Friends Collection and College Archives.

CHAPTER 4

Annice in Ramallah from 1935 to 1941

While Annice was at Pacific College, the Friends schools in Ramallah and area villages continued to do well. The total number of students there exceeded the enrollment at Pacific. Whether because of the amount of work required of her at the college, or a tug to return to the Holy Land, in 1935 Annice returned to resume her work at the Friends Girls School. That year was to be the last calm year for a while. It was as if the situation was about 'leven-thirty, approaching political and social midnight.

As Annice labored in Newberg, Jewish immigration to Palestine was increasing, owing to the rise of Nazism in Germany and the growing persecution of Jews. The number of immigrants had increased dramatically, from 5,000 in 1930 to 61,000 just five years later. Although the United States accepted only a small fraction of the Jews seeking refuge, the British in authority in Palestine were not so restrictive.

By 1935 the Zionist enterprise in Palestine had resulted in the establishment of a Jewish middle class living a life easier than that of the early Zionist "pioneers." Palestine now had Jewish cities, towns, villages, and colonies. World-class universities had been established in Jerusalem and Haifa, and Jews made up one-fourth of the entire Palestinian population—with the number of Jewish immigrants increasing by 10% annually. Only ten years earlier, the Jewish population had amounted to only one-tenth of the total.

The Arab population, aware of Zionism's political policies and aspirations, was not sympathetic to Jewish needs, and the British Government was increasingly being pressured to limit immigration. Meanwhile, Muslim Arab revolutionary cells had begun developing, and the Haganah—the paramilitary wing of the Jewish Agency—was arming itself with smuggled weapons.

*Proportional
seems
similar*

When two Jews were killed at a makeshift Arab checkpoint in April of 1936, violence spiraled into reprisal after reprisal and was met by a severe response from the British authorities. By the end of 1939 more than 5,000 Palestinian Arabs had been killed, and many thousands more had been wounded. Estimates of Palestinian Jews killed ranged from fewer than 100 to several hundred. The period from 1936 to 1939 became known as the second Arab Revolt.

This was a very difficult time for the schools under Friends care. Day students were exposed to all the unrest while boarding students, though somewhat insulated themselves, worried for their parents. Everyone knew someone in harm's way, and this caused a great deal of anxiety.

Ironically, the outbreak of World War II would bring relative calm to Palestine. In deference to the British war effort, Jewish and Arab forces ceased hostilities, and the war itself never came fully to Palestine.

This was the situation that met Annice on her return. She had stepped out of college work that must have felt overwhelming at times, but which was a world away, literally and figuratively, from the troubles in Palestine. Her experience teaching Dramatics, however, might well have been good preparation for what would be happening on the world stage.

WORK AT THE SCHOOL

Not much had changed at the Girls School or in Ramallah while Annice was away, although the enrollment had been affected by the region's political difficulties. Ramallah had become a center of resistance to British policies, and families were nervous about sending their children to board there. Enrollment still included many students from well-to-do families. Even while most people in Ramallah went about on donkeys or camels, students arrived at school in cars. The Muslim girls, though, were still representative of a conservative culture. They came to school with black veils over their faces.

Ramallah was still a small village, and the local culture reflected that. Women wearing traditional long embroidered dresses, heads covered with shawls, walked about with huge jugs of water or baskets of produce on their heads. Peasant men tended olive trees and worked their small strips of land outside of town—when they weren't in the coffee shops. Nor had the climate changed. Summers were dry and hot, but it was cool inside the stone buildings. And "cool" barely suffices to describe the insides of those buildings during the rainy winter. There was still no central heating in Palestinian houses, and chilblains were common.

Annice's duties were similar to those of her previous time at the School. In addition to teaching, they included getting the girls up at 6:00 A.M., helping with breakfast, monitoring study hall and after-school activities, administering Saturday baths, and examining heads for lice. One duty was now added, however: Annice was appointed treasurer of the Ramallah Mission. As such, she had to "keep the books" of the Mission and maintain accurate accounts of the salaries paid by the Boys and Girls Schools and the Board of Missions, expenses related to the Mission's work, staff travel, and maintenance of Mission facilities. Her monthly correspondence with the Board of Missions in Richmond indicated just how difficult that task often was. Financial constraints at the Schools and on the Board meant that every penny had to be accounted for. One series of letters, for example, was concerned with an expense of $2.06 related to a staff member's application for a permit!

Annice's first few months back at the School went smoothly. She was pleased with the work of Victoria Hannush, the principal of the Girls School, and also with the work of the Schoonovers. She reported on their pastoral calls with staff teacher and translator Na'ameh Shahla, and she appreciated Kermit Schoonover's sermons in the Friends Meeting's worship services. Annice was especially pleased with Kermit Schoonover's frequent mention of Jesus as the Son of God and emphasis on Jesus' way of life. Her approval, however, would wane in coming months.

Annice expressed growing concerns about other staff. One teacher, she felt, was incapable of putting herself on the level of her students, and as such was more fit for a position in a college. Annice was pleased that this teacher would be leaving. She described one staff member as "flighty," another as "in a daze," and yet another as questionable in his "temperance" concerning alcohol. She also had concerns about Khalil Totah, the secretary of the Friends Mission who also served as principal of the Boys School and who had assumed oversight of the Girls School as well. Reporting to the Board of Missions, Annice wrote that Totah was incapable of hearing criticism and was becoming too dictatorial.[29]

Christmas of 1935, however, brought the usual programs at the School. Annice enjoyed a return to the worship service at Shepherds' Field in Bethlehem and a lengthy vacation that accommodated both Latin and Eastern holiday observances. She spent some of the vacation time creating a garden and rock wall in front of the Home Economics cottage; she also traveled in the coastal regions of Palestine. One outing took her to the home of a Girls School student north of Jaffa, in a rural area inhabited primarily by Bedouin, where she enjoyed the hospitality of a traditional sheikh and his family. However, this "vacation" was unexpectedly extended for six months, from April of 1936 into the fall, as the Arabs had called a general strike in response to the immigration policies of the British Government.

Classes resumed when the strike ended, and Annice wrote, "There are times when most of the thrill and glamour of being in Palestine fades out and one is buried in the routine of ordinary school teaching."[30] She described activities that included chaperoned trips to the cinema, various games, plays, and a wildflower competition. Their home economics studies were even turned into an extracurricular event of exhibiting their sewing handiwork and selling cakes, cookies, and candies they had made. At the end of the school year, the students participated in planning Commencement exercises.

That summer Annice oversaw a tennis club for girls and taught extension courses in villages to instruct girls in domestic work so they could have opportunities to work for hire. She also had the chance for

---

[29] Annice does not mention it in her letters, but tension between Khalil Totah and the Board of Missions led him to resign his position. The controversy resulting from his falling out with the Board led to a split in the Friends Meeting, with those siding with Totah eventually leaving the Meeting, and those more supportive of the Board's conduct of the School and Friends work in Palestine remaining. The long-term impact of that separation was that the bilingual members of the Meeting, with closer ties to American Friends, felt comfortable with worship being conducted in English; this meant there was little chance of attracting a local population to join. When many of those members left for the U.S. for further education or better economic opportunities, membership was depleted and not replaced. This had an adverse effect on the long-term sustainability of the Meeting.

[30] June 6, 1937, letter to Merle Davis, Annice Carter Microfilm, MR-157, Earlham Friends Collection and College Archives.

The faculty of the Boys and Girls Schools in Ramallah in 1937. Annice is in the second row, second from the left.

some travel and especially enjoyed a trip to Hebron, where she visited the traditional glass factory. She commented on seeing "the very oak of Mamre" under which Abraham supposedly sat. On the return to Ramallah, she visited "Solomon's Pools," which actually were Roman-era reservoirs near Bethlehem that had supplied water to Jerusalem. She also visited Rachel's Tomb in Bethlehem, a monument erected by the British Jewish philanthropist Sir Moses Montefiore.

Before a summer spent back home in Indiana in 1938, Annice enjoyed the Girls School's May Day activities that drew more than 400. One of the events was the Tolstoy play, *What Men Live By*. There were songs, dances, a kindergarten orchestra, and more home economics exhibits and bake sales. The concluding celebration was the singing of the School song as students arranged by height spelled out F.G.S., with little boys forming the periods. A few weeks later was Commencement. Annice was responsible for making the patterns for the five graduates' dresses and sending them off to the dressmaker.

Back in Ramallah after her time at home in Indiana, Annice was faced with growing political difficulties and worry about missing budget vouchers from the Board of Missions. When those drafts finally did arrive in December, they included a check for $4,500 for the building fund and

$918 for auditorium chairs. Those monies were designated for a new auditorium at the Friends Boys School.

By the fall of 1938, Annice was concerned enough about the Schoonovers that she wrote to the Board of Missions that she hoped they would go home soon, although she didn't detail what the issues were.[31] She was also ready to have Khalil Totah give up his oversight of the Girls School and recommended that in the future there be an American secretary of the Mission. Annice felt that, if there were to be another Arab principal of the Boys School, there should be an Arab oversight committee.[32]

Other problems occupied Annice's thoughts, including the threat of a literal occupation of school buildings by British troops. Only State Department intervention in 1936 prevented the British from requisitioning School property. As political tensions in the region continued to increase, the number of soldiers sent to Palestine grew to more than 20,000, and on different occasions the Government looked to the Friends Schools for housing. Khalil Totah managed to keep the Boys School building from being taken over by allowing army tents to be set up on the School's soccer field. From September through November of 1938, the Royal Irish Fusiliers lived in the tents there. An attempt to house soldiers at the Girls School that same year was prevented only by the Board on Mission's appeal to the U.S. State Department and the British Colonial Office in London.

Annice also was faced with the task of finding a replacement for the worn-out kitchen range at the Girls School. She finally located one that the School could afford, but it was broken as it was unloaded in Jaffa. She ordered another one, and it was broken as it was being handled in Haifa!

December of 1938 brought concerns over how to celebrate the Christmas season at the School amid the uneasy situation in the region. Because of the uncertainties, the students had not been told of any plans for the usual gifts and observances. Annice noted that one Muslim student

[31] The Schoonovers finally departed in February of 1939, leaving Swift House, the Mission house, vacant. Soon, various items at the empty building "walked." That necessitated Annice's hiring a man for $10 a month to reside there. While it was a non-budgeted item, Annice was pleased that the man was working hard improving the grounds and tending the garden at Swift House.

[32] Annice's thoughts about Khalil Totah are contained in letters from September 3, 1938, and May 1, 1957, Annice Carter Microfilm, MR-157, Earlham Friends Collection and College Archives.

insisted that, at least, there be a Christmas tree, and some of the little students wrote to Santa asking for gifts for others.

What Annice had kept secret from the students was that, while in the States that summer, she had purchased little gifts at the "Five and Dime"—204 of them! In addition, each student received a bag of nuts and a tangerine or orange. Christmas programs were held, but they had to be put on in the afternoon rather than the evening, owing to a British-imposed curfew from 5:00 P.M. to 5:00 A.M.

At the conclusion of the Christmas programs, students were dismissed for the holiday. Special permits had to be obtained from the British authorities for two buses to take students home in the direction of Haifa and Jaffa. Buses then brought students back after the break, with some students remaining at home because of the worsening conditions. Seventy-eight boarders came back to the Boys School; 58 to the Girls School.

In June of 1939, Annice reported to the Board of Missions about a different issue. She had discovered that teachers at the Girls School were receiving an annual salary of $600 while at the Boys School the salary was $650. It turned out that Board appointees had been told the salary was $650, but word hadn't gotten to the Girls School, and its budget could not cover the extra money. Merle Davis responded that Quaker rectitude demanded payment as promised, and the discrepancy was corrected.[33]

That fall, the School celebrated a Jubilee for its 1888/89 founding, with "old students" attending. The ongoing violence of the regional conflict prevented a large attendance, but Annice was pleased that funds were collected that would go to the School's relief efforts in the villages.

Annice reported that, in spite of the regional conflict as well as more mundane problems, the Boys and Girls Schools were carrying on well. She was concerned about getting students to study more, stay quiet between classes, and obey school rules. There were also the usual worries about water and the need for a new cistern—a need that was finally satisfied only 25 years later when she was principal. On the positive side, there were new playing fields, new books for the library, and a new award to encourage English speaking. Annice hoped that the Schools were growing

---

[33] June 16, 1939, letter to Merle Davis, Annice Carter Microfilm, MR-157, Earlham Friends Collection and College Archives. Annice's concern about pay equity between the Schools was an issue she would address again when she served as principal in the '50s and '60s.

better citizens who could help build a more peaceful future—a task she felt was of growing importance.

Ironically, as the war in Europe began, the conflict in Palestine calmed down, and Annice's reports from Ramallah were about busy but pleasant summers, good enrollments, ordering books, ongoing relief efforts in the villages, and even finally getting a good cooking range. The problems pertained to the usual budget concerns, the water supply, and managing furloughs so that the Schools would remain properly staffed.

Annice herself was due for a furlough in 1941, but so was Khalil Totah, and the Board of Missions reported that no replacement home economics teacher had been found. Furthermore, missionaries in Kenya had delayed their furloughs and were "in line" ahead of Annice. Board funds could not cover the transportation for everyone. The passage by ship that had cost Annice a little more than $100 in 1935 now cost more than $800. Annice was willing to forgo her furlough in favor of the Totahs', but in April of 1941 she received a cable from Richmond, "Board approved furlough."

Annice did indeed return home that year, although the war's disruption of transportation led to concern about evacuations and indecision about whether to stay or go. Eventually, Annice's decision was made for her by the illness of her father and a cable asking her to return to Russiaville.

POLITICAL CONCERNS

One thing that had changed since Annice's 1929–32 term of service was the growing unpopularity of Americans, owing to President Roosevelt's perceived favoring of the "Jewish side" in the question of Jewish immigration and nationhood. The violence that Annice had experienced in 1929 expanded into a protracted revolt against British policies, with Ramallah eventually becoming a "rebel center." Following the General Strike[34] of

---

[34] As Arab concerns about Zionist aims for Palestine increased with the influx of Jewish immigrants, a general strike was called in April of 1936 in Nablus. It affected labor, transportation, and businesses, and rapidly spread to the rest of Palestine as the Arab population protested British policies. Initially a grassroots protest, the strike became organized by a central Command and was extended for six months. *Popular Resistance in Palestine: A History of Hope and Empowerment* (Pluto Press, 2011) by Mazin Qumsiyeh describes this strike and more than 300 other forms of primarily nonviolent Arab resistance over the centuries.

1936 that caused a six-month closing of the Schools, Annice shared her understanding of the situation in a letter to the Board of Missions:

"About the first, last, and only topic which is thoroughly discussed by all is that of the Arab-Jew situation and the long-continued strike." She continued by citing an article countering Zionist Organization president Chaim Weizmann's argument that Jews were in Palestine as a right and not at the pleasure of Great Britain. The article claimed that Jews had been in Palestine only temporarily—and only by the grace of neighboring powers—and went on to state there had not been a significant population of Jews in Palestine for 2,000 years. Meanwhile, Arabs had called Palestine home for the past 1,400 years. The article also reminded that the Balfour Declaration of 1917 had guaranteed Arab rights, which Jewish claims to the land clearly infringed on.[35]

Annice further described how the Arabs, having resisted for 18 years, were dismayed that Christians in England and the United States actively favored Zionism. She foresaw the imposition of martial law by the British Government. She told of two 17-year-old Arabs sentenced to death for possessing arms; of cities placed under curfew; of the dynamiting of houses in Nablus, Hebron, and Lydda because ammunition had been found or shots fired; and of the destruction of whole villages in the North, as the British seemed intent on crushing the Arabs.

"Arabs are agreed that they cannot carry on another strike," Annice wrote in a subsequent letter. "But, at the same time, they are determined to hold their country from the Jews. The Jews are just as determined to keep on until they gain Palestine as a National Home. All are waiting for the report of the Royal Commission."[36]

That Commission was formed in 1937 as the British authorities had become increasingly frustrated with the situation. The inquiry into possible solutions was headed by Lord Peel (thus, the Peel Commission) and ultimately recommended that the country be divided between Jews and Arabs. The Arabs opposed the plan, as they believed the "best parts" of

---

[35] September 24, 1936, letter to Merle Davis, Annice Carter Microfilm, MR-157, Earlham Friends Collection and College Archives.

[36] June 6, 1937, letter to Merle Davis, Annice Carter Microfilm, MR-157, Earlham Friends Collection and College Archives.

the land would be given away, and the Jewish minority would be given an amount of land much greater than what they currently owned.

The partition plan was not everything the Zionists wanted, but it was far more than what they had, and their response was positive. Arabs, as could be expected, found the partition plan unacceptable and responded with both violent and nonviolent protests. In response, the British arrested many Arabs and exiled several hundred, including many leading citizens. That quieted things for a little while, but writing in a February, 1938, issue of the *Friends Missionary Advocate*, Friends Boys School principal Khalil Totah noted that, while the country was externally somewhat quiet, there was strong internal unrest and that the Palestinian problem was far from settled.

Annice's description of the growing tensions went further than Totah's. In a January 1938 letter to the Board of Missions, she compared the growing British military presence with events in Italy, Germany, Japan, and Russia. She believed the situation was a "boiling cauldron."

> We are still having retaliating murders and bombings. We are expecting a little disturbance in Ramallah now, because an elderly Jew who has lived in Ramallah for many, many years was shot last night and is in the hospital in serious condition. Rumors are conflicting, with some believing it was a Muslim attack for there being a Jew in Ramallah, and others holding that it was in retaliation for a mother killed in a Jewish bus bombing several weeks ago. You can hardly imagine the feelings of hatred and injustice that seethe in the hearts of the Arab people. Neither can you imagine the terrible fear that fills the heart of each Jew. Jews we talk with feel that Arabs are heartless and ignorant heathens. Arabs, on the other hand, consider Jews as greedy and grasping.[37]

Annice's comments appeared in that fall's issue of the *Friends Missionary Advocate*, with the additional note that the Schools were still carrying on with good enrollment and that she believed they were building better citizens for Palestine. The Schools, she said, strove to instill in students the Quaker ideals of brotherly love, peace, and justice.

In May 1938 Annice wrote again about the local situation:

[37] January 25, 1938, letter to Merle Davis, Annice Carter Microfilm, MR-157, Earlham Friends Collection and College Archives.

May
1938

The Jews refuse to see any wrong in forcing the Arabs out of their country.
The Arabs refuse to give up their country without an attempt to keep it.
And the English are glad for an opportunity to keep large military forces
in this part of the world. . . . It is difficult to say anything about the political
situation because rumors are numerous, and the truth is difficult to detect.
It seems the whole world is a boiling cauldron that needs to be cooled
with straight thinking and just dealings.[38]

She continued by citing a recent visitor who said that the Arabs say
Allah has promised the land to them, while the Jews say Jehovah had given
it to them. Since the two are one, it would seem that God will have to
settle it with Himself!

But Annice didn't write only political commentary; she also noted that the
cisterns were full and there had been a netball competition at the Girls School!

Annice took a brief break from the tensions of the Middle East by
returning to Indiana during the summer of '38, but those tensions were
waiting for her when she returned in September. She described the
conditions as a bit worse than when she had gone home, and reported
that there had been Arab attacks on the British near Ramallah. But while
she worried about the impact this might have on enrollments, she didn't
feel any particular danger yet.

In the September issue of the *Advocate*, Khalil Totah was pleased to
report that the promised new auditorium was being constructed on the
Boys School campus,[39] but he also reported that the political situation
had worsened. A bomb planted by a Jewish group had killed 40 Arabs
and wounded 50 others. "We venture out of Ram Allah only when we are
obliged," he wrote. "But life here is normal—it is an oasis of peace."

Coming to teach in Ramallah that fall was Nancy Parker (later
McDowell), a recent graduate of Goucher College who would be teaching
biology at the Girls School. Although she spent only one year there, her
2003 book *Notes from Ramallah, 1939* gives a keen sense of the growing
turmoil in the region. Parker's narrative tended to be more descriptive of
the dangers than were Annice's or Khalil Totah's.

---

[38] May, 24, 1938, letter to Merle Davis, Annice Carter Microfilm, MR-157, Earlham Friends
Collection and College Archives.

[39] This was later named the Khalil Totah Auditorium. For a long time it was the largest
auditorium space in Ramallah and El-Bireh.

In Parker's account, Ramallah was becoming a hotbed of Arab resistance to the British, with rebels taking control of the town in spite of the presence of British soldiers and government ministries. British response to the resistance was increasingly brutal. After a British commander was killed elsewhere, 170 houses in an Arab village were destroyed in retaliation. When the fight came to Ramallah, it was even more lethal.

In the fall of '38, a firefight between the British and rebels broke out around the Girls School. Rebels ran through the campus as British machine gun fire was answered by Arab rifles. Teachers and students had to run for cover as bullets whizzed by. At the end of the day, British planes flew over Ramallah dropping bombs that killed 80 Arabs.

As the revolt continued in the region, curfews were imposed on all roads, and land mines were placed in strategic areas. The interruption of transportation meant food shortages in town and at the Schools. Arabs who were caught with weapons were shot. Soon a large number of British soldiers were encamped in Ramallah, with the attendant shooting, flares, explosions, and arrests. Sandbags were placed at windows in the Schools to protect the inhabitants from bullets. By October, there was a curfew in town from 7:00 P.M. to 5:00 A.M. Among the casualties of the fighting was the father of one of the FGS girls.

It was this situation that Annice, Khalil Totah, and others described, in reports back to the U.S., in terms such as "It's peaceful here," "Ramallah is an oasis," and "It's worse in Europe."

In December of 1938, Annice wrote again for the *Advocate*. She expressed thanks for the financial support coming to the Schools and gratitude for the interest in Friends work in Ramallah. She then went on to say, "It is true conditions in Palestine are more serious and critical than at any previous time. We are hoping a just and fair compromise can be made. The Arabs are desperately fighting for what they call 'The life of their country,' and we are hoping Great Britain may realize this." She then commented that school was going along nicely and that she hoped conditions would permit the year to continue without any trouble.

Writing in the same issue of the *Advocate*, Girls School principal Mildred White reported that postal and telephone service had been closed by the British, and that Arab rebels had come to the government buildings near the Boys School and carried off typewriters. An Arab leader had been killed, and in response a general strike had been called. When the father of the Shahla girls at the FGS had fallen ill and needed to go to the hospital, staff at the School spent the whole day trying to help them find some men who would dare to break the strike to get him to the hospital.

Nancy Parker reported that it was unsafe to go into Jerusalem's Old City—Arab East Jerusalem. Light-skinned people were suspected of being the new European Jewish immigrants and were spit at—at best. Even Bethlehem was dangerous, but that didn't keep staff from the Friends Schools from attending the Christmas observances there. The only way they were able to return to Ramallah after visiting the Shepherds' Field worship service, however, was in the British Yorkshire regiment's open machine gun truck! The soldiers had seen the women hitchhiking along the road and insisted that they get on board.

Arab resistance lessened in March of 1939 after a British White Paper laid out a "solution" to the troubles. The British government had grown less supportive of the Peel Commission's partition plan, and the White Paper mapped out a different direction. Palestine would be granted independence in ten years; Jewish immigration would be allowed for five years until it resulted in Jews being one-third of the total population; Arabs and Jews would govern jointly; and no Arab land would be sold to Jews.

Annice reported that the White Paper eventually caused another flare-up of violence, with renewed Jewish bombing campaigns which, in turn, brought a violent Arab response. "And here we are in the same old condition," she wrote.[40] One of the results of the renewed hostilities was the postponement of the annual sessions of Near East Yearly Meeting.

April brought another wave of violence when an Englishman was shot in Jerusalem, which resulted in more travel restrictions and curfews. Arab drivers' licenses were revoked, and Arab leaders were rounded up and imprisoned. Acts of revenge occurred throughout the country.

In May, the Mandate authorities affirmed the White Paper's conclusions, including the restriction of Jewish immigration, and Annice reported, "The Jews have been active since the news was released. They are calling it robbery. The Immigration Office in Jerusalem was bombed and burned. I suppose they are trying to dispose of records so that the thousands of

---

[40] March 1, 1939, letter to Merle Davis, Annice Carter Microfilm, MR-157, Earlham Friends Collection and College Archives.

illegal immigrants cannot be deported. We will probably have a gay time with the Jews for a while at least. We are hoping the Government will see fit to search and restrict the Jews as they have been doing to the Arabs."[41]

Conditions had not improved by early fall of '39, and Annice reported that most of the violence was of Jewish origin, with bombs in one of the broadcasting offices causing several deaths. "Bombs seem so heartless," she wrote. In addition, money was scarce as Arab businesses were affected. Still, Mildred White had held a four-week summer Vacation Bible School, and Annice had held a tennis camp.

With the outbreak of war in Europe, however, conflict in Palestine came nearly to a complete halt as both Arabs and Jews saw cooperation with the British as the best way to realize their hopes. The impact on the Friends Schools was positive. The Girls School had an enrollment of 194 students, increasing to 218 in the fall of 1940. Until the end of the war, Palestine was actually something of an "oasis" while the fighting raged elsewhere.

One of the benefits was an end to curfews, and in October of '39 Annice could report, "Things are going along very well now. We do not have curfew and are inviting the Boys School staff down for a moonlight supper on the Home Economics Cottage roof. We think we may be able to have some social life this year."[42] This was no small accomplishment, given that the Girls School campus was a mile away, literally down a steep hill!

RELIEF WORK

As a result of the extended revolt of 1936 to 1939, which exacerbated other conditions impacting the Arab population, relief efforts began in earnest in the fall of 1939—especially in the impoverished rural villages. In a report to the Board of Missions, Annice outlined what had been done already with funds received from the United States. Clothing and comforters had been purchased; 70 comforters had been made and

[41] May 18, 1939, letter to Merle Davis, Annice Carter Microfilm, MR-157, Earlham Friends Collection and College Archives.
[42] October 26, 1939, letter to Merle Davis, Annice Carter Microfilm, MR-157, Earlham Friends Collection and College Archives.

distributed in villages; and quinine had been supplied to the village of Ain Kinya to combat an outbreak of malaria. She also described the situation of two girls who were unable to attend their Greek Orthodox School. There was a strict school dress code, and the girls had only one ragged dress apiece and didn't have the required black apron. Annice gave them the material and instruction for making the aprons, and they were able to return to school.

On another village visit, Annice and others from the Girls School visited two villages and distributed bags of oranges to the children, a gesture meant to gain the confidence of the sometimes skeptical villagers. In one very hilly village, they were able to convince the *mukhtar* (leader) of the village to secure a donkey to carry the oranges to various houses. While there, they assessed the conditions needing further aid and found sore eyes, untended wounds, and empty olive and oil containers. With cloth and rubbing alcohol, they addressed some of the injuries. "It is hard to describe the conditions," Annice wrote in a letter to the Board of Missions, "because there is nothing in the States for us to compare with them."[43]

During the Christmas vacation of '39–'40 Annice participated in further visits to villages to survey the needs, and reported some of the findings in a February submission to the *American Friend*:

> In one home there was a naked infant wrapped only in a corner of its mother's head scarf. One couple lived in a 5' X 6' hovel with only one straw mat and a dirty comforter; the man's only work was occasional blacksmithing, and he accepted food in payment. A mother and two small children were alone and without support because her husband was in prison for life on account of having a weapon. Another woman's husband had been killed by Arab rebels, leaving her to care for their children and her husband's aged mother. There were many cases of eye disease and blindness. Many women were widows, as they had married young to much older men. There was no money, no work, and no support. The villages had no doctors, and prospects for the people were very discouraging.[44]

---

[43] December 10, 1939, letter to Merle Davis, Annice Carter Microfilm, MR-157, Earlham Friends Collection and College Archives.

[44] February 28, 1940, letter to Merle Davis, Annice Carter Microfilm, MR-157, Earlham Friends Collection and College Archives.

Annice reported that the Schools had distributed aid to 150 families from donors, under the proviso that no aid was to be given to Ramallah families; reliable aid workers visited homes; names of recipients were recorded; and preference was given to widows and orphans.

In an article submitted to *The American Friend* in May 1940, Annice commented on these relief efforts, beginning with references to Matthew 4:25 and Luke 9:1–2, passages that describe Jesus' visits to villages.

"When the first great Teacher and Physician trod these paths and visited these villages, he was grieved by their conditions and tried to change the laws and customs to give them a chance at life." She then reported on the $2,200 received from Friends in the U.S. for relief, but said that it would have no lasting impact unless accompanied by education and a focus on health.

"The oppression of the past centuries, the hardships of the recent disturbances, and the common belief that everything is sent by God," Annice wrote, "have combined to produce a people not strong enough to come through hunger and want with sufficient ambition to seek a better way. Poverty and ignorance always have a detrimental effect upon a people."[45]

While dispensing the needed aid, Annice was reflecting an attitude characteristic of a political belief that she was raised with in her Hoosier home: "getting something for nothing" had a tendency to reduce a person's willingness to "do for themselves." In later work for her county's welfare department and in addressing the needs of refugees in Palestine and the poor in Africa, Annice would consistently display this belief. Nonetheless, she was remembered by people in both Palestine and Kenya for her quiet acts of kindness and generosity.

By February of 1941, Annice and the School's relief work had realized one of their goals. After long negotiations with the British authorities, they succeeded in opening a health clinic in the village of Beit Ur near Ramallah. A nurse had been appointed, and Annice was pleased that her home economics students were writing term papers about child care that they would be presenting to mothers in the villages. Those students were also helping her care for a newborn whose mother had died three days after

[45] May 3, 1940, letter to *The American Friend*, Annice Carter Microfilm, MR-157, Earlham Friends Collection and College Archives.

childbirth. Annice wondered, though, if it would be kinder to let the infant die rather than be subjected to the hardships of village life.

THE FINAL MONTHS BEFORE
LEAVING RAMALLAH IN 1941

Although Annice had been granted a furlough, it was not clear whether she would be returning home in the summer of '41. Two matters complicated the decision. For one, as the European war increased in intensity, the Board of Missions was recommending individual discretion among its missionaries regarding evacuation. For their part, the missionaries in Ramallah had decided to stay in Palestine for the time being. In a letter to Annice's father, Merle Davis shared that report but added, "We take it, however, that Annice will be coming home on furlough this summer."[46]

Annice was not so sure. The other complicating factor was the escalating cost and complexity of transportation during wartime. In just a few years, ticket prices had quadrupled. Passage over the normal routes was restricted because of the war, and Annice did not want to be stuck in South Africa or India for weeks, waiting for a ship to come. "I would rather be stranded here," she wrote to Richmond.[47] She was willing to forgo her furlough in favor of the Totahs. Furthermore, she was hesitant about leaving, as were so many others, since it would leave the School short-staffed. She confessed that the only reason she was eager to return home was because of the failing health of her father. But she wasn't sure how he was doing, as he had dictated that his health was not to be discussed in letters to Annice.

The issue would soon be resolved.

---

[46] June 19, 1941, letter from Merle Davis to Charles Carter in Russiaville, Indiana, Annice Carter Microfilm, MR-157, Earlham Friends Collection and College Archives.

[47] July 22, 1941, letter to Merle Davis, Annice Carter Microfilm, MR-157, Earlham Friends Collection and College Archives.

CHAPTER 5

Annice at home between 1941 and 1957

In September of 1941 Annice received a cable that her father was ill and wanted her to come home. The news set her in motion to arrange departure as soon as possible.

"Soon" was difficult. The war complicated everything, and communications and travel options weren't what they are today. As a U.S. citizen living under British occupation she had to get permits in Jerusalem from the U.S. Consulate and the British Administration, arrange transportation on military conveyance that allowed limited seating for civilians, obtain the paltry amount of U.S. currency the British were allowing out of Palestine, and pack her luggage not only for the three seasons she would experience in her long voyage but also to account for the possibility that the military aircraft might have to dump luggage if required to lighten the load in a war zone.

Being Annice, she got it done, but not without many difficulties. The first was getting the cash needed out of Barclays Bank in Jewish West Jerusalem. She was at the bank early on a Friday to get the funds needed for her flight the following Tuesday. The teller said her money would not be ready until Tuesday morning, as the next day was the Sabbath, and the bank was closed Sunday and Monday for a "bank holiday."

"Oh, no," said Annice. "I have to have the money now. When does the Central Exchange [the clearing house for cash transfers to banks] close?" She was told 12:30 P.M. that day. "You will have my money in two hours," directed Annice.

Annice left the bank at 12:45 with her money!

But on the appointed day when she returned to Jerusalem to check in with the Cook Travel Agency, she was told her seat had been canceled, and she would have to wait another ten days. Returning to Ramallah, she occupied herself sewing blackout curtains, helping in the office, and assisting with other duties at the Girls School.

Finally, two of her colleagues drove her to Tiberias, where she boarded a sea plane that had landed on the Sea of Galilee. The first leg of her flight took a circuitous route to avoid German attacks and landed on the Nile in Cairo. She then hop-scotched across Africa in another military plane, seated initially next to a British Major who had been on one of the last boats out of Dunkirk, had barely escaped death on Crete, and had been fighting Rommel in North Africa. He was on his way to drive the Italians out of Abyssinia.

It took five days to get from Cairo to Capetown, South Africa, on account of re-fueling and planes not being able to fly at night when bombers were in the air. Although often terribly ill from "evening land sickness," altitude sickness, and the heat, she maintained her self-deprecating sense of humor. When the plane made a sudden descent from 7,000 feet to a few hundred feet, she told the steward, "People who know me are aware that I do not like sudden changes." And of her night in Khartoum, she said, "I always thought that the description of Hell was based on the Jordan Valley in August. I now know that it is Khartoum in October."

Annice enjoyed watching Africa's big game from the plane as the pilot would fly low for passengers to see, and she enjoyed the intrigue of the various places they stopped for the night. One of the stopovers was in Kisumu, Kenya, where she tried to contact staff of the Friends Africa Mission in the Western Province. She was unsuccessful, but some saw her name in the hotel registry a while later and wondered why she hadn't come to see them!

In Capetown she waited in a hotel room for the cable that would inform her that the ship had arrived in port for her trans-Atlantic trip. When it did arrive, it was the New York, the ship a steward on her plane had pointed out to Annice as her probable next conveyance.

Zig-zagging across the ocean to avoid German U-boats, Annice finally arrived home, where she was able to help care for her father in the last two years of his life.[48]

---

[48] Details of this harrowing journey are in a March 1942 letter Annice sent to family. The summary here hardly does justice to the challenges she faced on the trip. Her journey from Ramallah to Capetown alone is described in seven single-spaced typewritten pages. Sadly the remaining pages about her journey home from South Africa have been lost.

INITIAL ACTIVITIES BACK IN INDIANA

Annice reported to the Board of Missions that she had arrived home after the long and harrowing journey and was looking forward to a December 7 visit to Russiaville by Merle Davis, the Administrative Secretary of the American Friends Board of Missions. He would be attending the Honey Creek Quarterly Meeting of Friends. Annice noted that her father was a bit better but not able to walk or help himself much. Later, Davis wrote to her that he had enjoyed the visit, meeting her parents, and having a long discussion with her. Evidently, that conversation had something to do with Board of Missions business, as he said he would look forward to seeing her at the upcoming Executive Committee meeting in Richmond. She would, indeed, eventually become a member of that committee.

While home, Annice continued to work on treasurer's reports for the Mission, covering the last months she was in Ramallah, and began to receive invitations to speak in Friends churches. Merle Davis had written to the Friends meetings of Western, Indiana, and Wilmington Yearly Meetings about her availability, and the responses came in abundance. By March of 1942 Annice could report that her speaking schedule was "breathtaking." She did, indeed, speak throughout Indiana, into Ohio, and as far afield as Tennessee and Iowa. She was in demand for youth conferences and missionary society meetings.

Annice's father Charles died of bone cancer in April 1943, and Annice remained in Russiaville to live and care for her mother in the farmhouse that Charles had built on the edge of town when he turned the home place over to Annice's brother Walter. Annice's other brother, Oakley, lived next door and continued to farm the land that he and Charles had purchased together.

Conditions were challenging at home, not only owing to her father's illness. Wartime rationing had started and it was challenging for Annice to find substitutes for scarce food items. On the farm tires had to be carefully maintained, as rubber was needed for the war effort. The draft had taken some of her younger nephews off their farms to do conscientious objector work, while older ones received deferments for their agricultural work. It wasn't uncommon for yellow paint to be splashed on telephone poles and fence posts near those farms where there was suspicion of "cowardice."

Descendants of Charles and Milley Carter in front of the homeplace in Russiaville, Indiana, in the early 1940s. Annice is the fourth from the right in the third row.

Annice wrote letters to her nephews to encourage them in their stance as conscientious objectors.

Although she remained on the farm, Annice did not have a hand in the farm work. Instead, she took a job with the county welfare office in Kokomo, eight miles away. In a May 28, 1945, letter to Levi Pennington, her friend and former Pacific College colleague, she noted that she was staying busy with that employment and was being introduced to child welfare work. Commenting on the latter, she wrote, "I have great sympathy with numbers of our children in their efforts to overcome the influence of inefficient parents."

In the same letter, Annice shared that she was keeping in touch with "some of the girls at Pacific," and went on to say, "I can't seem to feel much encouraged about present trends such as the San Francisco Conference [a conference of countries that fought against Germany and Japan, at which a Charter of the United Nations and a Statute of the International Court of Justice were agreed upon], the renewed effort for permanent military conscription, etc. Also the threatened uprising against the French in Syria."

By 1945, Annice was beginning to receive requests to return to Ramallah. Principal Victoria Hannush was scheduled for a furlough, and Annice was asked if she could come for a year. She had her mother's permission, and Annice said that she would be willing to cover her own travel expenses, consistent with a short-term appointment. With wartime

Annice ca. 1950s.

travel still difficult, however, it was decided that Annice should wait a year and come in 1946.

When the request resumed in 1946, Annice replied that if an answer were needed immediately, it would have to be negative. Care for her mother would have to be decided by the whole family, and she had accepted several duties in Western Yearly Meeting. She told the Board of Missions that she would be praying for wisdom and guidance. Nonetheless, in a July meeting the Executive Committee of the Board approved her return, and Merle Davis wrote to her, "Are you ready to give us your reply? We very much hope that you will return to Palestine early this fall."[49]

[49] July 23, 1946, letter from Merle Davis, Annice Carter Microfilm, MR-157, Earlham Friends Collection and College Archives.

Annice with her siblings in the 1950s. l-r: Annice, Oakley, Achsa, Walter, and Nora.

Milley Carter and her children in the early 1950s. Front row l-r: Oakley, Milley, and Annice. Back row l-r: Nora, Walter, and Achsa.

Annice at her parents' house in Russiaville, ca. 1950s.

Annice responded, "I am very sorry to report that I have been unable to get favorable support from my family to allow me to feel free to return to Ramallah."[50] She went on to ask that her name be removed from the list of candidates. It made her sad to do so, she said, as it was difficult to choose between two duties. She still hoped to return to Palestine someday, but for the time being she believed it would only be on a personal trip to bring back her trunks.

ACTIVITIES FOLLOWING HER DECISION NOT TO RETURN TO RAMALLAH

Annice wrote in her January 1, 1950, Christmas letter that she had a Jewish assistant in the welfare office who expressed a love for Christmas, and when Annice asked her how that could be, she was told that it no longer had religious significance. That prompted Annice to look for evidence and found that most Christmas cards and decorations featured holly, evergreen trees, reindeer, and Santa Claus rather than scriptural references.

After sharing more about the secular nature of the holiday festivities, Annice went on to write, "Perhaps you can tell that six years in the Howard County Department of Public Welfare has done something to my thinking. I am concerned about the part the Church has played in bringing about the present condition: delinquency, lawlessness, lack of personal integrity, increasing use of alcoholic drinks, the desire to get rather than give. . . . If through our laxness, we have helped produce the above, then our responsibility is great to do something about it."

Ending this 1950 Christmas letter, she commented that she was still living at home with her 83-year-old mother and, in spite of many job offers in other places, considered it her duty to stay at home. That duty ended with her mother's death on February 2, 1955.

In her December 7, 1956, Christmas letter Annice mentioned having taken a "part-time" job in Kokomo at Cuneo Press, the press that printed *Good Housekeeping Magazine*. Although supposedly part-time, her work proof-reading averaged 40 hours per week!

---

[50] July 24, 1946, letter to Merle Davis, Annice Carter Microfilm, MR-157, Earlham Friends Collection and College Archives.

Annice outside Russiaville Friends in the early 1950s with pastoral minister Bill Wagner.

Annice was also kept busy doing "pulpit supply" for Friends meetings without pastors, continuing to do guest speaking at Quaker gatherings, visiting Friends meetings and the Friends Academy in Tennessee, attending the conference of the United Society of Friends Women (USFW), and serving on the USFW executive committee. Additionally, she was the editor of *Friends Missionary Advocate* magazine from 1952 until 1957 and served on the American Friends Board of Missions. Attending the Missions Board meetings in Richmond, Indiana, afforded her the opportunity to connect with former colleagues from Ramallah.

FINAL MONTHS BEFORE RETURNING TO RAMALLAH

In January of 1957 Annice moved to Georgetown, Illinois, to live in the Friends Meeting parsonage in lieu of a pastor and to serve the Meeting as Pastoral Secretary while another minister brought the Sunday sermons. While there, she received a request in April from the Board of Missions to return to Ramallah. Interim Administrative Secretary of the Board R. Ernest Lamb wrote that Friends Girls School principal Anna Langston's father was very ill, and Anna needed to return home.

Annice responded that it would be difficult for her to arrive in Ramallah before the end of the school year in order to overlap with Langston. As with other civilian travelers, her passport had been confiscated in 1941 to ensure that she would remain in the U.S. and out of a possible war zone. Annice was further concerned that she was not a school administrator. "The only thing I can hope to do is to hang on and sit tight and attempt to hold things together until permanent workers return," she wrote. "Although I have a deep desire to return to Ramallah and to observe the present situation, I certainly am not looking forward to the experience at this particular time."[51]

Addressing the assumption that she shouldn't have much trouble returning to the Girls School, given her previous experience there, Annice noted that so much had changed in the intervening years that she would be like a new person there. She expected to do the best she could with the advice and counsel of others, "and I am aware that I will need plenty of counsel."

On June 10 Annice received a letter from the Board of Missions saying simply, "Hooray. You have your passport!!!!!" But then on June 26 the Board wrote to Georgetown Friends saying that Annice couldn't leave yet. They had been unable to find transportation for her before September. It was beginning to look like the summer of 1935 all over again.

Then on July 1 Annice received a letter from the Board saying that their travel agent was holding a cabin on the S.S. *Excalibur*, sailing August 9 and due in Beirut August 28. The cost would be $515.00 plus $2.00 tax. Lamb told her that the Board would cover her travel expenses above whatever USFW might offer.

But even those travel arrangements would change. Annice instead sailed July 26 on the S.S. *Exeter*, and on August 15, 1957, she was back in Ramallah.

---

[51] April 15, 1957, letter to R. Ernest Lamb, Annice Carter Microfilm, MR-157, Earlham Friends Collection and College Archives.

CHAPTER 6

Events in the Middle East
while Annice was home

The relative calm in Palestine during World War II masked plans already underway on the parts of both Zionists and Arabs to force the British out and realize their respective national dreams. With the end of the war violence erupted again. As with the second Arab Revolt of 1936 to 1939, the cycle of attacks and reprisals led to terrible bloodshed and acts of terrorism. The difference in post-war Palestine, however, was that the Zionist forces were well-trained, well-equipped, well-funded, strategic, and motivated by the horrors of the Holocaust. They also far outnumbered any organized Arab response.

The British Mandatory government tried in vain to root out the insurgents, arresting and executing many. In response to one such action, on July 22, 1946, a Zionist underground paramilitary group, the Irgun, led by future Israeli Prime Minister Menachem Begin, bombed the wing of the King David Hotel in Jerusalem that housed the offices of the British administrative headquarters. Ninety-one people were killed, including a 1945 Friends Boys School graduate, Charles Mogannam.

With violence escalating, the British government announced in February of 1947 that they would be leaving Palestine and would let the United Nations (UN) determine its future. In November, UN Resolution 181 called for partition—a repeat of the Peel Commission's recommendation. The plan for dividing Palestine into a Jewish state and an Arab state was rejected by the Arab League and the Arabs of Palestine. In their eyes, it was unfair to create a Jewish state on 56% of British Mandate Palestine when Jews made up 33% of the population and owned far less than 10% of the land.

British withdrawal was set for May 14, 1948, and in anticipation of that date both Zionists and Arabs set about to improve their chances in the aftermath. More terrorism, more bloodshed, and on both sides more fear

Nakba

of possible annihilation. In the fight for Palestine, the Zionist forces had the advantage—and a plan, Plan Dalet, which outlined the intended expansion of lands the UN Partition Plan would allot to a Jewish state.

Part of Plan Dalet was to punch a corridor through to Jerusalem from the coastal plain. In the UN plan, Jerusalem was intended to be an international city, not claimed by either side. To create such a corridor, many Arab villages had to be cleared of their population, and one way to do that was through terror. On April 9, 1948, fighters from the underground Zionist groups Irgun and Lehi (led by future prime minister Yitzhak Shamir) massacred the village of Deir Yassin on the outskirts of Jerusalem. More than 100 men, women, and children were killed, with a warning to inhabitants of other villages that the same fate would befall them if they didn't abandon their homes. Nearby Lifta heeded the warning, and residents fled. In 2023 the abandoned buildings of Lifta still stood as a stark reminder of those dark days. Deir Yassin was razed, and the Jewish suburb of Givat Sha'ul occupies that site today.

On May 14 as the British Mandatory authority lowered its flags, David Ben Gurion announced the establishment of the State of Israel in the partitioned areas of Palestine and those places conquered by Zionist forces. The United States was the first country to recognize the new state. May 14 is celebrated in Israel as Independence Day and observed by Palestinians as *Nakba Day*, "The Disaster."

A year of fighting ensued, as what became the Israel Defense Forces continued to press for additional land, and armies of the Arab League sought to protect Palestinian Arabs in harm's way and stop the advance of the Israeli military. Most of the American staff at the Ramallah Friends Schools were evacuated, some going to the Gaza Strip, where AFSC had been asked by the UN to respond to a crisis as Palestinian refugees flooded into the Strip. AFSC also assisted Jews who were affected by the fighting. Eventually the AFSC work in Gaza was replaced by the United Nations Relief and Works Agency (UNRWA).

School staff who stayed behind in Ramallah worried about being caught up in Zionist terrorist operations and were relieved by the arrival of the Arab Legion, British-trained forces from Transjordan. Although these were no match for the Israeli forces advancing into some areas of the

1949

EVENTS IN THE MIDDLE EAST WHILE ANNICE WAS HOME

partitioned Arab territories, they did keep Ramallah safe and occupied East Jerusalem as Israel claimed West Jerusalem.

During the first months of the fighting, Friends Schools facilities were pressed into service as a hospital, offices for the Arab Medical Association, and housing for refugees. The Friends meetinghouse in Ramallah became home to nine families totaling 58 persons, even though there were no kitchen or bathroom facilities. For two years the meetinghouse remained in use as refugee housing and a temporary school. Remarkably, in spite of ongoing hostilities, the school year started as usual in the fall.

As Israeli forces sought to establish a Jewish state, refugees flooded into Ramallah and other West Bank towns and villages. Eventually 750,000 Arabs were forced to flee their homes. Until the 1960s, those remaining in the territory that became Israel were held under martial law. More than 530 Arab villages were "depopulated," some by massacres such as Deir Yassin and, later, Lydda. Others were left vacant through the threat of slaughter, voluntary abandonment in the hope of returning after the fighting, or "temporary" displacement as Israeli army units occupied villages for strategic purposes. "Temporary" almost always became permanent.

When separate armistice agreements were signed in 1949 between Israel and the countries of Egypt, Lebanon, Transjordan, and Syria, Israel's territory had increased. Israeli forces occupied an additional 22% of Palestine, including the western part of Jerusalem and the corridor leading to it from the coastal plain. Egypt occupied what was left of the Gaza Strip, and Transjordan occupied East Jerusalem and the reduced West Bank. As a result of the fighting, Israel lost more than 6,000 troops; the Arab armies' losses were 3,700; and there were 13,000 Palestinian casualties, mostly civilians.

Ralph Bunche, the U.S. diplomat who mediated the armistice agreements, was awarded the 1950 Nobel Peace Prize for his work. In a private conversation with Israeli pacifist and former kibbutznik Joseph Abileah, Bunche admitted that the Partition Plan had been a disaster and that the UN should have pursued Abileah's suggestion of a confederation of Arab states and a Jewish state.[52]

[52] Related by Joseph Abileah to Max Carter in Ramallah in 1971. In 2014, Abileah's 2x grand-niece Rae Abileah co-led an Interfaith Peace-Builders trip to Palestine and Israel with Annice Carter's 2x grand-niece, Maia Carter Hallward.

71

Following the armistice, all the countries involved consolidated their holdings amid persistent tension between Israel and the Arab states. With Egyptian leader Gamal Abdel Nasser seeking to solidify his stature as a leader of Arab opposition to Israel, hostilities simmered between the two countries. With the addition of Cold War intrigues and Soviet influence on Egypt and Syria, the region was once again a tinderbox.

In 1956 Egypt nationalized the Suez Canal, setting in motion a crisis that provoked a British, French, and Israeli military response. Israel occupied Gaza and the Sinai Peninsula, and although the three countries' military objectives were largely achieved, pressure from the U.S., the Soviet Union, and the UN led to Israel's withdrawal, and Nasser was strengthened politically. Israel finally pulled out of the Sinai in early 1957.

A few months later, Annice returned to Ramallah, this time as principal of the Friends Girls School. The Ramallah she stepped into was a very different place than the sleepy village she had left in 1941. Swollen by refugees, the village had been transformed into a bustling city. It had expanded into the countryside beyond the 1910 Friends meetinghouse, creating a new, modern business and residential area that extended past the Boys School, melding with the village of El-Bireh.

CHAPTER 7

Ramallah 1957–59

In July of 1957 members of Annice's family saw her off at the Kokomo, Indiana, train station as she began her return journey to Ramallah. In New York she boarded the Italian line *S.S. Exeter*, which she described as all first-class and a rather ritzy way for her to travel. She wasn't used to formal champagne dinners and sometimes forgot to turn over her glass when the steward was pouring the bubbly! On one occasion she let the full glass remain untouched throughout a meal until a woman at the table couldn't take it any longer. She asked Annice if she were going to drink it—and if not, could she have it?! Annice welcomed her to it and observed that this was the woman's fifth glass, and that she became quite "hilarious."

Annice enjoyed the long voyage and the opportunity to sleep into the late morning, relax, read, and visit the various ports along the way. In Barcelona she experienced another encounter with drinking that amused her. Exploring the city with a group of shipmates, she was taken along on a version of "bar-hopping" as they tasted the various wines of the region. Annice turned her glasses over this time and focused on watching people and taking in the occasional folk dance. Commenting on some of the people she observed, she wrote, "A drunken American is just as revolting in Spain as in the USA."[53]

After arriving in Beirut Annice took a plane to Jerusalem and arrived in Ramallah on August 15. She hit the ground rrunning—she was immediately asked to bring that Sunday's message at the Friends Meeting. Afterwards she invited a visitor back to the Girls School for tea and scones, where she was appalled to find that the parlor had a thick layer of dust and that many of the dishes were cracked and chipped. She was quite upset that, as she expressed in letters, the standards had relaxed.

She was also concerned that the School had not been having cake and cookies very often! With a new stove in place, however, Annice saw no

---

[53] Letter, August 7, 1957. Private collection of Sarabeth Marcinko.

reason not to have them frequently. And she very soon saw to it that new dishes were purchased.

Annice also found that much had changed in Ramallah. The village of 5,000 that she had left in 1941 had become a city, its population swollen by refugees from the 1948 war. Ramallah had expanded well beyond its old limits and reached all the way to the neighboring village of El-Bireh a mile away. In place of the narrow alleyways and paths she first encountered, there were now wide streets and lovely landscaping. Where donkeys had been the primary mode of transportation when she came in 1929, there was now a city bus service. Going out at night for the first time after her arrival, she was amazed by the crowds and bright lights. It bothered her that the culture of the city appeared to be changing. "I find that we can no longer call Ramallah a Christian village. Everything is open and going full blast on Sundays."[54] She didn't very much like the change.

But it was more than dishes, cookies, and a changing culture that concerned her as the new principal of the Girls School. She was immediately faced with the problem of replacing a math teacher who had been enticed away to teach in Libya at a higher salary. A kindergarten teacher had become engaged and would soon marry and move to the United States. The teachers she did have were unwilling to take on extra-curricular activities, something the teaching staff had been willing to do 16 years before. Her office assistant had moved to Beirut. The account books were a mess, and she heard that there had been issues the previous year with the administration. Parents were complaining about children who had not been promoted. There were problems everywhere. She wondered what she could take on and what she should let go. When she wasn't being tugged to the social whirl of friends and former students wanting to see her, all her time was being spent in the office with very little to show for it, given the constant interruptions. She was at work by 6:30 A.M. and didn't leave the office until 8:30 P.M. most days.

The first two weeks after her arrival were a great trial. She described the work as "crushing," and it affected her nerves and digestion. Becoming sick to her stomach one day, she fainted in the bathroom, fell, and broke a front tooth. Still, Annice's humor showed through. In letters home, she noted that her hair usually became oily when she was under stress, but it

[54] Letter, August 18, 1957. Private collection of Sarabeth Marcinko.

Annice with her home economics class, late 1950s.

didn't in Ramallah! She credited the soft cistern water and noted that she hadn't washed her hair in two weeks.

But with school to start in mid-September, she hunkered down and attended to all that needed to be done: rearranging schedules to compensate for the missing teachers; instructing two little-employed men on the staff to sand, paint, and varnish desks and chairs and whitewash classrooms; and collecting fees and convincing some families on scholarship to pay more as she learned of their improved financial status.

Finally, the School opened with 320 students. It remained hectic, but a routine settled in. In addition to her office work as principal, each week she taught eight hours of home economics and one of Bible. Though she was not one of the "dorm duty" teachers, she still felt a responsibility for the boarding section and checked regularly on the students, dealing with sickness, bed-wetting, and weekly clothes washing. There were the ongoing obligations of balancing the books, collecting fees, dealing with parental complaints, and even once having to calm an angry Saudi Arabian Vice-Consul when his son was being sent back a grade. Annice prevailed.

There were periodic electricity blackouts to deal with, and wood to buy for the fires that heated water for weekly baths and clothes washing. As the cold and rain descended in late fall, temperatures in the low 40s greeted Annice when she went to the office in the morning, but fuel was too expensive to have regular heat. She relished her hot water bottle and blankets at night—but chilblains were a constant companion. She dreaded the easterly winds that brought the coldest weather.

Preparations for a Thanksgiving meal served by Jelileh, the School cook, provided a welcome break, as did helping with the various Christmas programs. The week of holiday that she took after Christmas was a blessing, but she quipped that it would have been more wonderful if she hadn't kept remembering all that needed to be done.

Annice reported that the first week of the new semester went well, even with a new project of opening an English-speaking school at the Girls School. This came about in response to the needs of children of workers at an oil drilling company from the United States. The major problem was that the children didn't like the local food and wouldn't eat vegetables. Annice chalked it up to their being from Texas.

There were other issues less taxing than those that had greeted her first few weeks as principal. But one she had to deal with was taxes! She needed the help of a man in the government tax office to calculate the Jordanian withholding rules. Another was the surprise visit of representatives from the Department of Education. Annice treated them to hospitality that included letting them smoke, serving Arabic coffee, and giving them a full tour. They left satisfied.

Another time government inspectors came to the School, concerned that classes up to third grade mixed boys and girls. Annice responded to them that the boys were unaware of girls until about the age of 16—and then the task of the School was to try to keep them out of each other's way!

While the semester was off to a good start, Annice did admit that it had been unwise for her to take on teaching four classes amid the ordeal of collecting fees, dealing with what she considered an over-emphasis on grades, and handling the recurring problems of running a boarding school. She was resigned to the task, however, commenting that "This school and its problems will be here long after I am gone." She did get some relief from her workload when Evelyn Smuck, the wife of the Boys School principal, volunteered to teach two of her home economics classes.

February brought a special outing with the boarding students to Jericho and the Dead Sea. Annice had the girls pay a little of the cost of the excursion, and she covered the rest herself. She also covered most of the

Annice at the Dead Sea with her students, late 1950s.

expense for the *knafeh*[55] dessert the students wanted for the Eid ul-Mi'raj observance. She was less generous about the cost of school uniforms, especially with those who had previously received clothing free but had failed to offer thanks.

Throughout the remainder of the semester, Annice continued to deal with the minutiae of being the principal. She was perturbed by the pettiness of some of the boarders and expressed that she'd "like to shake the socks off of some of them," but she tried to ignore their attitudes. There was a concern that discipline at the School had slipped, harming its reputation. She wanted to change the emphasis on rote memorization. There was work to be done on appealing to donors in the U.S. for scholarship funds.

There were also small victories. Annice had a 9' X 12' concrete platform poured and had students paint the outline of the continent of Asia on it with the various national boundaries. She had the swing set repaired, purchased a new net and balls for volleyball, and made plans to have a see-saw installed. But her attempt to get teachers to lead the girls in calisthenics was a flop. She decided to get upper-level girls to lead them the next year. More successful was her institution of supervised co-ed mixers and social evenings to teach "courtesy."

[55] An iconic Palestinian dessert made with spun pastry, soaked in a sweet syrup and rose water, and layered with hot cheese and topped with nuts.

The semester ended with a July graduation, but Annice was perturbed by the stiff petticoat that one graduating girl wore as she sat on a high platform in the front row of chairs! The petticoat wouldn't bend over her knees. "Yes, I know I'm getting old," Annice admitted.

Still, affection for her students was evident in Annice's writing. She was proud of the School's history of serving the educational needs of girls, both Christian and Muslim, and noted that with the addition of the Boys School in 1901 the Friends Schools had helped develop high educational standards in the country and had sent out graduates to take positions of responsibility in a complex society, and to stand for right and justice. It wasn't just educational standards that the Friends Schools improved. In one letter, Annice reported that one of the graduating girls was already married, and three more were engaged. Education, she said, gave the girls better prospects for offers of marriage.

"Getting old" or not, Annice was asked by the Board of Missions to stay another year. Anna Langston, on furlough from the position of principal, needed to remain in Indiana to care for her ailing father. Annice was sympathetic to the situation, having faced the same thing 16 years before. But she worried that an extension of her assignment would interfere with her hope to spend some time serving in Kenya after Ramallah.

During the summer before the new school year, Annice supervised the painting and plastering of classrooms and fretted over the fuel shortages that meant limits on electricity, over the low water level in the cistern, and over the fact that the political situation in the region had discouraged U.S. teachers from coming. She spent a great deal of time with the financial accounts of the School, and although she claimed that she was not good at keeping books and was careless in financial matters, by the end of the academic year the School had a slight surplus.

The 1958–59 school year got off to a good start. Enrollment was again good, but this did mean that some classrooms had 38 students. There were continuing concerns about the shortage of water, and fuel was still too expensive to justify using heaters when it turned cold. What fuel Annice could afford was needed for cooking. By December, however, she "weakened" and brought out a kerosene heater for the staff room. Later in the year, she also gave in to heating the library so that students, who had been suffering from chilblains and swollen feet, could study there during exam week.

Something else was heating up, too. A teacher had developed a "crush" on Annice and was making up stories about going out dancing with her. Sharing this news in a November letter, she proclaimed, "I can't have that rot."

Less personally troubling, but still a bother, was that the local garment factory reneged on making costumes for the Christmas pageants. Annice set to work helping make the costumes herself. She was also bothered by talk of getting a "mission car," which she was convinced would primarily be used by the Boys School staff. And when this car was actually at the Girls School, and the Boys School needed it, Annice wondered, "Do you think the car would drive itself up to the FBS?"

Annice also continued to be upset about the laxness of discipline that had crept into the Girls School over the years. She described jealousy, cheating, and even fighting. "They have gone too far," she wrote.

In spite of the previous school year ending in the black, finances continued to be a worry. Sixty of the 330 students were on scholarship, most of them refugee children, several of whom were also receiving free lunches. UNRWA aid provided only basic staples for refugee families. Nonetheless grateful for the financial assistance funds that did come to the School, Annice wrote to donors, "And may our Master who said, 'Inasmuch as ye have done it unto the least of these my brethren, ye have done it unto me' give you your just reward."[56]

Following the well-costumed Christmas plays, the usual Christmas Eve visit to Bethlehem, and a much-needed holiday break, Annice welcomed students and staff back to the School in January, noting that one teacher was ill, a housekeeper was absent, another staff member had the flu, and there was too little rain. The biggest concern for her, however, was that a Muslim girl had become engaged over the holiday, and she knew that also meant an immediate marriage—to a man the girl had never met before. Annice told the girl and her family that if she wanted to continue to board, she could have no contact with her husband. The girl was fine with that arrangement, knowing that, if she became a day student, she wouldn't be allowed by her husband to complete her education.

Later in the semester, however, Annice softened her stance a little and allowed the girl to go home for an occasional visit.

[56] Letter, December 10, 1958. Private collection of Sarabeth Marcinko.

She did not soften her attitude about appropriate dress for the girls, however. "Swishy petticoats" had come to the region, and students were coming to school in what she described as "fashion plate attire." Some of the parents were appealing for the adoption of a uniform to counteract the expense of the fashionable dress, but Annice was initially resistant. She thought it was not "Quakerly," but she was especially concerned that many of the refugee children were clothed from the bales of clothing sent over by AFSC.

Finally deciding to go with uniforms, Annice found a suitable blue cloth for the jumpers. When the local garment factory wouldn't make them, she set up a "factory" at the School and hired a dressmaker to produce the dresses. Joking about the decision, she wrote, "At the zenith of a girl's attainment, I demand that she appear frumpy and old-fashioned. What a tyrant!"[57]

Later in the year, Annice took on another clothing project. Of it she wrote, "I have known for some time that I have little sense, and now I am showing it again." She purchased 100 yards of blue cotton material to match the uniforms and set up another "factory" with a seamstress to make 165 pairs of shorts to go under the girls' smocks when they were playing games or doing drills.

Annice continued to be concerned about the School's income and found that she had to be tough in collecting school fees. She was willing to be lenient to a certain extent, but after one family kept making excuses about failure to pay for their girls, she pulled them out of their exams and sent them home. The fees arrived later that day. On other occasions, though, Annice quietly used her own funds to pay a student's fees and to balance the School budget.

A little money was also added to the School's coffers through a small business that Annice set up in her office. She purchased Kleenex and girls' sanitary products at wholesale, selling the items to boarders at a little over cost.

The school year ended with a graduating class of 17—and continuing "adventures." A girl was stung by a scorpion, there was a bad case of cheating, and a staff member fell down 22 stone steps. Everyone survived, though, and Annice turned her attention to summer projects of resurfacing

[57] Letter, January 4, 1959. Private collection of Sarabeth Marcinko.

the basketball and tennis courts, hiring staff for the coming year, and working on class schedules. All this while packing to leave for her much-anticipated time in Kenya.

ANNICE'S ENCOUNTER WITH A CHANGING CULTURE

As Annice noted upon her return to Ramallah in 1957, the little village had become a bustling city. Much had changed in the 16 years since she had last served at the Girls School, but there were also sturdy elements of the Palestinian culture that remained. Some disturbed Annice, and others pleased her.

She enjoyed the respect given older people, characterized by her being called *Sit Annesah* (grandmother Annice) by people in the street. But she wasn't a fan of the "force-feeding" so typical of the abundant hospitality. She commented that she enjoyed large, formal gatherings for meals—as nobody was urging her to take more food! She loved attending traditional weddings and watching the graceful *dabkeh* dancing. An economy that couldn't provide affordable heating oil, however, was not a favorite! She complained constantly about the frigid winters, the chilblains, and the freezing rooms at the School.

There were other issues Annice had with the culture. She did not appreciate young men gathering around the gates of the Girls School when the girls were out on the grounds. When she was alerted to this phenomenon, Annice would stay outdoors most of the day. She was also concerned about some of the traditional women's feeling of embarrassment about their own dress in relation to the increasingly "European" dress of others. Two of the mothers of graduating seniors didn't come to a tea celebrating the girls because they themselves wore the embroidered peasant *thobes*.

Other peasant traditions still vied with the increasing modernization of Ramallah. The municipality was widening the streets around the Girls School to accommodate the heavier traffic in the city. In the process, the walls surrounding the campus had to be dismantled and later rebuilt. The problem was that while the walls were down, local shepherds brought their flocks to graze on the grass at the School! Annice found herself playing what she described as a "Cold War" game with the municipality

Annice in the traditional cross stitch *thobe* of Ramallah during her time as principal of the Friends Girls School late 1950s/*early* 1960s.

and the shepherds. Sharing the experience in a letter to her girlfriends in the U.S., she commented, "Oh, gals, this is a great life."

The major change, of course, was the flood of refugees resulting from the *Nakba*.[58] Even in 1957 many of the refugees lived in circumstances that shocked Annice. Visiting the home of one of her scholarship students, she found eight children, the parents, and the grandmother living in a one-room house on UNRWA rations. Their Sunday dinner consisted of fried potatoes. Another home was even worse: mother, father, and two children lived in a room measuring six feet by eight feet, with just a curtain for a front door, a metal roof, and no windows. Annice commented that under such circumstances she herself would fold up and quit, and she wondered how she could sleep that night.

It was apparent that the refugee camps were becoming permanent. Israel refused to allow refugees back to the homes they had fled. Tents were being replaced by small one-room adobe or cement houses. Land rented for the camps proved too small to accommodate the expanding population, and the camps were becoming crowded and unsanitary with no infrastructure to handle the numbers living there.

Annice found it discouraging and marveled at the physical and mental fortitude of the refugees. She wondered if there must be a spiritual quality that came to their rescue and gave them strength. But she also remarked on the problem of fathers losing their authority as the bread-winner of the family when the families had to depend for food on UNRWA rations. As a result of this loss of self-respect, many men had become abusive. Annice noted that some of the girls from these abusive situations were on scholarship aid at the Girls School. "I would not have you think that all the problems of this country are economic solely," she said. "But economic problems do bring others even more difficult to solve."[59] Her experience in the Howard County Welfare Office manifested itself in other observations.

During a visit to a refugee camp in Amman where one of her poorest students lived, Annice again found a home with only one room—and only one bed. But still the mother insisted on providing suitable hospitality. She

[58] While Israelis celebrate the establishment of their state in 1948 the way people in the U.S. observe the Fourth of July, Palestinians refer to their expulsion from what became the modern state of Israel as the *Nakba*—the "catastrophe."

[59] Letter, August 18, 1958. Private collection of Sarabeth Marcinko.

sent one of her boys to get a little *bizir* (seeds and nuts) to offer Annice before the requisite Arabic coffee. Annice ate only enough to be polite, leaving the rest so the children could have a treat when she left.

One way Annice responded to such situations was through her own financial assistance. In addition to quietly covering the expenses of some of the School's refugee children and raising scholarship money for them, she used discretionary funds to respond to their physical needs. On one occasion, she used a $25 gift to purchase a large quantity of panties for the refugee girls.

At the same time, aspects of Annice's upbringing in staunchly Republican Indiana and her experience working in the welfare office in Howard County influenced her response to the refugee issue. She felt that too many had become dependent on assistance. Refugee girls on scholarship expected the same aid year-to-year, even when their family circumstances had improved. She told one parent, a former student of hers, that while she did understand that the woman was a refugee from Jaffa, she also knew that this parent now made more money than Annice did as principal of the FGS! Tongue-in-cheek, Annice suggested that maybe the parent should help her out!

While acknowledging the economic difficulties, Annice believed that it was important for parents from the camps to pay at least part of their students' fees in order to retain some self-respect. Again reflecting her experience in welfare work back in the U.S., she observed that, while some assistance was necessary for the refugees, it was creating a sense that the world owed them a living, and that this was the normal result of charity.

Most of the students at the Girls School, however, came from families that were better off. Annice enjoyed visiting those with traditional olive presses, a family in Nablus that owned a soap factory, and even a properly short funeral observance. She commented that attending a funeral is very trying any time, but going to a Muslim one in a village was almost impossible, given the separation of men and women, the wailing, the bitter coffee, and the length of time the visitation took.

Becoming better acquainted with Muslim customs was another change for Annice. There had been a few Muslim students at the School before, but the influx of refugees brought far more. In addition to Muslim weddings and funerals, there were the Muslim holidays, not all of which she fully understood yet. Of Ramadan, the month of fasting, she commented that shop and office hours were shortened so people could spend much of the day sleeping—and then spend the night in revelry.

Annice took all these changes in stride, but there was one thing she found to be a great tribulation. In a June letter from 1959, she shared the tragedy that in the market all oranges were "GONE"! There were apricots and apples, "but it doesn't take the place of oranges!"

THE POLITICAL SITUATION

When Annice first served at the Friends Girls School, Great Britain held a Mandate for Palestine and was struggling to maintain order between Zionists, who wanted a national homeland, and the indigenous Arab population, which feared that Jewish immigration was a precursor to losing their homeland. She arrived during the height of an Arab revolt against British policies. Annice's second assignment in Ramallah came during the second Arab Revolt, specifically against British immigration policies and the Peel Commission's recommendation that Palestine be partitioned.

By 1957, Israel was not only well-established as a modern state on 78% of what had been British Mandate Palestine, but it was already a military power and an important ally of the West during the Cold War. Jordan's occupation of the West Bank and East Jerusalem was also entrenched. Meanwhile, Palestinian refugees continued to wait for the world to respond to their plight and their desire to return to the homes they had fled.

This was the political reality Annice encountered upon her return, and she was not shy about sharing her feelings about it with her friends back in the U.S. In one of her first letters from Ramallah, she described taking a bus ride along a road in the Palestinian highlands. She could see the Mediterranean and Israel's coastline a mere 40 miles to the west. "I watched the sunset over the sea and Israel, but they could not keep the lovely colors from coming over to Jordan."[60] In October of 1957, Annice related the experience of visiting a Friends Girls School family in Qalqilya on the border with Israel. She watched an Israeli on a tractor plowing a field that had belonged to that family—and for which they had not been compensated. In another letter, she described a trip to the north in Jordan

[60] Letter, September 1957. Private collection of Sarabeth Marcinko.

during which she could see across into the Jezreel Valley and Sea of Galilee area of Israel. "It certainly seems incredible how the Jews managed to get so nearly everything desirable."[61]

Annice was not shy, either, about sharing her perspective with other Quakers working in the area. When a staff person for AFSC's program in Acre, Israel, visited the Girls School for a few days, Annice reported, "We do not get along too well because he is an admirer of Truman [who was the first to recognize the new state of Israel in 1948] and leans too heavily on the side of Israel to suit me."[62]

Annice often related stories of the situation faced by Palestinian refugees as a result of the formation of the state of Israel. Many of the refugees in Ramallah had fled Jaffa, and as was typical of so many Palestinians, they had kept the keys to their houses, assuming they would soon be returning. She wrote about one widow who had packed food for the trek from Jaffa to Ramallah but not family heirlooms. Annice marveled at the woman's ability to laugh about it ten years later.

In a 1958 letter to the Quaker C. H. Greene of Wilmington, Ohio, Annice laid out her analysis of the Arab/Israeli conflict, summarized as follows:

Arabs are antagonistic towards the U.S. for supporting the British in establishing Israel and not opposing partition. Historically, Arabs and Jews lived together as brothers, and when Jews were persecuted in Europe, they were welcomed here by the thousands. But then came the Balfour Declaration of British support for a Jewish homeland in Palestine, even after the Arabs had been promised the region for free Arab states.

When the Arabs became aware of the threat to their hopes, they protested increased Jewish immigration, and by 1922 there were Arab attacks on Zionist projects. They were not against Jews as a people, but Zionism as a movement that was demanding a political state for one religious group. The year 1929 saw the first large-scale violence, and then in 1936 there was a united Arab strike for six months. By that time, however, Jewish immigration had reached such numbers that there was no way to stop it.

Meanwhile, the United States didn't want to take in Jews who were suffering in Europe. But Jews convinced many Christians that the Zionist

61 Letter, July 1959. Private collection of Sarabeth Marcinko

62 Letter, October 29, 1957. Private collection of Sarabeth Marcinko.

movement was the fulfillment of biblical prophecies, and were able to influence public opinion to such an extent that the Jewish narrative, and not the Arab one, came to be the dominant story. Annice commented, "We allowed the Jews to tell us that they were not taking land that was used and that they would be able to get better production and it would really help the Arabs rather than hurt them. It is never safe to take sides until you know both sides."

Neither the Zionists nor the Arabs wanted partition. The Arabs saw no reason to divide the country, and the Jews wanted it all. In the ensuing war of 1948, the Jewish army, supported by Western powers, had munitions. The Egyptian and Iraqi armies were not very effective. Jordan's Arab Legion was well-trained and kept the Israeli army from taking all of the West Bank and East Jerusalem—but they lacked sufficient munitions.

Count Bernadotte was killed when he tried to negotiate a truce during the war, but Ralph Bunche completed that mission. Jerusalem, intended in the partition plan to be an international city, was divided into Jewish West Jerusalem and Arab East Jerusalem. An irregular boundary cutting through the country was not recognized by either side and would be a constant source of trouble. Arabs were not allowed to have any claims to property in Israel, but Jews kept Hebrew University and the Hadassah Hospital in what became Jordanian territory.

Palestinians are close to the land and won't accept compensation for their lost property, anyway. They believe they wouldn't receive a fair price for it, and besides, they want to return. "They dream of a return just like the Jews have kept the dream alive throughout the centuries through their religious ceremonies."[63]

Elsewhere in her letter to Greene, Annice again displayed her deeply rooted Midwestern Republican sensitivities about welfare programs. She was opposed to social welfare that doesn't require something to earn it. That applied, in her opinion, to the work of UNRWA. The organization was doing good work, she believed, but they needed to develop industries. She related how Israel helped their people with well-trained European Jewish expertise and U.S. money. On the other hand, Annice wrote, the Arabs didn't have that technical know-how, and trained people from the Arab world didn't come because the West Bank and Gaza were crowded with refugees.

[63] Letter, February 23, 1958. Private collection of Sarabeth Marcinko.

Annice's comments about the Arab/Israeli conflict were not her only observations on the geopolitics of the region. She became principal of the Girls School just after the Suez crisis of 1956, and she recognized its ongoing effects. Although Egypt and President Nasser had been defeated in the previous year's war, Nasser's popularity had only increased, and he was capitalizing on this with his attempt to unify the Arab states. It was causing some realignment of nations' loyalties, and news of unrest was being noticed "back home." In a November 1957 letter, Annice assured her family and friends that there was no need to worry about her safety. She wrote that things were in good shape in Ramallah, although there were rumors of trouble between Turkey and Syria. Annice didn't think it would affect Israel and Jordan, owing to the importance of tourism to the area. She believed it would remain quiet locally at least through Christmas.

In early 1958, Annice noted the new union of Egypt and Syria, which precipitated a new federation of Jordan and Iraq. She and Boys School principal Harold Smuck were summoned to a meeting in Ramallah to plan a public celebration of the creation of the United Arab Federation. After a delay in establishing the day of observance, the celebration was finally held at the city's *manara* (a traffic circle and central gathering place). Annice was amazed by how orderly it was—and that the event began on time. Of the new political alignment, she commented, "I am quite interested to know what it will mean for us, but no one knows yet. It is quite an experience to be in on the beginnings of such a move."[64]

Annice continued to assure people back in the U.S. that all was calm and safe in Ramallah, while reporting in her letters in the spring of 1958 that there was serious trouble elsewhere, especially in Lebanon and Iraq. Of the troubles in Beirut, she wrote that "it doesn't affect us down here." She was especially confident of that because Israel was preparing to celebrate its 10th anniversary, and "they are desirous of having many tourists visit. It is usually Israel that initiates border incidents."[65]

That confidence continued even through a coup in Baghdad and the July landing of 15,000 U.S. Marines in Beirut to prop up a pro-Western government there. Pro-Nasser forces in Iraq had murdered King Faisal, and the West was worried about Nasser's alignment with the Soviets. Annice

[64] Letter, February 16, 1958. Private collection of Sarabeth Marcinko.
[65] Letter, May 23, 1958. Private collection of Sarabeth Marcinko.

didn't think this would lead to much, as most Arabs didn't favor Russia. Her main worry was that it might disrupt the upcoming school year. While others were fearful of what might happen, she kept writing that it was quiet and safe in Ramallah. Annice was grateful for people's prayers, "but we are okay. It all seems so difficult to believe the accounts of all the unrest and political happenings in the area because it all seems so normal here. The major problem is that the theaters are closed in mourning for King Faisal, and movies are what people depend on for entertainment."[66]

The U.S. Consulate in Jerusalem regularly checked on the Americans at the Schools, something that was easy to do, since the Consul General often attended Quaker worship in Ramallah. There was some concern that U.S. citizens would be evacuated, but Annice felt this would be unnecessary. Nevertheless, she organized a trip to Jerusalem with colleagues to fit in visits to important religious and historical sites in case they were told to leave.

When school resumed in the fall of 1958, Ramallah was still quiet and peaceful. The main concern was food shortages and high prices brought about by the difficulties in Lebanon, Syria, and Iraq. But Annice was also receiving inquiries regarding a *Time* magazine article about a Girls School graduate who had been caught up in the region's political intrigue. Annice acknowledged that a young woman named Nadia, a student at the American University in Beirut, was on trial in Amman for a terrorist bombing in Jordan. Nadia admitted to carrying a bomb intended for King Hussein; but, she testified, she had been tortured, stripped naked, and threatened with rape if she didn't carry out the mission.

Throughout the remainder of the school year, Annice's only concern about regional unrest was what effect the troubles in Lebanon might have on the annual sessions of Near East Yearly Meeting. Friends in Lebanon might be prevented from traveling to the meetings scheduled for Ramallah.

RELIGIOUS ISSUES

Among the many changes in Ramallah since Annice's previous time at the Girls School was the influx of Muslim refugees. It affected the culture of the city, and it also had an impact on the Friends Schools. With a Muslim government in power, the Schools adopted a schedule of Fridays and

66 Letter, July 27, 1958. Private collection of Sarabeth Marcinko.

Sundays off to accommodate both Muslims and Christians, with classes held on Saturdays. Annice was clearly not completely in agreement with the change, but she didn't make a fuss about it since the staff used Fridays for cleaning, giving baths, and other chores. Annice also noted that the Arab history curriculum was really "Mohammedan" history. After using that word in an early letter, however, she consistently wrote "Moslem" in subsequent communications. She didn't indicate why she changed to the preferred term, but evidently she was learning.

Annice was pleasantly surprised when Muslims came to the School on Christmas Day to wish the Christian staff a Merry Christmas. She was also interested to see that it was the Muslim students who took the most interest in decorating the classrooms for Christmas, and that two Muslim girls volunteered to be Mary and Joseph for the pageant. It made an impression on her to see how excited Muslims were about the Christian holiday.

It is not clear from Annice's letters to what degree she had attempted to understand the deeper, spiritual meaning of Islam. During the Muslim month of Ramadan, a period of fasting and introspection, she commented that girls could fast at the School if they had a note from their parents. "The less fuss made about it, the fewer girls fast," Annice wrote. "Most of it is done to call attention to the fact they are good Moslems."[67]

Describing a month-long emphasis for the Young Friends group on how different religions view peace, Annice mentioned that a Muslim boy involved in the program would be presenting how Islam teaches about peace. She admitted that "all I know about their peace principles is that if any man dies in a holy war, he goes straight to heaven. And they believe in spreading Islam by the sword. I am interested to see what Jamil tells us about it."[68]

Although she gave no indication that she ever attended Friday prayers at a local mosque, Annice did interact with a variety of the religious faiths in the region. She attended the Samaritans' Passover feast in Nablus, visited a Baha'i community in Jordan, went to a number of weddings and engagements in different traditions, and even had the Young Friends group do a month-long study of Buddhism, Confucianism, and other world religions. Her commentary on the experiences were often humorous—and

67 Letter, March 8, 1959. Private collection of Sarabeth Marcinko.
68 Letter, November 1958. Private collection of Sarabeth Marcinko.

typically reflected a preference for her Quaker faith. At a Greek Orthodox wedding, however, she noted that the chanting of scripture by the priest reminded her of "the sing-song of the old Quakers."

When Annice was invited to a Greek Orthodox celebration of the baptism of Jesus at the Jordan River, she declined, preferring to attend to tasks at the School. Her colleague Lois Snyder did go, however, and described the ceremony as "dunking" a jeweled crucifix in the water, supposedly making the water holy for a time. Annice said that Lois didn't think much of the ceremony and that "her Quakerism is showing through."

Of the Anglican Easter service at the Garden Tomb in Jerusalem, Annice said that she preferred the Easter worship based on silence at the Ramallah Friends Meeting. It seemed more appropriate to her than the Anglicans' "ritualistic service." She did accept an invitation to the investiture of the new Anglican bishop, commenting, "whatever makes a bishop"— perhaps signaling her preference for the Quaker polity devoid of bishops.

Upon visiting the Saint George Monastery in Wadi Qelt near Jericho, Annnice again stated her Quaker preferences: "It is hard for a practical Quaker to understand why they go to all the labor of building a big monastery on the side of a precipice like that. I am sure that prayers in a more accessible place would go as high."[69]

A feature of the monastery was a cave which was supposedly Elijah's hideout after he fled from King Ahab and Queen Jezebel, and where the Bible describes the prophet being fed by ravens. Annice was fascinated to hear her colleague Wadi'a, the FGS Arabic teacher, give a different interpretation of that biblical passage. According to Wadi'a, the Arabic word for raven is very similar to that for peasant, and she believed that God had actually sent Arab peasants to feed Elijah.[70]

Annice was also often critical of Quakers of a certain type. Hearing about a Friends Meeting in Indiana Yearly Meeting that criticized FYM's missions for not being "evangelical" enough, she commented that nothing in FYM or Quakerdom was ever good enough for them. She identified the

[69] Letter, February 1959. Private collection of Sarabeth Marcinko.
[70] This interpretation is also related by Abuna Elias Chacour, the Melkite priest who founded the Mar Elias Educational Institutions in I'billin, Israel. In the church on the school campus there is an icon of Elijah being brought food by an Arab peasant while a raven looks on from a branch overhead.

Meeting's pastor as having come from a California "tabernacle meeting," referencing the holiness/revivalistic Quakerism that had developed among some Friends in Southern California. Other pastors in the Yearly Meeting, she complained, were coming from colleges affiliated with denominations that also emphasized a holiness/revivalistic theology. "I am completely fed up with the old cry for converts. We have a few missions here who work for converts and get them. Then they are very much like a lot of the people at home who make such a cry about being saved and sanctified but they can do dirty, mean tricks. . . ."[71]

Annice "[didn't] want to set [her] eyes on" anyone claiming to be without sin in a time as complex as then. Concluding her response to friends who had shared the account of this criticism of FYM's work, she wrote, "Now you know how I feel about that tripe."

Annice directed other criticism at local Friends who, she felt, did not display proper Christian behavior. Quite often that behavior was related to "Sunday observance." She was upset when work was being done at the School on a Sunday, and she even criticized the clerk of the Meeting, Jirius Mansur, for seeing people in his medical clinic on a Sunday. When he responded that it was proper to attend to a person's medical needs on the Sabbath, Annice said that he should then contribute his fee to the Meeting. As at other times, she recognized that her attitude was in the minority. "I could live a much easier life if I would only close my eyes to lots of things that are wrong," she wrote.[72]

Overall, though, Annice was pleased with the Friends community in Ramallah and was very active in it. She appreciated sitting in the quiet of the old stone meetinghouse, but she certainly did more than just sit. She led the Young Friends group and was often called on to bring the prepared message in worship. Among her goals for the Meeting was increasing members' understanding of stewardship, and some of her messages focused on that topic. When the weekly offerings increased by a few cents, she was quite pleased with herself.

Worship at the meetinghouse was not her only spiritual outlet during the week. Annice instituted a daily practice of meditation with staff in the parlor of the Girls School. The time began with a reading from the daily

71 Letter, February 7, 1958. Private collection of Sarabeth Marcinko.
72 Letter, October 29, 1957. Private collection of Sarabeth Marcinko.

devotional *The Upper Room*, followed by 10–15 minutes of silence. She hoped the time would introduce the practice to the many new and young teachers who had so little background in Quaker silence.

Annice was also pleased to be able to rub shoulders with some of the leading Friends of the time as they passed through Ramallah and attended Yearly Meeting sessions. Her letters mention Elmore Jackson of AFSC, Landrum Bolling of Earlham College, Herbert Hadley of the Friends World Committee for Consultation (FWCC), the Replogles of FYM, and others. While not commenting on the impact of meeting worldwide Friends, Annice certainly expanded her worldview through such encounters.

Annice's personal faith is revealed not only in her response to other religious traditions and her "old-fashioned" ideas about Sunday observance and abstinence from alcohol,[73] but also in concrete statements about her theology. While her Christianity was definitely expressed more in action than in doctrine, she did have a theology, and she recognized that it didn't always conform to the image of a missionary that many held. When she was asked to do a "missionary emphasis" for a publication of the evangelical Oregon Yearly Meeting, she confessed that she wasn't quite sure how to go about the assignment for those particular Friends.

When people told her that it must be a thrill to know she was walking where Jesus once did, Annice admitted that she often forgot about it in the routine of her work at the School. But she did reflect on the "footprints" of Jesus and the lines of an old hymn, "Judean hills are holy, Judean hills are fair, For one can see the footprints Of Jesus everywhere." For Annice, the important "footprints" were acts of kindness and mercy. "His footprints are found not only in Jordan but wherever we are doing His will and living according to His teachings."[74]

The pastoral countryside of Palestine, though, could inspire Annice. Upon hearing a shepherd's flute once, she reflected on how it illustrated for her the fact that "Jesus shepherded his flock as he walked those hills— and is still shepherding the flock by giving followers inner peace and security through Jesus' calm and protective presence."

[73] Annice's teetotalism was so well known that when the U.S. Consulate in Jerusalem hosted Americans for cocktail and "eggnog" parties, there was always lemonade provided for her and her staff.

[74] Letter, January 26, 1958. Private collection of Sarabeth Marcinko.

In one statement reflecting her Christian faith, she wrote to the women of USFW, "Let me join with you in re-dedicating ourselves to do the will of our Father. And may we all feel constrained to live so close under the protection of His love that we will draw upon that Spiritual Power available to us, so that we will be able to identify those temptations to compromise and do the good instead of the best, thereby becoming living witnesses for our Master."[75]

TRAVEL AND PERSONAL THOUGHTS

When the work in Ramallah allowed it, Annice liked to travel. Sadly, with the creation of the state of Israel, many of her favorite places, such as Galilee, were inaccessible. The political changes in the map of Palestine also affected Jerusalem, and on her first trip there since 1941 she was disoriented by the division between East and West, the barricades, and the new traffic patterns. She had to wander about the Old City for some time until she found the familiar Jaffa Gate, and then she could re-orient herself.

In addition to concerts in Jerusalem at churches and schools, receptions at the U.S. Consulate, and official meetings, Annice attended various religious observances such as the Palm Sunday procession down the Mount of Olives, and visited the holy sites of the three Abrahamic faiths. Her letters home described the pools of Bethesda, the Lithostrata with its etchings of games played by Roman soldiers garrisoned there, the Via Dolorosa and various processions along it, the Holy Sepulchre and its five competing Christian denominations,[76] and the Haram al-Sharif/Temple Mount area holy to Jews and Muslims. On a visit to the Dome of the Rock, she saw the rock from which Mohammad was said to have ascended into

---

[75] Letter, April 16, 1959. Private collection of Sarabeth Marcinko.

[76] Annice described the Holy Fire ceremony of the Greek Orthodox and how the flame that emerged from the Holy Sepulchre on Orthodox Easter was spread to the hundreds gathered in the church and then carried to churches throughout the country. But she didn't go to the foot-washing service on Maundy Thursday, claiming that she was "too busy and too lazy." She also admitted to not understanding the symbolism of the jeweled umbrellas featured in the Abyssinian Easter Saturday night services. Of her observance of pilgrims carrying crosses along the Via Dolorosa and stopping at each "station," Annice quipped that she didn't know how they had determined where Jesus set his cross to rest for a few seconds.

the heavens, and which some believe was a part of the Jewish temple. Under the Al-Aqsa Mosque, she toured Solomon's stables.

Annice also enjoyed trips to Jerusalem for souvenir shopping. She had a favorite shop on the Christian Quarter Road, the Oriental Bazaar. It was owned by graduates of the Friends Boys School, and most of her nieces, nephews, and grand-nieces and -nephews have a string of olive wood camels that she purchased for them there. While not shopping or touring, Annice liked the occasional splurge at a Jerusalem restaurant. One time, she went all out and had a six-course steak dinner with all the trimmings. She justified the indulgence, though, by reporting that it cost only $1.10.

Other excursions took Annice throughout Jordan, including Amman, Jerash, Petra, and Aqaba; to Lebanon for Near East Yearly Meeting in Brummana, and on visits to Beirut, the Bekaa Valley, and coastal towns; Damascus; Hebron and the Cave of the Patriarchs and Matriarchs and the Oak of Mamre;[77] to Jericho for warmth during the cold Ramallah winter; to the caves of Qumran and the Essene "Dead Sea Scrolls" community; and even to a "swanky" hotel on the Dead Sea.

There were the Christmas Eve services in Bethlehem and Shepherds' Field in Beit Sahour, which she claimed were "almost too civilized now for me." Several times, Annice accompanied Friends Schools staff and visitors to the Northern West Bank to see Samaria Sebastia (biblical Shechem), Nablus, and Jacob's Well. She especially enjoyed seeing how new visitors to the site of Jesus' meeting with the Samaritan woman would sit on the lip of the well and scoot around to be sure they sat in the very spot where Jesus sat. Annice would then tell them that the current stone structure above the deep well was several feet above whatever Jesus had sat on!

A three-day vacation at biblical Emmaus afforded time for leisure reading and resting. "I got NOTHING done," she wrote in an August 16, 1958 letter. She went on to say that the vacation must have done her some good, as she was "going full steam ever since" back at the School.

Annice needed the time away from the concerns of her work. Confiding to her friends in the States, she frequently mentioned her exhaustion from the strain of running a boarding school and providing leadership in the Friends Meeting. There was the constant pressure of arranging schedules,

---

[77] About the oak under which Abraham supposedly sat, Annice commented, "Is it really 4,000 years old?"

supervising teachers, monitoring boarders, overseeing meals, keeping the financial accounts, teaching, grading, hosting guests, programming for Young Friends,[78] keeping the minutes for various organizations to which she belonged, including Near East Yearly Meeting, and even worrying about rainfall sufficient to fill the School's cisterns and to assure harvests that would keep food prices low. Her work schedule was punishing, but citing her "old-fashioned" work ethic, she pushed on. "There's no rest for the wicked," she said, "and the righteous don't need any."

When others didn't do their jobs Annice would step in, even sweeping the floors with the distinctive Palestinian brooms without handles—since wood was so scarce. She handled complaints from all quarters, including conferences that rented the School's facilities and expected special treatment. Hosting a UNRWA group once, she fielded negative comments about the food. "We were given only $1.14 per person per day," she wrote, "and meat is expensive. When someone had asked in arranging the conference what kinds of food we would serve, I glibly replied that we would use steaks, roasts, and chops mostly. They must have believed me."[79] Still, to accommodate "fancier" tastes, Annice often spent hours in the kitchen preparing acceptable meals herself.

Suffering from fatigue and nervous exhaustion, Annice experienced occasional blackouts. The tooth she broke when she fainted in the bathroom required several subsequent trips to a dentist in Jerusalem. When she finally went to a physician in Ramallah about her health, he told her she needed to take a week away from the School. In a snide comment to her friends, Annice said that wouldn't solve the issue of the doctor's sister-in-law, a problematic teacher at the Girls School.

Beyond the work at the School, there was also the physical exertion of climbing the hills around the School. There was no escaping the vertical in walking to and fro. The winter cold didn't help, either. Although Annice noticed that the stores in Ramallah were carrying better clothing for the weather, she commented often on the toll the cold took on her. The win-

---

[78] Among Annice's "old-fashioned" ideas was her concern about the socializing that so often was the focus of Young Friends activities. She described herself as an "old crank" in her insistence on careful oversight of the mixing of the boys and girls, having friends from "outside" attend programs, and functions that were not spiritual in nature.

[79] Letter, August 23, 1959. Private collection of Sarabeth Marcinko.

ter cold brought chilblains, and fuel costs prevented her from adequately heating her office and bedroom. After one beautiful snowfall, she commented that the thrill was lessened by the chill of an unheated house. She chided her family in Indiana about being able to rest after the harvest season and warm themselves in heated homes: "If anyone offered me a job with the privilege of a heated bathroom, I would be sorely tempted."[80]

In addition to the travel which took her away from some of the cares and concerns, Annice also found some simple pleasures. She started going to bed with a book after supper, and not getting up until 6:30 A.M. She enjoyed special meals on occasion, particularly with the "comfort foods" from back home. Pork and steaks were especially desired. Even there, however, Annice experienced some disappointment. Going to Jerusalem once for a steak dinner on her birthday, she found she had to settle for chicken. On another occasion, with her mouth set for a Sunday dinner of pork steak and gravy, the School cook burned it. Annice teased her about it, but later apologized.

Dealing with difficulties, Annice displayed a wry sense of humor and a good deal of continued self-deprecation. Although she felt she was not qualified to be principal in the first place, she said that she was fortunate in having followed someone who had not been that great as an administrator. "That is sure good for me. It is not so hard to follow a person who did not do so well."[81] Another time she thanked the women of USFW for their support, adding that she hoped her trial-and-error methods weren't causing too much harm to the School.

At times, though, the pressures got to her, and she "went on the warpath," as she described it. Feeling that she needed to be "more normal," she found comfort in a sermon Harold Smuck preached in worship. Speaking of the common idea of the mild and gentle Jesus, he cited passages indicating that he was also firm, hard, and forceful. "It was a real encouragement to me," she noted, "but I still think I should attempt to reach the mild and gentle standard."[82]

A major blow to Annice was a cable received in July of 1958 reporting that her sister Achsa had died. She tried to go about the business of the

---

80 Letter, February 15, 1959. Private collection of Sarabeth Marcinko.

81 Letter, January 19, 1958. Private collection of Sarabeth Marcinko.

82 Letter, August 23, 1959. Private collection of Sarabeth Marcinko.

School, but felt keenly aware of being far from home and family at such a time. She wanted to go to the Mount of Olives and Garden of Gethsemane for solace. "It is so hard to really believe Achsa is gone. I am trying my best to adjust to it."[83]

Of great consolation to Annice were her friendships "back home." Among "the gals" who meant so much to her, one in particular was quite important. Mina Emily Seidler was from Annice's own ancestral Quaker community and often hosted her when she was on furlough. Annice confided that she thought of Mina Emily "dozens of times a day" and was deeply grateful for her friendship. Although she admitted to unloading on her friend, Annice said it was just what she needed.

Another regular correspondent was Mildred White. She was at the Girls School when Annice first arrived in 1929 and subsequently served as principal for many years. In addition to sharing a Hoosier farm background with Mildred, Annice could share with her about the trials and tribulations of their common experience as principals.

Having extended her time in Ramallah beyond what she had originally expected, Annice learned early in 1959 that Anna Langston would be coming that fall to replace her as principal. Reflecting on her two years in the position, Annice noted with understated pride that enrollments had increased; she had established an English-speaking section for non-native residents; her Arabic had improved to the point of understanding most conversations and being able to speak quite a bit; and that, although when she had arrived in 1957 the Girls School had only about $400 in cash on hand, causing Annice to be worried sick, she would be leaving more than $6,000 in the School's coffers.

It had been a successful two years, but Annice was looking forward to a break and to traveling to Kenya for the experience of Friends work there. As Anna Langston's arrival continued to be delayed through summer, however, Annice kept up the work of preparing for the new school year.

---

[83] Letter, July 25, 1958. Private collection of Sarabeth Marcinko.

CHAPTER 8

Annice in Kenya

In August of 1959 Annice was preparing to leave Ramallah for Kenya, East Africa. One Hoosier Quaker would be replaced as principal of the Girls School by another Hoosier Quaker, Anna Langston. FYM in Richmond had received word from African Friends that they wanted Annice there at the "earliest possible moment." In a letter to the Penningtons, Annice said, "I am glad for the opportunity to go to Africa . . . but I do not like getting ready to go."

THE FRIENDS AFRICA MISSION

The Friends Africa Mission that Annice was entering had begun in 1902 when three Quakers connected with the Friends Bible Institute and Training School in Cleveland, Ohio—Arthur Chilson, Edgar Hole, and Willis Hotchkiss—landed in Mombasa, took a train across the country to Kisumu, and then traveled by foot to Kaimosi. Motivated by the same evangelical zeal that sent Eli and Sybil Jones to Palestine, their intent was to find an area where no other Christian group had established work. Kenya's Western Province was such a place, and eventually the work of these three and others resulted in meetings for evangelical worship, as well as the construction of a saw mill and establishment of hospitals in Lugulu and Kaimosi, vocational and agricultural schools, and a Bible Institute. By the time of Annice's arrival, there were more than 350 Friends schools in the country. The British colonial administration had divided Kenya into four districts, one each assigned to Anglicans, Roman Catholics, Methodists, and Quakers; Friends were assigned the Western Province.

In 1946 African Friends took charge of their own Yearly Meeting, with FYM remaining actively involved. The move towards national autonomy, as exemplified by this change, was not yet being encouraged by the British authorities, however, and from 1952 to 1956 the Kenya Land and Freedom Army engaged in a rebellion against the British. Known as the Mau Mau rebellion, the uprising cost thousands of lives. For propaganda purposes the British characterized the rebels as savages and provided horrific, exaggerated accounts of massacres of Christian missionaries. Those reports made sensational headlines in Western countries.

The rebellion was crushed in 1956, leaving only pockets of resistance. Native Kenyan majority rule was finally established in January 1960, and over the next three years Kenya transitioned to independence, completed in 1963. Once again, Annice was an eyewitness to uprisings, resistance to British rule, and a desire for independence.

ANNICE AT THE MISSION

Through all the years that Annice worked for the American Friends Board of Missions, she developed a deep interest in the work in Africa. She had been disappointed in 1941, during her trip back to Indiana from Ramallah, that although she had a stopover in Kisumu near the Quaker Mission, she was unable to connect with any of the staff. Now was her opportunity, and she looked forward not only to the experience but also to the possibility of a leisurely trip from Ramallah, visiting new places in Africa, and possibly even joining in a safari. The leisurely part, however, wasn't to be.

While still in Ramallah awaiting Anna Langston's delayed arrival, Annice learned that she was needed in Kenya in mid-September instead of the later date she had anticipated. It meant that she had to fly, taking just about the same route that she flew in '41—only without military escort and with more freedom! Owing to disturbances between Israel and Egypt, not unlike the military maneuvers in '41, the plane had to hop from Jerusalem to Amman to Beirut and then to Cairo. Annice was excited to see the Nile in full flood, but even more excited to meet former Friends Girls School students in Cairo. During her layover in the city, Annice was pleasantly surprised that a 1932 FGS graduate recognized her on the street and hosted her at home with several other FGS alumnae.

In an October 6 letter home, she announced, "arrived in Kaimosi, and I'm not worth shooting!" She said that her intent was to keep her eyes and ears open, to talk little, and to try not to make quick appraisals of the work. "But you know me!" she wrote. She did share one clear opinion: "I've been here 40 hours, and am deeply disappointed that I haven't seen a single monkey yet." She was fascinated by the bird life and noted that she had already taken to baking, one of her first products being a Hoosier pineapple upside down cake.

Already, though, Annice was learning of some of the difficulties at the Mission. She was surprised by how large the staff was—and how scattered it was throughout the Western Province. Staff members weren't always fully acquainted with the work going on at the various centers, which led to some misunderstandings. Annice was also experiencing the different sounds of Africa. She was curious about the drumming she heard each Sunday from across the valley. She had heard that it was only a "beer party," but she was curious to know if it might be a religious sect.

Annice immediately entered the social whirl, which she noted required getting used to strong tea that was half milk. Other things were even more difficult for her. "I tell you, this is like nothing I've experienced before," she admitted. A number of the young students at the Mission school were pregnant. The girls collected and ate ants. She wondered if she would ever feel at home. Leaving Ramallah had been more difficult for her than she expected. Annice felt rooted there, and this new situation, in which she had no control over the undisciplined students and the scant supervision of the dorms, was upsetting to her.

Writing to the Penningtons, Annice admitted that she was still "quite ignorant" about what was to be her work in Kenya, although she knew that she was to teach in the Girls Boarding School in Kaimosi, where Pearl Spoon, another American Friend, was principal. She soon learned that her duties would be "and others as assigned."

Part of that assignment was assisting Pearl in the office. She compared her work there with the last part of Matthew 8:9: "Do this, and the slave does it." Annice was an enormous help to Pearl, but she didn't always feel appreciated.

Other duties were quickly added. Shifts of boarding duty and putting the girls to bed required an average of two miles walking at night while checking on the girls in the dorms. Annice tried to get the girls to be quiet at bedtime in spite of all the "tricks" they played to hide their conversations. Annice was wise to them, however, and commented that it was to her advantage that "girls are girls the world over, and there are not many unique tricks."

She also took on study hall supervision, teaching a religion course on famous Quakers, and seventh-grade English—even though she protested that she knew no grammar. At least she did find some amusement in the girls' writing. In Bible class, a girl wrote, "God created Evil out of Adam's rib."

By November Annice's schedule was full: helping with the Christmas play, making costumes, leading field trips, continuing to help in the office, cooking for pitch-ins (sometimes seven in a week!), buying food, cleaning, and even stocking the student canteen and supply cupboard. Her letters home quite often mentioned cooking chicken and noodles, as well as doing a lot of sewing. Given all the sewing classes she taught and the clothes she made for herself, for other staff members and their children, for the girls at the school (she once made all 67 dresses for the girls' graduation ceremony), and for women in the community, she was very protective of her scissors! She shared in a letter that a girl once wanted to borrow them to cut her hair, but Annice gave her an old razor blade instead.

By her second year in Kenya, Annice was carrying an overwhelming teaching load of 35 classroom hours each week: two Bible classes, four sewing classes, one English, one science, and one drama. Coordinating the Dramatics Club meant directing several programs. In addition to her teaching, dorm duty, and assistance in the office, Annice also worked on planning for the annual sessions of the Friends Africa Mission, served on the finance committee, and was the recording clerk for the meetings of the Mission.

Early on she expressed some feelings of hurt about all her work being taken for granted, but in a letter of Sept. 26, 1961, she noted that Pearl Spoon had finally said, "I do not know what I will do when you go home. You have been a great help to me."

It all took a toll. She ended one letter home with, "I think I shall go to bed . . . I seem to get sleepy earlier than usual. Maybe because I am tired."

Annice's work extended beyond the Kaimosi campus. She was called on occasionally to preach, both in the weekly services and elsewhere. When asked to preach on Palm Sunday because she had been in Jordan, she commented, "How much can I get out of walking the same route Jesus did?" At Christmas, she spoke to several thousand in Lugulu, using Luke's text and the theme, "And let us go even unto Bethlehem and see."

She led a rural women's group in sewing and bought thimbles, needles, scissors, a tape measure, and other supplies for the women. Her letters detailed all the corrections of bad sewing she had to make while the women were learning the skill. The rural women were beginning to want to wear bras, and she helped them, in spite of their timidity. Some, she said, "have been courageous enough to ask me to help them make knickers." Annice described, with a hint of humor, some failed attempts by the women at making French seams in their undergarments. But as much as she enjoyed sewing and making dresses, she expressed real envy of the people on staff who received the new drip-dry dresses from the U.S.

Other work involved fund-raising for a student who had been accepted to Berea College in Kentucky and for another who wanted to attend Pendle Hill in Pennsylvania. When some of the girls expressed the desire to earn their own spending money, Annice taught them how to embroider items to sell.

Annice's letters were filled with descriptions of life at the boarding school, which housed 200 girls in fairly primitive conditions. She appreciated eating with them from time to time, as that was the only way she got to experience the local cuisine. Staff meals were "Midwestern." The girls' meals typically consisted of a sweet potato for lunch and meat stew, greens, rice, bread, and tea for supper. She didn't think the native diet had enough protein, fat, or calcium—but it did have enough starch. The home economist in her always came out!

She commented on the practice of the girls going barefoot and not wearing sweaters. Although they didn't mind getting rained on, they were very protective of their hair and put books over their heads if caught in the rain. Most, she said, wanted to go to college in the U.S., but she couldn't imagine them there.

Observing Kenyan life beyond the Mission, Annice described a visit to a teacher in her traditional mud-and-wattle, grass-roofed home, which she found very comfortable. She was amazed that, on the roads and on public transportation, she often saw women carrying 12 to 15 baskets of produce at a time.

As for her own accommodations and food, she expressed appreciation for her roommate Mildred Henry, a graduate of Friendsville Academy in Tennessee. Their living quarters were more modern and comfortable than those in Ramallah, and she relished having a toaster, better-quality beef, and the availability of fresh fish, something she didn't have access to in Palestine, "as Israel took all the coast and the Galilee," she explained. She missed the oranges of Ramallah but was enjoying the strawberries, pineapples, and mangoes.

TRAVEL IN AFRICA

Despite the workload, during breaks and vacations Annice had the opportunity to travel around Kenya, and she clearly enjoyed the experience. Not being "in charge" as she had been as a principal, she didn't feel as tied down as she had in Ramallah.

On a trip to the Great Rift Valley, she noted its contrast with the northern end of the Valley—the Dead Sea and Sea of Galilee with which she was so familiar. She also got to get all muddy pushing the car out of a ditch.

One special outing was a five-day excursion with friends Mildred Henry, Mabel Dorrell, and Mabel Hawthorne via steamer around Lake Victoria, with stops at various ports. While on shore one night, they were able to take in a movie, which started at 9:00 P.M. and didn't get out until after midnight. "Imagine me getting to bed at 1:30 A.M.!" she wrote to friends in the U.S., commenting that the only ill effect of the lack of sleep was that, the next day, she was even less patient with little annoyances.

She described Victoria Falls as "unbelievable; beyond description." Touring the Goli Goli Valley at night, she commented on seeing constellations new to her, including the Southern Cross. Even the new Soviet "rocket" orbiting the earth could be seen.

With friends from the School, she visited Yala Falls in Kenya and Murchison Falls in Uganda; drove to Nairobi and Eldoret; went to Lake Nakuru to see the famous pink flamingos; and, with her friend Lois Snyder, visiting from Ramallah, she flew to the Serengeti Plains in Tanganyika. Her letters described the zebras, hartebeests, wildebeests, gazelles, monkeys, elephants, and giraffes she encountered. She told of one "thrilling experience" of pulling her car to the side to allow a giraffe to pass slowly across the road. On one outing, she told of identifying 64 different species of birds.

Because of all her travels and the need to purchase supplies for the Mission, Annice finally bought a used Ford Anglia, which often suffered from vapor lock. On one trip, she got stuck in the mud four times in 30 miles. With her freedom to travel, she took advantage of as many opportunities as she could, as she noted that she didn't expect ever to be "in these parts" again.

There were also letters from family and old friends to brighten her days. Before her May 13 birthday in 1961, she received greetings from Mildred White, who knew that Annice's schedule would have her on duty at the school on her special day. "I hope the day will bring some lovely thing for you. Something like anemones from Jiffnah [a village near Ramallah] in an empty baklava tin, all pink and white and blue and lavender. That was one of the nicest surprises I ever had on my birthday in Ramallah."[84]

In spite of the enjoyable outings and learning opportunities in her new location, Annice's main concern was the workings of the Mission and interactions with staff. And she was not overly pleased, much of the time, with either. Her initial intent to just watch, listen, and not express an opinion was soon set aside!

OBSERVATIONS ON THE MISSION AND MATTERS OF RELIGION

Annice commented on the quirks of the staff. About Logan Smith, head of the teacher training school who was leading the Mission staff in a weekly study of the Book of John, she quipped that at the rate he was going through it, she wondered if he'd get the whole book finished before the time came for her to leave Kenya! About not being offered rides for the mile trip to the place where those study sessions and other meetings were held, she said it was "thoughtlessness."

But she was especially concerned about how the staff conducted and acted at the regular meetings of the Mission. For one thing, she found the meetings took longer than in Ramallah, where things got done more often in informal conversations. Moreover, she found the Mission meetings tense; someone was always waiting to attack. She missed the more friendly and pleasant business meetings in Ramallah. She was displeased with how high-strung and "flighty" some of the staff were. Over time, she found the meetings becoming less tense, but she was becoming disillusioned with the

84 May 3, 1961, letter from Mildred White, Friends United Meeting Wider Ministries Records.

Mission. As her undefined term of appointment dragged on without her hearing from Richmond about when she might leave, she commented that "they may just want to leave me here to rot."

Annice was also not a fan of the male leadership at the Mission, and refused to be a pushover. In a letter to her friend Mina Emily Seidler, she encouraged her to be the same in her home Friends church: "I know the ways of New London Quaker men. Don't let them determine things." She also made known to FYM her feelings about the staff at the Mission, but admitted to Mina Emily that "I have done most of my opposing sort of under cover, as I do much of my work. I'm also not sharing all the details of the tension here with my family, as some are not as loyal to FYM as others."[85]

Annice's critique of the staff was not limited to the Mission. She was pleased with Glenn Reece as general secretary of FYM, but was adamantly not in favor of Fred Reeve if he were to be considered as the administrative secretary of the American Friends Board of Missions (AFBM). With others on the staff, she was opposed to Reeve's re-appointment to the Mission itself. She liked him personally but felt he was too "ambitious" and tended to "go solo." When he was re-appointed, she was impressed by the staff's willingness to cooperate with him, the work being more important than the individual. Still, she felt burdened by the feelings that the staff expressed to her in confidence about Richmond's staffing decisions, some saying they were upset enough that they were ready to leave Friends. Annice wasn't ready to give up on Friends yet herself, but her critique of Reeve continued.

Annice was especially concerned about tensions among Reeve, Logan Smith, and Herbert Kimball.[86] It was bad enough that Kimball was forced out as head of Friends Bible Institute in '61, leaving a void in leadership as standards declined. Logan Smith and Roger Carter, Head of the Teacher Training College, resigned.[87] She was also "peeved" by Reeve's expressions of delight that FYM was being taken over by "big business men" such as

[85] Letter to Mina Emily Seidler, May 7, 1961. Private collection of Sarabeth Marcinko.

[86] Annice does not go into great detail about the reasons for the tensions, but they included lack of collaboration by the leadership of the Mission and differing attitudes about American/ African relations.

[87] Carter resigned when his suggestion that Africans be included in governance at the Mission was rejected.

Willard Ware and Delbert Replogle—while acknowledging that "there are still some religious folks still involved."[88] Beyond these things, Annice also disagreed with Reeve's assessment that the Africans were ready for freedom.

Her letters detailed changes coming to the Africa Mission, including the combining of the men's and women's teacher training colleges. A high school would be developed out of the intermediate school, and a demonstration school would be built for the training college. A new nurse's home was going up at the hospital, and a search was on for a replacement for the doctor leaving on furlough. The work was too great, she believed, even for two doctors.

To her friends back in the U.S., Annice confided that she was convinced the AFBM should prepare to close the work in Kenya.

So, what were Annice's thoughts on the Mission and missionary work? How did she express herself religiously in Kenya?

At one evening worship service, a Dr. Peter Green spoke about "The Purpose of Mission." Annice was unimpressed, disagreeing with much of what he said. His emphasis was on how missionaries have had to toil and suffer for the sake of mission. Annice didn't think her work had ever required her to give up pleasures and wealth.

When there was talk of opening mission work in Turkana, she was opposed to it, given that there was so much still to be done on current projects. Yet at the same time she felt the Mission was too concentrated on schools, should do more extension work, and should get out from "centers." She believed that each missionary should be required to work with a local group, just for closer relationships and for "inter-racial morale."

It is difficult to figure out Annice's personal religious beliefs. She didn't express herself in terms of "saving souls" or "converting people to Christianity," or even in the typical language of personal piety so familiar in the Wesleyan-influenced Quakerism of her upbringing.

---

[88] The tendency towards appointing successful businesspeople to important positions in Quaker organizations was widespread in the 1900s. Two scholars at the University of Virginia, Isaac May and Andrew Taylor (a graduate of Guilford College), wrote a paper in 2021 entitled "Quakers and Social Power" in which they argue that in the early part of the 20th century, Friends came to prioritize economic and professional status markers in appointing their denominational leaders.

In one of her letters, she noted that Billy Graham was leading a Crusade in Nairobi, but "it's no fun to take these girls to a revival as they always think they should respond to every altar call. I was assigned as a counselor to the teacher training students who went forward, but I foxed them by telling them I would be right here at school and they could counsel with me at any time—and that I would be watching them."[89] By "watching them," she didn't mean to see if they were expressing themselves in "holiness" language, but to see whether they were "behaving" as Annice felt Christians should.

She was not interested in attending the revivals led by Friends Bible Institute students in the area; she felt it more important to support the services at the Mission. Annice was concerned when she heard about new staff arriving who were "anti-modern" in religion.

When one of the girls claimed to be having visions of God telling her that the girls needed to repent, Annice wasn't impressed. She read them Luke 11:23-25 and scared them about the idea of evil spirits wandering about. She compared their "confession" with the "Catholic idea" of "repent and then sin some more."[90]

Annice was upset about the girls doing laundry on Sundays. She took it as a sign that the School's Christian instruction was not effective. "I can't see that we are getting much practical religion across to them, and maybe no theory, either."[91] In an argument with British Friend Roger Carter, she urged him to clamp down on the students who were "breaking the Sabbath" with their washing and ironing, but Carter wasn't that concerned about it. Annice also disagreed with Carter's wanting to loosen restrictions on contact between the male and female students. Annice felt that would be like "throwing them into the deep end to learn to swim." About a prospective teacher at the Mission, Annice said she should be discouraged from coming, as she had attended a beer party and dressed inappropriately.

After her argument with Carter, Annice sewed two dresses on Sunday, calling this "getting my ox out of the ditch," a reference to Luke 14:5. The power had been out for the previous several days, and she had to get them done.

89 Letter, February 29, 1960. Private collection of Sarabeth Marcinko.
90 Letter, July 18, 1960. Private collection of Sarabeth Marcinko.
91 Letter, June 1, 1961. Private collection of Sarabeth Marcinko.

Annice's sentiments clearly bent towards orthopraxis rather than orthodoxy. In one letter, she complained that "some are disregarding Christian standards of behavior." But she had an understanding of what the "Truth" is. Commenting on a visiting Quaker doctor named Frank Lepreau[92] who spoke at the Mission prayer meeting, she noted his belief that we cannot determine absolute truth, using as examples different cultures' practices of polygamy, liquor, and slavery. Annice's rejoinder was that there is, indeed, a way, and it is in the light of the teachings of Jesus. In further response, she led the chapel programs the following week on "truth."

Annice commented about Roger Carter's thoughts on religion: she said she would be speaking at an evening service, but that this would be difficult owing to Carter's disapproval of saying anything definitively. She wasn't impressed with his belief that holding to one interpretation of religious truth smacked of intolerance.

Most of Annice's comments regarding religion were about Christian behavior and not often about particular Quaker expressions of it. But Annice did show frustration when Quaker process was not properly used—even while describing unprogrammed worship at times as "meditation." She was concerned that Mission business meetings did little discernment, with the clerk typically taking too much control over what was approved. She disagreed with the habit of calling for "approval" of items without asking if there were any "disapprovals." She even used the phrase "sense of the meeting" for Quaker business process rather than "consensus." When Pearl Spoon's dog died, Annice suggested a "Quaker-style memorial service"—one gathered according to the practice of silent worship. Presumably, not "meditation"!

Annice was also concerned about Benjamin Wegasa's advocacy for a separation in East Africa Yearly Meeting so as to set up a Yearly Meeting in Lugulu. By contrast, she praised Benjamin Ngaiya as "honest and independent" and was impressed by his belief that Africans could contribute more money to the work.

---

[92] Frank Lepreau was a graduate of Harvard Medical School and was in Kaimosi for two months, seeing if it might be a fit for his interest in serving in Africa, inspired by the example of Albert Schweitzer. He found that it wasn't, especially for his family.

Annice's Quaker world had expanded far beyond the limits of her exposure to the one brand of Friends in her part of Indiana. She attended the unprogrammed worship conducted by the British Friends at the Mission, and she was acquainted with a variety of Quakers who visited in Kenya and Ramallah. The list of such visitors was a Who's Who of prominent Quakers of the time. It included Landrum Bolling, D. Elton Trueblood, and Sumner Mills from her Hoosier homeland, but the nature of her work also brought meetings with a host of international Friends.

That was especially true when she was involved with hosting the 1961 Triennial of Friends World Committee for Consultation (FWCC). As much as she enjoyed such gatherings, she was worried as this one approached. There were 150 people expected. Kenya was in a drought, so the river that provided energy for generating power was too low to guarantee sufficient electricity. Would there be enough food for all those people? She had to make 300 sheets and 150 pillows stuffed with coconut fiber. She was upset by the "101 things" FWCC listed that they needed for the gathering, and wondered who had invited all those people—and who would bear the expense and work. There was also the problem that all salad vegetables would have to be soaked in disinfectant and all drinking water sterilized—even the water used for brushing teeth. Cooking would be done in big tubs over fire boxes. Fortunately, 30 school girls assisted her in the preparations.

Annice was offered the opportunity to be a delegate from Western Yearly Meeting to the Triennial but declined, saying it was more important to prepare the food than attend sessions. When FWCC delegates arrived, she commented on what a "funny crowd" it was, not the least aspect of which was their very diverse requests for tea, coffee, and food. Her girls wondered if they were even Christians, given that some didn't say grace before meals!

In the end, she felt that the Triennial went well, and she was pleased to see such Friends as Douglas Steere, Leonard Kenworthy, George Scherer, Errol Elliott, Oscar and Olive Marshburn, John Pipkin, and Ward Applegate. But she wasn't overly convinced by Fred Reeve's statement that many of the delegates had been converted to enthusiasm about the evangelistic approach to missions: "I doubt if any impression was made on Douglas Steere."[93]

[93] Letter, September 19, 1961. Private collection of Sarabeth Marcinko.

Annice may have used "evangelistic" simply to mean a more Five Years Meeting rather than Friends General Conference" mode of missions. In another letter home she described how she was helping with the revival services at Friends Bible Institute, but commented that Fred Reeve was not attending because he "can't stand the evangelistic meetings." Asking, perhaps rhetorically, she wrote, "Am I seeing clearly or blinded a bit by my own self-righteous pride?"[94]

THE POLITICAL SITUATION

Kenyan politics also occupied Annice's attention. She was keenly aware of the major political changes taking place and worried that Kenya's drive for independence could result "in another Congo." In an October 19, 1959, letter to the Penningtons, she wrote that England was trying hard to keep Kenya from descending into the troubles in Congo, but "most of these Africans are still too close to tribalism to take over a modern type of government carried on for the good of all. It is also very difficult to find one who will be honest enough to work for the good of all and be dependable. . . . It is even difficult for Friends church members to be morally honest. It is a real disappointment."

In an October 23, 1960, letter, she commented on the upcoming Kenyan elections, which some felt would bring little change while others believed they would demonstrate a great demand for immediate independence. "With the very low standards of honesty, I cannot feel very hopeful about any stable government carried on by Africans," she wrote. Her Christmas letter of December 11 mentioned the elections again, as well as the belief of many that they would bring independence. "A great number are shouting UHURU (Freedom) whenever they see Europeans on the roads. They are building up some queer ideas of what freedom will bring to them." She described some of those "queer ideas" as free schools, no taxation, no Europeans, big houses for Africans, and plenty of money. They believed that they would be able to take over the big houses the Europeans would be leaving behind. The Tiriki people expected to take over the Friends Africa Mission as private property.

94 Letter, October 22, 1961. Private collection of Sarabeth Marcinko.

"Of course, there are many educated, Christian Africans," Annice wrote, "who know that these things cannot be, and are very eager to have a long period of adjustment and training so that African Government can go on in an orderly, wise manner. From experiences in other countries we will just have to go easy and see what happens here. We do not anticipate very much chaos."

She was concerned about Fred Reeve's and the Mission executive committee's intention to meet with Jomo Kenyatta, then out of prison for his alleged participation in the Mau Mau uprising and living under British administrative restrictions in remote Northwest Kenya. Annice worried about what these Friends might promise him while representing Friends in East Africa. When the delegation finally did meet with Kenyatta, the headline in the paper read, "Quakers urge Kenyatta release."

When elections were held in March of 1961, Annice commented that some people would not participate until Kenyatta was released from his confinement. She expressed some informed understanding of those dynamics: "The effort to get Kenyatta released seems to be a joint project of the Kikuyu [Kenyatta's tribe] and the Luhya tribes. Many people fear it will again emphasize tribal loyalty rather than national loyalty. The majority don't want him released."[95]

Throughout Annice's time at the Mission, she continued to be concerned about the changes that Kenyans expected with independence, and its possible impact on Friends' work in Kenya. She shared her thoughts with the Board of Missions back in Richmond. In a July 1961 letter, Mission Board director Norman Young alluded to previous communication from Annice in which she claimed it did no good to write to him. He expressed concern about this perception and disputed it, noting his awareness of difficulties at the Mission and acknowledging the fear of FYM "dictatorship."

"You realize," Young wrote, "that with the near approach of freedom for Kenya the principal task we have as missionaries and as a Mission Board is to prepare our African Friends to take the responsibility which is bound to be thrust upon them when that happens."[96]

Annice commented on other "political" events unrelated to the elections. She acknowledged hearing of UN Secretary-General Dag

95 Letter, March 5, 1961. Private collection of Sarabeth Marcinko.
96 Friends United Meeting Wider Ministries Records.

Hammarskjöld's death in a plane crash in Africa. It made her worry about the future of the UN, which was an interesting sympathy, given the negative feelings about the UN among some in her family.

She also reflected on workers at the Mission expressing interest in unionizing—a movement that was gaining momentum in the country. Annice opposed it; Fred Reeve was more open to it, believing that, by their opposition, Protestants were losing ground to Catholics.

INTERACTION WITH THE CULTURE

Annice's thoughts on Kenyans and independence revealed some of her inclinations regarding Africans, as well as race in general. There were other instances in which she reflected attitudes common in her time. Anticipating her first Christmas in Kaimosi, she expressed how she wasn't getting in the Christmas spirit. It wasn't just that it was warm: "All these black girls taking the part of shepherds, Wise men, Joseph and Mary, etc. does not give me a Christmas spirit."[97]

Annice's description of the girls might be considered inappropriate by more culturally sensitive standards. She was intrigued by their appearance, and wrote in one Christmas letter to family and friends, "I get quite a chuckle out of seeing these girls use their hair for so many different things. It is so curly and wooly that they keep it cut very short. And, of course, they all have black, black hair. Because it is short and wooly they can hold most anything on top of their heads."[98]

She mentioned that because classes were "segregated" between missionary students and African students, some in the U.S. were hesitant to donate funds. Annice didn't see the point of the hesitation, though, as the African children would require a great deal of work to catch up with the white students. She found the standards of education were not very high at the Mission. She wasn't afraid, therefore, to teach any of the subjects—except English, because in the British system in use there, punctuation and spelling were different from what she was familiar with.

Until the end of her time at the Mission, she continued firmly to believe that the African students and American students should be separated,

[97] Letter, November 18, 1959. Private collection of Sarabeth Marcinko.
[98] Letter, November 30, 1959. Private collection of Sarabeth Marcinko.

with Africans receiving an "African education" and American students an American one.

Annice commented on the number of girls pregnant out of wedlock, and the African men who had impregnated them while the men were already married. "There are lots of problems" was a common refrain of hers. While making dresses for graduation, Annice found that one girl had increased 1½ inches in bust size, and reported this to Pearl Spoon. Indeed, the girl was pregnant. Pearl confronted the young man at his home. There was another girl, too, that Annice suspected of being pregnant.

Her view of the girls' cultural and educational training was that they didn't get as much as the men and couldn't think beyond the immediate moment to outcomes: "I think that is one reason so many get into trouble. They decide for the moment and not for nine months hence."[99]

After again helping girls fix their badly sewn dresses, she expressed her frustration that Africans "have mighty little ingenuity and initiative." Another time, she wrote that she found Africans in general to be very wasteful. While expressing real fondness for the girls, she found them to be "worse gabbers" than Arab girls. She was also bothered by the girls' lack of discipline. She tried to keep them from "running around," but colleagues told her it was pointless. Annice was upset with their lowering hems so the dresses would "swish" about their ankles. She got them to hem the dresses up, but she was disappointed by their having disobeyed her instructions in the first place.

Annice also struggled with the culture's different ideas about stealing and lying. It was not considered stealing to take someone's dress if they had three good ones and the taker had none. Anyway, the person should have given from her surplus. This ran right up against Annice's upbringing regarding honesty: "I feel that I am unable to even touch the problem."[100]

When Reeve's car was stolen in Nairobi, she commented on the amount of thievery at the Mission and around the country, and went on to say, "I wish the Africans would just tell us if they want us to go home without making it so miserable for us."

[99] Letter, November 14, 1961. Private collection of Sarabeth Marcinko.
[100] Letter, December 11, 1960. Private collection of Sarabeth Marcinko.

Still, Annice was very fond of the girls and was pleased when one of the recent graduates who had been married invited Annice for a meal and ate with her husband—something the women usually didn't do.

And she did try to gain an understanding of Africa. She was reading John Gunther's *Inside Africa*. Further evidence of Annice's learning about the culture was in her concern about the impact of drought conditions on the Maasai. An extensive lack of rainfall had led to the death of thousands of cattle. The cattle were too precious for the Maasai to kill for meat; they had a procedure of draining blood that, mixed with milk, was their main diet. Annice was very concerned and was glad to learn that one of the Friends Africa Mission's gardeners was helping them learn how to grow vegetables.

Additionally, Annice was disturbed that graduates of the Friends Bible Institute who became pastors were typically not paid by their churches. They had to find other sources of income to support their call into ministry.

In letters Annice sent home, she revealed a great deal about her thoughts on the Mission, on other staff members, on religious ideas, and on Africans. She also revealed much more about herself than many who knew her could recall learning about her. In person, she was fairly tight-lipped about herself, while freely expressing her opinions about others!

She really missed good popcorn—and mentioned it often. Annice loved having sweet corn, as it reminded her of Indiana, and she enjoyed the occasions when she could get liver. It was a special treat to prepare "home" meals: pressure cooker roast beef; potatoes; carrots and onions; Jello-O salad; and mince pie.

She enjoyed gardening and planted corn, beets, asparagus, and celery. It was a way she kept in touch with her farm roots—and she kept her brothers informed about farming practices in Kenya. Her letters contained frequent commentary about drought, rainfall, and their effect on crops and wildlife.

PERSONAL THOUGHTS

A special pleasure for Annice was hearing news from home. Her letters to friends in the U.S. contained news she heard from her family. She delighted in learning that Leland, widower of her sister Achsa, was getting re-married at the home of former Russiaville pastor Mary Hiatt. Annice liked receiving the *Russiaville Observer* newspaper and keeping up with events and people back home. She received a magazine article about her nephew Theoren Chapman's new grain drying set-up on his Bloomingdale farm. She commented on sister Nora's breaking her ribs and on brother Walter's surgery, and expressed interest in the crops on her brothers' farms. In a January letter to her brother Oakley she wrote, "I hope the crops are in and that there's nothing to do but sit by those nice, steady heating systems and enjoy yourselves."

There are hints of her plainness and frugality. She made a new dress for Easter, the first in 35 years, but noted that even with a new dress, she wouldn't wear it on Easter so as not to "join the Easter parade."

On occasion her letters slip in a surprise about her openness to "new ideas in religion." She was keenly interested in hearing Roland Brown speak during his time in Africa, as she was curious about his Camps Farthest Out project—noted for "new thought," mysticism, the use of Quaker silence in prayer, and world peace.

Annice also admitted to weaknesses and idiosyncratic character traits. She wasn't patient with colleagues who complained constantly. "I complain and criticize people, not things," she said, and commented that people need a good sense of humor.

Her foot became infected, and Mission doctor David Hadley operated on it under anesthesia. When she felt "woozy" afterwards, she said she was "ashamed of myself." But she quite often talked about how tired she was, how she was "literally dragging," and how "low" she felt. One time, noting how wrung out she was after a difficult week, she wrote, "I've shot my wad."

Annice admitted to her sometimes peevish ways. "I've been just plain contrary all day" and provoked colleagues, she once wrote. When she got a new housemate who talked a lot, she commented, "it's wearing on me." Another time, she noted in a letter, "I'm getting cantankerous." Upset by plans to convert half of the house she was staying in to a student union, she said she wouldn't live there with students hanging out with no supervision.

She recognized at one point that she was giving others the "cold shoulder" because she was tired. She went on to comment that several on the staff would be glad when she finally left. Fatigue seemed to be a constant companion, and she was especially despondent on one occasion when all the drama costumes had been stolen, and she was contemplating the weariness of having to make new ones.

With a touch of the humor she said people needed, she commented once about wanting a copy of the Western Yearly Meeting Quaker Lecture: "It's by someone I usually don't agree with, but I always like to see what he says—and what I don't agree with."

Annice also didn't take herself too seriously as a religious person. She admitted to not being a fan of so many prayer meetings and religious services. "It does not leave much time for one to get into mischief," she wrote.

There was even a hint of an activist streak in her. Concerned with the number of rhinos dying for lack of water, Annice expressed a readiness to join in a campaign by Coca-Cola to provide water.

Annice's letters also revealed how ready she was to leave the work in Kenya. Midway through her time there, upon learning that Lois Snyder would be leaving Ramallah and returning home, she wrote in a June 1961 letter, "I sure wish I was taking that trip with her." She was upset that Richmond had no word for her on when she would be going home. Still, in signing off on one of her Christmas letters, she wrote, "May the joy and satisfaction of an inward peace be with you all throughout the Christmas season and the New Year. May the Love of God surround us all."[101]

But she also wondered what she would do for a job upon returning home, as she didn't have the "crutch" of Social Security. But still she claimed her main concern was for Friends Missions, about which she was finding more and more to disagree with: "Maybe I was born 30 years too soon." This would become a regular theme in her assessment of how she related to the mission philosophy in Kenya and Ramallah.

Annice anticipated leaving Kenya in 1961 and planned to travel home by boat via the Far East. She looked forward to stops in India, Australia, Fiji, and Honolulu, finally traversing the West Coast of the United States with stops at Seattle, San Francisco, and Los Angeles. Thoughts of visiting various FYM mission fields on the way home were scuttled, however, when it became clear that travel to Cuba was not possible.

---

[101] Letter, December 10, 1961. Private collection of Sarabeth Marcinko.

As it turned out, leaving the mission in 1961 also didn't work out. The Board of Missions was having trouble finding replacement staff for Kenya, and Annice was asked to stay through the end of the school year in December.

When school finished that December, Annice wrote to Richmond that she was ready to return to the U.S. and requested that the Board of Missions help pay her transportation home and purchase the car she had bought. Norman Young agreed to provide $670.99 to cover travel and freight and $400 for her car.

By January of 1962, Annice was preparing to leave, even though no replacement had been found yet. It felt odd for her when school resumed mid-month, and she wasn't preparing for classes. But with a teacher shortage, she anticipated being asked to substitute in some courses. Indeed, she was soon asked to fill in for an English class and noted the students' surprise to see her still there. One student blurted out, "Are you still here?" She responded, "No, I'm not here."

Willard Ware arrived in January to represent the Board of Missions in some land transfer and other business. Annice had issues with him as one of the "big business men" in FYM, but said in a January 18 letter that she vowed not to face him and discuss anything controversial—"rather an ambitious program for me."

By early February she finally was packed, and left for the anticipated journey home. She had purchased binoculars and enjoyed bird watching in India, where she also visited the Taj Mahal, New Delhi, Agra, and other sites. She regretted not being able to meet with Friend Ranjit Chetsingh and also expressed concern about India's struggle with Communist China.

Traveling with a Mennonite friend, she visited Ceylon, Sumatra, Singapore, and Saigon, taking in botanical gardens, museums, and more birds along the way. In Vietnam, she saw a vase that President Eisenhower had given the country's president, and she was fascinated by the women's dress: "They wore a sort of pajama pants with a dress that was very plain. The top was nicely fitted and had a high collar. The dress had no seam at the waist and had a front and back panel open to the waistline on each side."

Annice spent three weeks in Japan, including time in Sapporo and Tokyo. She was impressed by the industriousness of the Japanese and by how religious they were.

AN INTERLUDE IN THE U.S.

After three months of travel, Annice finally arrived back in Indiana, staying alternately at her brother Walter's home in Russiaville and with her friend Mina Emily Seidler in nearby New London. She commented that adjusting to life back in the States after five years abroad was "like pulling an old hat out after it has been on the shelf for years. You know how out-moded it can be, but you may not realize the changes that have come about which make it out-moded."[102]

There were new mixes and prepared foods in supermarkets, new beauty aids in the stores, and new terms and expressions derived from television and the space race. Annice found it difficult to settle in, especially having come from the mission field where people took religion more seriously than what she found was the norm "back home." The contrast was apparent especially at Christmas time, with the secularization of the holiday. Annice commented on the "grotesque balloon figures" at Christmas parades that had nothing to do with the real meaning of the season.

Annice did enjoy getting acquainted with 17 new grand-nieces and -nephews, however, and stayed busy with speaking engagements and various sewing projects. She wasn't ready for retirement but wasn't looking for a permanent job, either.

A November 24, 1962, letter arrived from Norman Young, Administrative Secretary of the American Friends Board of Missions, indicating that Annice's time in Indiana would be brief, and there would be no need for her to look for work: "The executive committee of the American Friends Board of Missions appoints you as principal of the Friends Girls School in Ramallah, replacing Anna Langston, who is on furlough for one year."[103]

Annice speculated at times that this sojourn overseas might be her last, but that would not be the case.

---

[102] Christmas letter, December 3, 1962. Private collection of Betsy Alexander.
[103] Friends United Meeting Wider Ministries Records.

CHAPTER 9

Annice in Ramallah 1963–1966

As Annice prepared to return to Ramallah, her interview with a local newspaper gave insight into her thoughts about service abroad. In the June 26, 1963, article in the *Kokomo Tribune*, the reporter began with the questions, "How can primitive people be happy with none of our luxuries? How can American missionaries endure separation from their homeland and from a high standard of living, for little, if any, pay?"[104] Annice's response was that, essentially, missionary work "gets in your blood" and that "primitive" people and conditions had become a large part of her life. She went on to imply that "primitive" is a matter of perspective.

She described the importance that "underdeveloped" countries assign to education and said that because it was so highly valued, teachers rarely encounter students who are there against their will. "I did not want to teach in America," Annice said, "where high school education is compulsory, because I was used to students who ALL wanted to learn."

Annice went on to note that many people abroad held a negative impression of Americans, owing to the behavior of some tourists and businesspeople: "We must show the people that we are interested in them and in their problems. We need to let them know that we are not out for what we can get but for what we can give and share." She went on to speak of how the issue of race in America also influenced Asians' and Africans' impression of the United States.

"People ask me how I can sacrifice so much. But really I've gained much more than I've given," Annice said, and then commented that the so-called primitive conditions she lived under didn't bother her, since "... my life has been such that I never got accustomed to things I could do without."

In the article, Annice pointed out that many of the people in Jordan (the occupying power in the West Bank at the time) were refugees from Israel, suffering high unemployment and needing UN assistance for

104 Judy Leas, "Missionary Says Problems Outweighed by Rewards," *Kokomo Tribune*, June 26, 1963.

food, clothing, and shelter. She described women doing needlepoint as a means of supplementing the family income and showed the reporter examples of their work. Annice also commented on the World Health Organization's effectiveness in almost eliminating diseases that had once been so devastating. She noted that modern agricultural techniques in the Jordan Valley were improving diets.

Annice talked about adjusting to the typical foods in Jordan and Africa, and said that she had to apply her home economics expertise to improvise making favorite foods from home. She laughed about a mincemeat pie she once made from meat, apples, pineapple juice, a local squash, and goat's milk cheese instead of cream cheese. She did admit to missing graham crackers and ice cream. However, Annice enjoyed the "one-dish" meals typical in Asian and African cooking: "A squash filled with meat, rice, and tomatoes is delicious. Or sometimes I brown meat, onions, and pieces of cauliflower and eggplant, cover with rice, and serve with yogurt."

She continued by undercutting Western stereotypes of the people with whom she had worked: "Many of us watch movies about savage tribes and think this is Africa, but this is false. And it's surprising to know that many Arabic ideas about Western cultures come from movies and movie magazines, not always the sources we'd like."

After commenting on modernizing tendencies in Africa and Palestine and noting differences in dating and marriage customs between the West and Asia and Africa, Annice expressed her hope for mutual friendship and understanding: "We must see their customs and standards as an outgrowth of their environment," and she warned against expecting their conformity to "our way."

Finishing the interview, Annice spoke of the rewards of her life's work: "travel, learning more about people, having new experiences, and trying new foods." The reporter noted Annice's conviction that, above all, a missionary must be sincerely interested in people.

Family and friends saw Annice off at the Kokomo, Indiana, train station in early August for the beginning of her return to Ramallah. Arriving in New York, she boarded a ship carrying flour and soybean oil meal—and 12 passengers—bound for the Middle East. A trunk packed with feather pillows, towels donated by USFW, cotton prints, and a variety of items for the School was also shipped. Again, her brother Oakley would take care of her affairs while she was away. She left, having applied to the Board of Missions for more scholarship money for refugee children in Ramallah. The AFBM executive committee responded with $1,300.

Writing from shipboard mid-Atlantic, Annice commented that it was the smoothest crossing ever and that the rest and food were luxurious enough that she had gained three pounds. She enjoyed touring the ship with the captain and took special note of the kitchen facilities and the engine room. But she was also thinking of the sessions of Western Yearly Meeting convening in Plainfield, Indiana: "I am hoping and praying that Western Yearly Meeting will be content to seek only spiritual growth so that she can be a real witness for Christ and his plans for dedicated followers in this day of need."[105]

Annice disembarked in Beirut and flew to Jerusalem, arriving at the airport three miles from Ramallah. Four years had elapsed between Annice's departure from Ramallah for her sojourn at the Friends Africa Mission in Kenya and her return as principal in 1963. During that time, nothing was happening on the West Bank that was quite as dramatic as Kenyan independence or the Cuban Missile Crisis. Jordanian rule had settled in, and Palestinians were fully involved in the government. Ramallah continued to grow as refugees took their place in society and Jordanian governmental ministries provided opportunities. The pleasant summer environment continued to attract tourists from around the Arab world to Ramallah, known as "the queen of Palestine."

While Ramallah and Jordan enjoyed a measure of stability, the West, engaged in the Cold War, was concerned by Egyptian President Gamal Abdel Nasser's growing popularity after the Suez war, and by his close relations with the Soviet Union. Nasser and others in the Arab world had a vision of Arab hegemony in the region, and Egypt's union with Syria as the United Arab Republic was a step in that direction. The confederation dissolved in 1961 after a coup in Syria, but many in the region held onto dreams of a pan-Arab movement. Quite a few Ramallah shops displayed portraits of Nasser rather than King Hussein of Jordan.

The apparent normalcy in Ramallah couldn't completely obscure the continued pain of the Nakba, the "catastrophe" of 1948. Any trip into Jerusalem provided reminders of the ever-present possibility of hostilities.

[105] Letter, August 16, 1963. Private collection of Sarabeth Marcinko.

Jordanian and Israeli pillboxes faced each other across the "no man's land" separating Jewish West Jerusalem from Arab East Jerusalem. The trial and execution in 1962 of Adolph Eichmann in Jerusalem captured the attention of many around the world and solidified the narrative of Israel's creation. Nasser's popularity could be attributed in large part to the hope that he'd be the one to redeem Palestine. The mixed attitude towards King Hussein, on the other hand, was connected to both his inability to confront Israel and the view that he, too, was an occupier.

Still, there was no organized resistance to either Israel's or King Hussein's rule. The Palestine Liberation Organization would not be formed until 1964, and the Popular Front for the Liberation of Palestine not until 1967. A common attitude in Palestine was that the world community would recognize the wrong done to the Palestinians and correct it.

Stability was good for the Friends Schools. The Girls and Boys Schools, considered the strongest in the West Bank, drew full enrollment not only from the original families of Ramallah but also from the families of many governmental bureaucrats, businessleaders serving the growing area economy, assimilated refugees, and others from the rest of Jordan and the Gulf. There were 40 boarders and more than 450 students in total at FGS as school began in the fall of 1963.

RESPONSIBILITIES AS PRINCIPAL OF FGS

Annice found that Ramallah had changed quite a bit during her absence. New buildings were going up everywhere, and although village women still dressed traditionally, the women and girls in Ramallah were keeping up with Western fashions. There was an abundance of private cars, and Annice was pleased that one improvement in the roads was a new route around the east end of the Jerusalem Airport's main runway. Previously, the road crossed the landing strip, and she recalled having to wait there upwards of half an hour so planes could land.[106]

106 Presently, the Jerusalem Airport is closed, idle since the Palestinian uprising (Intifada) of the late 1980s. The road around the east end of the runway now goes through the Qalandiya checkpoint at the runway's end. Described by Israel as an "international terminal" in the "security wall" Israel erected in the early 2000s, it is actually several miles inside Israeli-occupied Palestinian territory. Israel extended Jerusalem's municipal borders after illegally (according to international law) annexing East Jerusalem following the 1967 war.

King Hussein was having a home prepared in nearby Beit Hanina so he could spend more time in the West Bank. Growth and modernization were the norm. Among the students at the Girls School were girls from Ethiopia, Pakistan, Libya, Saudi Arabia, Kuwait, Armenia, Greece, Lebanon, Sweden, England, Canada, and the United States. Sadly, the coming years of Annice's service as principal of the Girls School would be the last relatively "normal" times for many years.

Several pressing issues met Annice upon her return to Ramallah. The first was that the Schools were celebrating a 75th Jubilee marking the 1888 opening of the Friends Girls School as a boarding school amalgamation of the various village schools of the Friends Syrian Mission. Preparations had to be made for dinner for 110 alumnae/i, as well as for tea and cake for 200, to be served after a program of talks by the Schools' principals and graduates. All went well, but Annice was bothered by the fact that the musical portion of the program didn't include any students from the Girls School.

Beyond the Jubilee, there were concerns about the faculty's teaching load and salaries, the constant struggle to deal with the organizational norms of Western countries while understanding the cultural norms of the Middle East, and a lack of sugar! Annice was already in negotiations with the government to help obtain sugar at a reasonable price, although she was not optimistic about their complying. Also, the departing principal had failed to complete the academic schedule, leaving things, as Annice described it, "in a mess."

More than the lack of sugar, though, Annice was upset about the discrepancy between salaries at the Boys School and the Girls School: "It is too bad that we cannot pay salaries on an equal basis with FBS, but most of ours run about a third less. I suppose we fall into the custom of the country and say girls are not worth as much as boys, but it seems to me to be unethical for Quakers."[107]

Another issue was the constant influx of parents wanting to enroll new students. While this helped the School budget, it put more pressure on teachers and staff. As classrooms became more crowded, the teachers told Annice they couldn't accommodate any more students. Still, she found it hard to say no, and after enrolling yet another student she admitted that

[107] Letter, September 15, 1963. Private collection of Sarabeth Marcinko.

"after I accepted one girl, I said that I would stand before the firing line at sunrise the next day, but it ended peaceably."[108] After starting the school year with a few more than 450 students, by the second semester there were 500.

Balancing these difficulties was an early October rain, which pleased Annice a great deal by bringing vegetation back to life following the long dry season. "I love to look out and see those pretty green spots now," she wrote to her family.[109] Later, wildflowers would appear, which always delighted her. As the early rains continued, she made sure that every drop was directed into the cisterns, even before the eaves and roofs had been cleaned and repaired.

Annice also delighted in some of the customs of the School, including the preparation of the fall harvest of olives for use by the kitchen staff. Nearly 300 pounds of olives were purchased, and she described their preparation. After being crushed with a rock on a flat stone, the olives were put in salt water. Later, they were washed and put to season in a solution including oil, lemon, and hot peppers. The process stained the workers' hands, Annice explained, the way working with walnuts did.

In November, Annice learned that Anna Langston would not be returning from her furlough, and Annice wrote to Norman Young of the Board of Missions to ask what his plans were for 1964–65, as "I would like to know." She was already thinking about the School's needs for the coming year, noting that although a Baldwin-Wallace student, Ginny Vigrass, would be coming to teach in the English Speaking section (children of English-speaking families), they would still need to find an English teacher for the upper classes who were learning English as a second language. And there was the need for more classroom space, as well as ongoing concerns about wages and benefits, supplies, and even water.

Finding that the girls had begun playing basketball, Annice tried to get proper backboards and the correct measurements for the basketball court. It had been many years since she had played for the Russiaville High School girls' team or coached the Pacific College women. She enjoyed this new challenge and added it to the list of things that a "Jack-of-all-trades" principal had to do. Adding to the challenges, however, was the lack of staff

108 Letter, October 27, 1963. Private collection of Sarabeth Marcinko.
109 Letter, October 30, 1963. Friends United Meeting Board of Missions Records.

to cover other tasks. Many were away for the olive harvest on their lands, so Annice had to help with the cooking and supervising of maintenance work in addition to her usual responsibilities.

November also brought the tragic news of the Kennedy assassination. Annice attended a memorial service for the slain president at St. George's Cathedral in Jerusalem.

Preparations for Thanksgiving offered a little respite—and some dark humor. The School's housekeeper had been raising a turkey for the staff dinner, but something killed it and left the bird half-eaten. Annice confessed to laughing out loud when she was told—and then apologizing to the grief-stricken woman. A celebratory dinner was held, nonetheless, but without turkey.

Annice dreaded the work that the end of the semester and the coming Christmas programs would require. She talked with each student who was failing with a grade of 60 or below—a total of nearly 60 students. There were two Christmas dinners to plan for and five school programs. The cold, wet weather also brought about a great deal of sickness among the boarders. Confessing to be "tired of practical nursing," Annice looked forward to the students being gone for the holiday.

When, indeed, the last student left for the Christmas vacation, Annice sat in the sun on the front steps of the main building and relaxed, later enjoying tea and visiting with the remaining staff. Her vacation included the usual Christmas Eve observances in Bethlehem, a more relaxed level of attention to school business, showing visitors around, planning for a book discussion group, an excursion to Lebanon, and trips into Beirut, Sidon, and Tyre.

Resumption of classes came soon enough, and with it the ongoing nagging problems facing Annice in her role as principal: collecting fees, dismissing some students, student homesickness, a girl falling down the stone stairs, too much emphasis on end-of-semester exams over daily work, and the constant issue of cheating on those exams. There were occasional instances of girls running away to see their boyfriends, the pressure of guests arriving to visit, and meal preparation. "I can never do anything without fort-leven interruptions," she wrote, "and it is sometimes discouraging."[110] Annice felt tied down by her duties and missed having a social life.

110 Letter, February 5, 1964. Private collection of Sarabeth Marcinko.

Annice was further discouraged by remembering that when she first arrived in 1929, girls were eager to learn, seeing attendance at the School as a privilege. Now, she felt, the girls attended only at the insistence of their parents. In her letters, Annice apologized for her "sob stories" and admitted to "feeling low" about it all. She even mentioned that she wasn't "feeling it" during the festive Easter season.

Needing a break mid-semester, Annice arranged to spend a day and a night in Jericho, where she simply relaxed in the sun and read.

The lure of Jericho was real for Annice. Although it was only 26 miles from Ramallah, the climate in winter was very different from Ramallah's cold. At 1,300 feet below sea level, Jericho could be basking in sun and warmth while Ramallah, at 2,400 feet above sea level, could be freezing in snow.

Although Annice grew up in the temperatures of Midwestern winters, the cold of Ramallah always bothered her. Three weeks of freezing weather—a record—in mid-February didn't help. "As I sat in silent worship in the stone cold meetinghouse with the temperature at 30 degrees, I was trying to pray for various Friends at home," she wrote in a letter, "but I had a hard time keeping the image of Friends sitting in warm meetinghouses out of my mind."[111] When her fellow Midwesterners were "glib" about their experiencing temperatures far colder than those in Palestine, she responded that zero degrees with heated houses couldn't hold a candle to 36 degrees in damp, unheated stone buildings.

Annice resented the families who moved to Jericho for the warmth in winter, which required their children to commute several hours a day to and from the School. She resented the American oil workers who provided heaters for their children's rooms in the English-speaking section of the School while the rest of the School remained unheated. But when guests arrived, Annice made sure to provide them with heated rooms.

Besides the quick trip to Jericho, Annice also "splurged" and bought a Dacron suit in Jerusalem to be "more dressy." To her "gal friends" in the U.S., she wrote, "Do you think such a financial splurge will help me to relax?"[112]

---

111 Letter, January 19, 1964. Private collection of Sarabeth Marcinko.

112 Letter, February 16, 1964. Private collection of Sarabeth Marcinko.

Annice confessed that the tensions of administration at the School were greater than before. She didn't know if she could hold up for as long as it might take to find a replacement. Nonetheless, when the executive committee of the Board of Missions unanimously decided in February 1964 to extend her appointment for another year, Annice accepted.

Although she agreed to serving another year as principal, Annice continued to express concern about the impact of an additional year on her own future. As she shared with the Board of Missions, "... my need to get home is the universal need of every missionary to have a little time to hold a more remunerative job for a few years in order to have a fair social security payment in retirement."[113]

With the next year decided, Annice continued the pressing work of finding teachers for the coming year. She needed faculty in English, physics, chemistry, home economics, biology, typing, and music. To one teacher who inquired about a position, she replied that the School sought to maintain high standards in academics and in conduct while trying to fit into the social standards of the country.

There were also important accomplishments to celebrate. In March of 1964, she accompanied a top student to Amman for an Arabic composition competition. She was proud of the girl's second-place finish and suspected that she probably was the top student, but first place had to go to a government school student, not one from an American Quaker school! Annice thought the consolation prize, however, was better than the top one. Her student got a set of binoculars, while the winner received Sheaffer pens. As an avid bird watcher, Annice valued the former over the latter.

As Annice prepared for the 1964–65 school year, her summer was busy. Besides the usual planning, there were political demonstrations, and the military and police were on alert. This threatened school openings, but permission came from Jordan to keep the Friends Schools open. A cistern needed to be built to guarantee an adequate supply of water for the Girls School. A constant round of guests required her to act as tour guide to Jerusalem and to take responsibility for getting them through the Mandelbaum Gate that separated Arab East Jerusalem from Jewish West Jerusalem.

113 Letter to Norman Young, February 12, 1964. Friends United Meeting Board of Missions Records.

In addition, Annice was concerned about the El-Bireh Municipality's plan to cut a road through the Friends Boys School property. The Schools opposed the project, but the road was constructed anyway, with some consolation that it was named Al-Friends Street. In other property matters, there was an issue about the payment of "rent" to the Jordanian Waqf (an Islamic endowment of property to be held in trust for a charitable or religious purpose) for the Girls School's land. Annice had always understood this to be a tax on school-owned property, but there were rumblings that the Waqf considered the property to be theirs.

All these concerns had Annice yearning for some time away from her work. She commented to Norman Young in Richmond that she needed some vacation before the summer got away from her, but there were few options for a getaway since Ramallah itself was the place where people went to get away from the summer heat. The city was filled with visitors, and she needed rest and quiet. Staff at the Friends Boys School had offered her the use of Swift House, the "mission house" next to the FBS campus, but Annice noted that staying there would require her to cook her own meals and do the cleaning—and that was no holiday! Finally, she did escape for a few days with colleague Lois Snyder to a hostel on the Mount of Olives in Jerusalem.

Somewhat rested, Annice was back at the challenges of being principal as the school year approached. She worried about the "extravagant" expense of $70 to pipe hot water from the Girls School kitchen to the guest bathroom. And then there was the possible added expense of the dietary needs of one of the new teachers. Larry and Nancy Shinn from Baldwin-Wallace College were coming as part of the Jordan Mission Project sponsored by the college, and Larry had a particular request for breakfast. He wanted two quarts of milk and up to four eggs at breakfast. Annice wasn't having it. She approved a small pitcher of milk and two eggs—on those days when there even were eggs!

The privation evidently did Larry Shinn no permanent harm. He went on to be the president of Berea College in Kentucky.

School got off to a good start that fall, although the Girls School was down to only 27 boarders, which hardly paid for the staff needed to maintain a boarding department. There was also the good news that USFW was sending $2,200 for scholarships. But more trouble was brewing with the authorities in Jordan. In a meeting with the Undersecretary of Education, Nuri Shafik, Annice was asked whether the School taught Islam to the Muslim students. She was unaware of the law that had been passed requiring this, even in private Christian schools.

Annice replied that there was no discrimination at the School between Muslims and Christians, and when a ruling had come down a few years earlier that Christianity not be taught to Muslims, the School changed to an "Ethics" class. Shafik told her, however, that the new law cancelled that out, and Islam had to be taught.

"What if the Board of Missions says no to that?" Annice asked. Should we close? Accept no Muslims? The Undersecretary didn't want either of those options and ended the discussion by suggesting further negotiations.[114]

In the letter to Norman Young in which she reported on the meeting, Annice commented that she was sorry it had been her, rather than the Boys School principal, Robert Bassett, with whom Shafik raised the issue: "You know my lack of diplomacy." She went on to say that she hoped the Board of Missions would confer with D. Elton Trueblood on the matter. The issue concerned her greatly, as one-third of her students were Muslim, and she didn't want to limit admission to Christians only.

Later, in a letter to Ardelle Cope, Annice shared her thoughts: "In a country where we cannot teach [the] Bible and our Christian witness, we must witness through living the teachings."[115] She went on to describe how there were citations from the Bible in assembly programs, and that both Christian and Muslim students referred to the Bible in the "Ethics" classes. The School owned translations of the Qur'an (Annice spelled it "Koran"), which the Muslim girls appreciated, as these were not in classical Arabic. Annice admitted not knowing the difference between classical and colloquial Arabic in the texts, as she didn't read Arabic. She went on to say that the most "evangelistic" message given in assembly had been by a Muslim student describing Christian mission work in the New York City ghettos.

114 Letter to Norman Young, December 17, 1964. Friends United Meeting Board of Missions Records.

115 Letter, November 26, 1964. Friends United Meeting Board of Missions Records.

The matter didn't surface again during the school year, and all went smoothly. This calm was interrupted, however, by an event 6,000 miles away. Annice learned that a major tornado—the largest in recorded U.S. history up to that time—had hit her home town of Russiaville on April 11, 1965. There were reports that the town had been "wiped off the map," and she learned that her home church, Russiaville Friends, was destroyed while more than 150 people huddled in its basement on that Palm Sunday evening. She was relieved by the news that no worshipers or family members had been injured. The homes of her brothers Oakley and Walter, located in town near the meetinghouse, were damaged but not totally destroyed, and neither they nor their wives, Delta and Arlie, suffered injury. Annice felt "far away" with the news and was concerned that her hometown would never be the same again.

At the same time, she pondered the fact that five of her aunts and uncles had died in the past two years, as well as a brother-in-law and a niece. Though she would have wanted to be home during this difficult time, she recognized that it was also a difficult time at the Schools, and there was work to be done by those with the wisdom to pilot the Schools through. Without naming herself as one of the "wise and sensible minds" needed, Annice knew where she needed to be.

With the end of the academic year came the difficulties of staff firings and student dismissals and the expected responses to them. For Annice, however, the decisions were "hard and fast." There were also more political rumblings, with demonstrations protesting Tunisian President Habib Bourguiba's recognition of Israel. But Annice also reported progress on a new cistern for the Girls School and plans for new toilet facilities. No one contested the need for the new toilets, but the cistern, with the necessary dynamiting of the layers of limestone and the inevitable work delays, became known as "Carter's Folly." It would, however, come to be recognized as a very wise decision.

Learning that the Board of Missions had decided not to teach Islam at the Schools, Annice visited again with the Jordanian Ministry of Education to inform them of the decision. She was in agreement, but the principal of the Boys School favored a compromise: arranging the Schools' schedules so that Muslim students could attend classes on Islam at the neighboring public secondary school.

There were other problems: the boarding girls had heard that bread and rice were fattening, so they didn't want to eat those foods, a staple of the diet. Jirius Mansur, the clerk of the Friends Meeting, was opposed to having a local advisory committee for the Schools, claiming that Arabs were too emotional, and this would get in the way of wise decision making. And there was the work day at the meetinghouse, during which she helped the students rake, pick up stones, and do other cleaning, leaving her, in her own words, "feeling like an old woman."

But "Carter's Folly," the cistern, was completed by late October, and the new toilets were almost finished.

A more serious problem was the renewed question of teaching Islam. Visiting in November, the Jordanian Inspector of Private Schools asked some of the Muslim students why they were at the Girls School. Their answer was that they wanted to improve their English so they could attend university in Beirut or the U.S. The Inspector admitted that he himself could have used such an education to speak better English.

Finding the funds to support needy students was a continuing issue. Friends United Meeting (the name change from Five Years Meeting around 1964) was having trouble raising enough to meet the demands of its mission fields in Ramallah, Jamaica, Kenya, and Mexico. In an attempt to appease Annice, the Board of Missions remarked that "God is fully aware of the needs." Annice felt that more publicity from FUM might help God along. Eighty-five girls were on financial aid, some of which was provided by UNRWA for the 30 girls registered as refugees. But most financial aid students were supported by Friends. Scholarships had also been given to the children of staff, but this was quite an expense to the School—and unfair, Annice believed, to the staff without children. That policy would be changed in the next year, reducing the subsidy to only a one-half scholarship.

Beyond that, as she complained, "guests, sickness, and discipline seem to take most of my time."[116] There was also a worry that mail was being censored and that she and Lois Snyder were under suspicion of "secret work" because of having been in Ramallah so long. At least, she said, the government was satisfied that the Schools were not cells of opposition to the government.

It wasn't all work and worry. Annice took some of the girls to the Boys School for a film on travel to the moon. The students enjoyed it, especially

116 Letter, November 5, 1965. Friends United Meeting Board of Missions Records.

for the mixing and mingling of the boys and girls! But she was unimpressed about all the "torture and trouble" that would be necessary to go to the moon, and she declared that "I for one do not care to go." There was also a concert at the FBS sponsored by the Goethe Institute. A woman sang to guitar accompaniment, and Annice's only criticism was that she struck a suggestive pose and kept it throughout the concert, all while wearing a very slinky red sheath!

Annice continued to confirm her self-diagnosis as an unrepentant puritan!

She also took 25 girls to Jerusalem, as many—even among the Christian students—had never visited the holy and historical sites. She especially liked taking people to the Church of St. Peter in Gallicantu, built over the supposed cell where Jesus was kept the night before his crucifixion. There were also the various religious holidays and even a holiday for the birthday of King Hussein (whom Annice proclaimed to be very nice). She commented in one of her letters that one of the approaching Muslim holidays was the Laylat al-Mi'raj[117] (she spelled it "Mirage")—although she confessed that she had no idea what it celebrated.

November brought the sad news of the death of her sister Nora's husband Lyman in Indiana. Annice worried about Nora, as she was "out in the country" and didn't drive. This situation underscored one of the sacrifices of those in foreign missionary service. Annice had also been in Ramallah in 1958 when her sister Achsa died.

Lyman's death prompted a mention by Annice in a letter that some of her staff had also lost family members and were wearing black, as was the local custom. She would let them wear it for a few weeks (the customary mourning period was 40 days), but they would have to take it off soon in favor of appropriate dress in the classroom.

As the Christmas season approached, Annice helped supervise donations and funds for the "White Gifts," a long-standing Friends Schools tradition of caring for the poor and needy in the community. After all was distributed, a poor elderly woman came to the Girls School seeking aid. Annice had to tell her that all the funds and gifts had been given out and they had nothing more. As the woman began to leave in tears, she turned

---

117 A feast day observing the Prophet Muhammad's ascent into the heavens where he communed with Allah and the prophets.

to show Annice her thin, unlined jacket and pointed to Annice's warm sweater. Annice took off the sweater and gave it to her.

"It was one of my favorite sweaters," Annice wrote home. "It had pockets, and pockets are hard to come by here."[118]

Following the many different observances of Christmas by the Latin, Greek, Armenian, and Coptic Christian communities, which necessitated a long holiday break, Annice faced further concerns in the new year. There was the poor family of a student who had lost their father in a work accident. Taking food to the family, Annice saw that they lived in a dark, one-room basement apartment.

And there was a concern about "slipping" standards at the Friends Schools in comparison with the public schools. Annice believed the facilities and curriculum had to be improved. She believed that the Schools must go co-educational, with the FGS campus being the elementary division and the FBS campus becoming the secondary school. Furthermore, she believed that there needed to be more American teachers who could stay for a longer period of time. Another recommendation to the Board of Missions was that an "over-all person," a Head of School, be appointed.

In those observations, Annice proved to be far-sighted: her recommendations were ultimately realized. Ironically, though, they didn't take place until the years following her death in 1988.

Norman Young responded to Annice's suggestions (which were echoed by the Boys School principal, Lloyd Brightman) by asking whether such great changes could be made by the new personnel who would soon be replacing the Schools' leadership. He also asked whether it might be time to consider ending Quaker education in Ramallah: "Is there still a mission to present the Christian message through education?"[119]

Annice was not opposed to the idea of closing the Schools. In fact, she suggested it in a report back to Richmond about having received further pressure from the Jordanian government to teach Islam. The Muslim Brotherhood was pressuring the Ministry of Education to enforce the law and require instruction in Arabic. There was a threat (although Annice believed it was only a threat) to nationalize the Friends Schools if they didn't comply.

[118] Letter to family, January 23, 1966. Friends United Meeting Board of Missions Records.
[119] Letter, January 17, 1966. Friends United Meeting Board of Missions Records.

There were alternatives, Annice believed, to closing the Schools. Muslim students could take instruction in Islam at government schools if schedules could be arranged. Or the Schools could accept only Christians. Annice preferred cutting down on the number of boarders, improving classroom facilities, going co-ed, and emphasizing excellent English preparation.

A government inspector returned to the school in March of 1966, continuing the pressure to teach Islam and adding that the School needed to offer 12th-grade exams in Arabic and hire an Arabic principal. He was upset that Annice did not speak with her staff in Arabic. Describing the situation to the Central Office in Richmond, she said that it felt like a noose tightening.

Harold Smuck, who had replaced Norman Young as the Executive Secretary of the AFBM, arrived from FUM the same month to help deal with the issue and meet with the government. He found that FBS principal Brightman was not opposed to teaching Islam, though Annice believed that teaching Islam at the School would compromise its mission.

Annice's proposal was to continue teaching in English, including giving 12th-grade exams in English, and to send Muslim students to government schools to study Islam. If that proposal were to be refused, she believed the Ministry of Education should be told that the Schools could take only Christian students; but she also knew that such a move would mean the Schools might forfeit their license. She told Harold Smuck that it wouldn't be such a catastrophe to close the Schools, as they had already accomplished their primary purpose.

Those advocating for the Friends Schools to remain open, even if they had to adapt to the Jordanian laws, argued that the Schools had a special atmosphere. That argument didn't carry weight with Annice. That "atmosphere," she believed, was the result of the Schools' Christian influence, Christian staff, and Christian teachings. Her fear was that if Islam had to be taught as an equal religion and if the Schools were prevented from making a strong Christian witness, that "atmosphere" would be lost. Annice's opinion was fixed: "I would prefer closing to becoming just another government school."[120]

In the same letter in which she described these discussions, she noted that her colleague Lois Snyder "is more logical." "I have rather definite feelings without logic," she added.

[120] Letter, March 13, 1966. Friends United Meeting Board of Missions Records.

Harold Smuck returned to Richmond without achieving any closure on these issues. Annice felt that he had been intimidated and flustered by the situation and by his conversations with government officials. She saw his return to the U.S. as a retreat and expressed her frustration by saying that if staff headed for Richmond every time they received an ultimatum from Jordan, they could have run up a big bill. She was very concerned about what might happen.

RELIGIOUS EXPERIENCES AND ISSUES

Annice enjoyed the varieties of religious expressions in the Holy Land. In her letters she described Jewish festivals, the Samaritan Passover, the Greek Orthodox and Coptic observances of Palm Sunday, and the various Christmas holidays and traditions. When the Pope visited in 1964, passing through Ramallah on his way to Nazareth for the dedication of the Church of the Annunciation, Annice was delighted that this visit encouraged greater unity and understanding between the Latin and Greek Orthodox branches of the Church. She hoped it would ease the tensions between the Church of the Holy Sepulchre in Jerusalem and Bethlehem's Church of the Nativity.

She was not pleased, however, with some of the changes to favorite religious observances. One experience she had always delighted in was attending the Christmas Eve celebrations at the Church of the Nativity and Shepherds' Field. "I am glad that I had the opportunity to attend the festivities of thirty years ago in Bethlehem," she wrote, "as the modern atmosphere and commercialism tend to spoil some of the experience. The thousands and thousands of tourists that come to this country now spoil the effect for the sincere Christian worshipers."[121]

Annice's relationship with Islam was more fraught. As indicated before, she opposed teaching Islam at the Girls School, preferring to close the School rather than obey the government's directive. She was annoyed by the Muslim holidays and confessed that she didn't fully understand their significance. She described the holy month of Ramadan as a time of fasting until sundown and then "carousing" through the night. She required a letter from parents to allow boarding girls to fast during the month, claiming that

[121] Letter, November 18, 1963. Private collection of Sarabeth Marcinko.

they fasted mostly for show, although she did admit that this might not be so different from the behavior of many Christians.

While there is evidence, over the course of her time as principal, that Annice developed a deeper awareness of and appreciation for basic Islamic principles, many of her comments are dismissive of the religion. In a 1963 letter, she wrote, "We are now hearing the call to prayer from this silly mosque which is near us. Perhaps I would not resent it so much if I thought it did any good, but no one pays any attention—I mean they don't stop and pray. This mosque is new since I was here before."[122]

Annice also made comments dismissive of Muslims' abilities in comparison with Christians. "The Moslems do not have the good, qualified administrators that the Christian population provides," she wrote in 1963, "They tried a Moslem principal for the Women's Training College but had to go back to the previous Christian principal."[123]

Annice was also concerned that one of her Christian staff members was dating a Muslim man. One evening she witnessed the young woman "stepping out" with him and called her into the office the next day to ask her about it. Annice expressed her opposition in terms of the difficulties such a relationship could bring and counseled the woman not to be so interested in young Arab men. "I have undertaken to try to explain to her the differences in moral standards between Christian and Moslem," she wrote. "But I fear I fail miserably. . . . I console myself by reminding me that she is 37 and old enough to make her own decisions. If I warn her and she does not heed, what more can I do?"[124]

She did acknowledge that some of the Muslim girls attended her religious discussion groups aimed at the Christian students, and that they participated enthusiastically in Christmas programs, especially enjoying the carols—as Annice noted, there really weren't religious hymns in Islam. Annice was pleasantly surprised when Muslim students chose the Tolstoy play *Where Love Is, There Is God* for a presentation. And although she had opposed the teaching of Islam at the Girls School, she was able to witness the first classes in Islam when she stayed into the beginning of the new academic year in 1966. She remarked that the girls had to learn to read

122 Letter, October 6, 1963. Private collection of Sarabeth Marcinko.

123 Letter, November 18, 1963. Private collection of Sarabeth Marcinko.

124 Letter, September 29, 1963. Private collection of Sarabeth Marcinko.

the Qur'an in a special way—a proper "sing-song." This reminded her of the way the older Quakers used to say their prayers. She also commented on Islam's opposition to translating the Qur'an into languages other than the original Arabic, which reminded her of some Christians' objection to translating the King James Version of the Bible.

Annice also looked forward to visiting the al-Aqsa Mosque and Dome of the Rock, two of the holiest sites in Islam, in the company of a Muslim grocer friend: "I will be glad to have a Moslem show us around."[125] "I am learning a lot about the religion," she wrote in her final letter home before her departure on September 9, 1966.[126]

If she was somewhat critical of Muslims, Annice was also unsparing in her concerns about Christian behavior. When a new principal came to replace Robert Bassett in 1964, Annice immediately wrote about him to the Board of Missions. In her communication with Richmond, she expressed concern that Lloyd Brightman frequently used the expression "Good Lord!" Annice was known to refer to "our Good Master" from time to time, but context was everything! She was told that FUM would talk with him about it.

Annice was also perturbed about Brightman's lack of punctuality, and she confronted him about both that and his language. She didn't accept his argument that he came from a different region than she did and that he had developed habits about time during his service in Africa. In describing the conversation in a letter to FUM, she admitted, "I have known for a long time that I seem to have had a rather puritanical upbringing, and it frequently shows."[127]

"Taking the Lord's name in vain" wasn't the only Commandment Annice was taking seriously. Work was proceeding slowly on "Carter's Folly," and the contractor had his Muslim employees working on Sunday. Annice wasn't appeased by the argument that their holy day was on Friday. "I struggle and struggle to uphold some kind of standards for Sabbath observance," she wrote in 1963, "but it is a losing battle."[128]

---

125 Letter, January 16, 1966. Private collection of Sarabeth Marcinko.

126 Letter, September 4, 1966. Friends United Meeting Board of Missions Records.

127 Letter, October 1, 1965. Friends United Meeting Board of Missions Records.

128 Letter, December 8, 1963. Private collection of Sarabeth Marcinko.

When a student from the Yale Divinity School applied for a position, Annice responded with the reasons she was skeptical about the student's appropriateness: "I am impressed with your training and skills, but the first thing that discourages me is your moderate use of tobacco and occasional use of alcoholic beverages. . . . The second thing is you have a hyper-acetic stomach. The above use and foods here would exacerbate it." [129]

Annice explained to the applicant that Friends have had a witness against alcohol and tobacco, even though other Christians in Ramallah might drink and smoke. In a classic Annice Carter tone, recognizable even in writing, she told the applicant that she was sure that a Divinity student would be careful in the use of such "narcotics."

The matter was resolved when the Yale Divinity School student responded that she smoked no more than a pack of cigarettes a week with no dependency, and that, as an Episcopalian, she would wish to participate in the rituals of the church, including communion with wine. Annice responded positively and invited her to come if her references were all positive. There is no indication in the correspondence whether the student did teach at the Girls School.

Annice was concerned about the need for more religious opportunities at the School for the Christian students: "I am beginning to wonder if I should try to start some kind of Christian study group, Sunday School class, or something on Sunday afternoons. We do not have very much deliberately Christian teaching for the Christian girls. Everything seems to me to be so watered down for the sake of the Moslems that I am a bit disturbed." [130] She did begin a Sunday evening religious study group for Christian girls in the School parlor. Using Quaker queries, the group focused on Christian conduct.

"Behavior" for Annice was apparently more important in Christian witness than the usual evangelical understanding of "witnessing." The American music teacher at the Girls School often complained to her that the Quaker witness in Ramallah was lacking: "She is unhappy with us because we are not evangelistic and refuses to accept the law that prohibits evangelization here. I maintain that her living witness is not as Christian as it could be." [131]

[129] Letter, June 2, 1964. Friends United Meeting Board of Missions Records.

[130] Letter, September 22, 1963. Private collection of Sarabeth Marcinko.

[131] Letter, June 22, 1966. Private collection of Sarabeth Marcinko.

Nor was Annice that impressed with expressions of Christian orthodoxy. When an American with an interdenominational youth project wanted to enroll his two young boys in the Girls School's elementary program, she wrote, "He wanted me to assure him that the boys would get nothing there that would undermine their deep faith." Annice told him that she could make no such assurance and went on to say, "I doubt that these boys have such deep faith and suspect that they are now little parrots repeating papa's views. It takes all kinds."[132]

Annice was also concerned for the Quaker community in Ramallah. In her 1963 Christmas letter, she commented that "the Meeting has been overshadowed by the Schools long enough. The services of pastors during their short intervals here has not led to the vital strengthening of the Meeting which is greatly needed. There is a great need for a real Christian witness, not necessarily in preaching, in this area dominated by Islam."[133] It was her opinion that the Friends Meeting was doomed unless a good pastor was assigned soon.[134] The Meeting's Sunday School program, under the leadership of Violet Zaru and Ellen Mansur, was serving as many as 400 Christian and Muslim children, but the adult membership continued to decline.

Annice's concerns for the Meeting extended beyond its spiritual condition. Sitting in worship in the spring of 1964 before Ramallah Friends were to host the Yearly Meeting, she noticed that the tall windows of the meetinghouse were filthy. She took it upon herself to wash all of them, which required perching on each window's stone ledge. At least her considerable height served her well.

RESPONSE TO POLITICAL CONDITIONS

In Annice's communications with her friends and family, she commented on the political situation in the Middle East, but her remarks sometimes

[132] Letter, August 14, 1966. Private collection of Sarabeth Marcinko.
[133] Letter, December, 1963. Private collection of Sarabeth Marcinko.
[134] Pastoral leadership at the Meeting continued to be short-term. By the 1980s, with the Quaker community continuing to diminish and the meetinghouse condemned because of structural problems, the Meeting moved to a room at the Girls School and adopted an unprogrammed form of worship. With renovations to the meetinghouse in the early 2000s, worship was moved back, but attendance by local Palestinians continued to drop.

were underappreciated. In a letter she received from an editor of USFW's publication, *Friends Missionary Advocate*, she was told, "We get so little real news about the political situation there . . . that I can't use many of your comments about that."[135]

When a summit of Arab leaders was held in Cairo in early 1964, Annice took note and expressed her appreciation for the friendlier feelings among the leaders. She had earlier worried about King Hussein's attendance at the summit, given his earlier opposition to pro-Nasser alignments. It took great courage, Annice believed, for him to appear in Egypt while his popularity was growing and support for Nasser was diminishing in Jordan.

With differences among the Arab countries smoothed over, it was Annice's observation that it was now the United States that was the main "enemy." The U.S. was backing Israel in its Jordan River diversion project. She further agreed that "Arabs have a point in objecting to the Jews making it possible to admit more Jewish immigrants when they refuse to allow the Arabs to go back to their own land."[136]

Annice did observe that, at Christmas time, Israel had agreed with Jordan to allow 3,000 to 4,000 Arabs who lived in Israel to travel through the Mandelbaum Gate separating Jewish West Jerusalem from Arab East Jerusalem to attend religious services. They could pass through only between 5:00 and 6:00 A.M. and had to be back through the gate by midnight on Christmas Day. She had gone once to observe the event and was touched by the emotional reunions of families separated by the hostilities between Israel and Jordan.

After the sessions of Near East Yearly Meeting were held in Ramallah in 1964, Annice approvingly shared an excerpt from the Yearly Meeting epistle: "The tensions and problems of the Middle East create frustrations, as well as opportunities, that are a challenge to the Society of Friends. We are hopeful that Meetings everywhere will feel the weight of this challenge, and seek to understand our difficulties, keep us in their prayers, and support projects in this area."[137] Annice added that few Friends had an understanding of what people were facing in the region.

---

135 Letter, June 12, 1964. Friends United Meeting Board of Missions Records.

136 Letter, January 1964. Private collection of Sarabeth Marcinko.

137 Letter, April 26, 1964. Private collection of Sarabeth Marcinko.

Following the Yearly Meeting sessions in Ramallah in 1966, Annice reported on a talk about the Quaker peace testimony given by Korean Friend Yoon Goo Lee: "He is concerned about the lack of the peace testimony in this area where Quakers should have a real peace witness. He knew that it would do no good to repeat the old peace arguments because the people here have a real cause for grievance. So he told stories of the things that happened to them during the Japanese occupation and the Korean War."[138]

His basic message was about returning good for evil, and Annice commented that she herself had consistently emphasized hating evil without hating the person doing the evil. She added the observation that, given their experience, it was hard for Palestinians to separate the deed from the person.

Annice's own views about the Israeli/Arab situation were definite, and she was not shy about sharing them with people "back home" who had a different understanding. Back in Indiana between her term of service in Kenya and her return to Ramallah, she spoke to a fellowship group at First Baptist Church in Kokomo. There had evidently been some disagreement with the pastor afterwards about how she presented the facts of the Middle East conflict. It took her a few months to formulate a response, and she sent her comments in a letter from Ramallah.

"It has been quite disturbing to me to know that a very prominent church leader in Kokomo is so firmly entrenched in the Jewish tradition that he upholds the Jewish idea of a superior and privileged people," she wrote. She went on to say that Christ had come to show that all may become "sons of God," citing a variety of scripture passages, including some that, unfortunately, have been used historically to blame Jews for the death of Jesus.

"I wish you could visit this part of the world and see the large plantations of oranges and citrus fruits owned and managed by Arabs before being taken over by the Jews in the setting up of the State of Israel. These groves are now shown as a part of the Jewish efforts to 'make the desert blossom as a rose.'" Annice then described the Arab refugees being forced from their land and Israel's refusal to allow them to return, even

---

138 Letter, July 3, 1966. Private collection of Sarabeth Marcinko.

while accepting indemnity payments from Germany for the Jews forced to flee that country.

"I do not wish to give the idea of being anti-Jewish," Annice continued, "although I am definitely anti-Zionist. I believe that Jews are a part of God's creation and have the same opportunity to become God's children through faith and works as have all other people. I believe that a political movement such as Zionism has no place in religious activities."[139]

Concluding her letter, Annice asked that the pastor accept her communication in a spirit of sincerity and said that writing the letter unburdened her of the concern, so she could "now continue my efforts among these Arab peoples, mostly Moslem, with a feeling of having carried out a commission." She signed it, "In sincerity and love."

Annice also reflected on politics elsewhere. Following the news of the Kennedy assassination, she wondered whether Lyndon B. Johnson, the new president, would carry on Kennedy's foreign policy and whether he planned "to soften the equal rights programs" of his predecessor.[140] Annice did not elaborate on whether or not she agreed with that foreign policy and "equal rights."

Following news of Kenyan independence, Annice weighed in with her assessment that "I have never had much confidence in Kenyatta being reformed."[141] When she had been at the Friends Africa Mission in Kenya, Annice had disapproved of some of the staff meeting with Kenyatta. She continued to associate him with the Mau Mau uprising of the early 1950s.

ANNICE'S TIME IN RAMALLAH WINDS DOWN

In the closing months of Annice's time as principal, she expressed a good deal of frustration. She disliked Jirius Mansur's suggestion as clerk that the Friends Meeting's mid-week worship be held in homes during cold weather, as the meetinghouse had no central heating. She reasoned that there were only a few homes able to accommodate the meetings—and each family would try to outdo the others with food offerings.

---

139 Letter to John Newsom, January 6, 1964. Private collection of Sarabeth Marcinko.

140 Letter, November 24, 1963. Private collection of Sarabeth Marcinko.

141 Letter, December 15, 1963. Private collection of Sarabeth Marcinko.

She was also upset with Jirius's expressed opposition to the Bible lessons that the Meeting pastor, Kenneth Shirk, was offering at the mid-week worship. Jirius said he attended the meetings to relax, not study. This bothered Annice a great deal, as Jirius had long been asking FUM to send a pastor to Ramallah, but now that there was one, he was unable to share leadership. Annice felt he had been "lead dog" too long.

Annice was frustrated about having to wind the School's five clocks each morning; frustrated about her broken typewriter; frustrated with the Boys School's deciding to break two days early for an upcoming holiday, meaning the FGS would have to follow suit; frustrated by an invitation to a gathering in hot Jericho that she didn't want to attend; frustrated with the lack of rain to fill the new cistern; frustrated that the FBS principal was negotiating with the government without her; frustrated that the FBS boys were doing Jordan's required military drills on School time and that an "Army Day" celebration with tanks, guns, and flags was held on the FBS playing field; frustrated that the Board of Missions had reversed itself and approved abiding by the Jordanian law about teaching Islam; frustrated that the Boys School principal believed the School couldn't refuse mandated military drills now that Islam would be taught, as Islam is not against war; and frustrated that FUM had known for two years that she would be leaving in 1966, but had not yet hired a replacement. Just frustrated all around.

Annice was happy to have the Boys and Girls School June Commencement exercises over with, but there had been some problems. The girls hadn't practiced their music enough, so the FGS offering was reduced to a trio. Annice had to amend one certificate, having left out a mark in the name "Mu sal'lam," an omission that made it into the name of a different person. There was a mix-up with the Minister of Education who was to hand out the diplomas, and ushers hadn't saved enough seats for VIPs, causing the District Governor to leave upset. Annice did note with some wry humor that she learned later of his attendance at the Bir Zeit Junior College Commencement, and commented, "They must have had a good seat for him. They are much better at protocol than we are."[142]

But there were positives: the issue with the *Waqf* about the status of the Schools' property had been settled to everyone's satisfaction. Robert

[142] Letter, June 19, 1966. Private collection of Sarabeth Marcinko.

Bassett was returning to be the principal of the Boys School. And a good rain came to fill the "Carter's Folly" cistern. Annice was even relieved that finally the decision about Islam had at least been made.

She agreed to stay into the beginning of the new school year, and began hiring new teachers, figuring salaries, paying food bills, supervising construction projects on campus, and handling boarding requests for the fall. Her last weeks continued to be busy. She met with the Minister of Education to devise a plan for 9th-grade girls who hadn't passed their exams. Annice wanted to encourage them to attend nursing school, given the region's shortage of nurses (and perhaps her old desire to have been a nurse?). The Minister wouldn't hear of it.

There were the sessions of Yearly Meeting to help with—even while maintenance work was being done in guest residences, covering their rooms with dust. Annice helped prepare meals while supervising the painting of windows and grills at the Girls School, tasks long put off. Later in the summer there were 36 French guests to look after, and 20 from Whittier, California, who needed attention and a presentation on "The Palestine Problem." "I can't remember that I have ever been so tired," she wrote to her friend Mina Emily Seidler.

In the middle of the summer Annice admitted that she couldn't keep it up any longer without a break, and booked four days at the Catholic Sisters Rest Home in Emmaus, where she simply did nothing but read and relax.

All was not drudgery and frustration, however, in her final weeks in Ramallah. She visited the Christian village of Taybeh, a few miles from Ramallah. This was the biblical home of Gideon, and she enjoyed visiting a church built on the traditional site where Gideon had laid out the fleece to test what he understood to be God's directive to him. Annice's host family asked her to read Judges 6 and 7, the passages describing that history, while at the church.

Annice also attended a lunch at the home of one of the U.S. Consular officials in Jerusalem: "We had the opportunity to drink beer before lunch and had a glass of something put at our places at the table. We wondered how our consular people can drink two bottles of beer and three glasses of wine and still do good work!"[143]

143 Letter, July 30, 1966. Private collection of Sarabeth Marcinko.

Other activities included helping to break in the new principal at the Boys School and reveling in the fact that the 9th-grade test results at the Girls School were better than those at the Boys School. But she was ready to "fade out of the picture now," as she expressed in a late August letter home.

Annice expressed that all the things she had achieved had been done not for her own credit but for the School, but she was justifiably proud of the improvements she had made in her extended "one year replacement." Others commented to her that she ought to stay another year so she could enjoy them. Her response was, "Don't you know there are enjoyable things in other places?"

Even Jirius Mansur, the clerk of the Meeting with whom she often disagreed, encouraged her to stay. He believed that the Schools needed American administrators, as he felt that one never knew where the locals stood. He wanted to know why she was leaving: "He admitted that I sometimes make him mad, but he knows where I stand, and that I keep my word, and when I am most firm it is for the good of the School. People are learning to appreciate me, and now I plan to leave. Jirius sometimes has very sane comments."[144]

By late August Annice had started packing and attended many "good-bye" teas and a celebratory meal of a favorite, *musakhan*,[145] at a Ramallah restaurant. She was disappointed, though, to learn that Meeting member Violet Zaru had declined the offer to take over as principal. Annice stayed busy with School details into the first week of school in September, still concerned that no principal had been named and that the interim principal, pastor Kenneth Shirk, lived too far away to be able to respond quickly in an emergency.

Departing in mid-September, Annice took a leisurely trip home through Istanbul, Athens, the Italian countryside, Vienna, Germany, Amsterdam, and London, finally flying KLM from London to the U.S. in early October. She probably thought once more that this would be her last trip abroad. Again, she was wrong.

---

144 Letter, August 14, 1966. Private collection of Sarabeth Marcinko.
145 Musakhan is a traditional Palestinian dish consisting of a large piece of flat bread soaked in olive oil, covered with cooked onions and sumac, and topped with pieces of baked chicken.

CHAPTER 10

Return to Ramallah in 1967

When Annice retired after the 1965–66 school year, Ohio Quaker Kenneth Shirk was named interim principal of the Girls School while also serving in the same position at the Boys School. Somewhat humorously, *Shirk* in Arabic means "idolatry," one of the great heresies in Muslim understanding. Though this didn't cause him any trouble in his position, managing both campuses during a time of growing tension provided difficulty enough.

Back home in Indiana, Annice was keeping busy. Shortly after her return home in the fall of 1966, she was in Richmond for the executive committee meeting of the American Friends Board of Missions. There was always deputation work to do, some of it with Lois Snyder. Annice also worked up a written virtual tour of the Friends Schools in Ramallah. It began with *Ahlan wa Sahlan* (welcome) and ended with *Mahsalamy!* (good-bye).

Annice's speaking engagements took her as far as North Carolina. She declared that many of the pastors there were more emotionally evangelistic than many Friends—although some could be of service in the mission field. When she wasn't traveling, she stayed close to home to help with grand-nieces and -nephews whose mother, Donna Chapman, had recently died in her 30s.

All this didn't seem to be enough to satisfy her, however. In a May 1967 letter to Harold Smuck at the FUM Central Office, she reported that she was rested and ready for any work, perhaps even at the Central Office. She wouldn't be available until September, though, since she would be serving as a counselor at the Quivering Arrow summer camp in Oklahoma—part of FUM's work in Indian missions. Harold responded with a suggestion of a possible position for her at the Quaker Hill Conference Center, next to the Central Office in Richmond. He also shared the good news that a new principal for the Girls School in Ramallah had finally been hired: Peggy Paull from California.

Meanwhile, troubles in the Middle East would affect all those plans. Tension was building between Israel and the Arab states, and mid-May of 1967 saw the beginning of a chain of events that would lead to the Six-Day War in June, even though most likely neither Israel nor the Arab governments in Egypt, Syria, and Jordan actually wanted war.

The Soviets warned Egypt of intelligence indicating that Israel was planning to attack Syria. In response, Egypt moved troops to the Sinai border with Israel, while telling the UN to remove its peacekeeping forces from the border. Israel itself had refused to have UN forces on their side of the border.

Egypt then closed the Straits of Tiran to Israeli shipping, and Egypt, Syria, and Jordan signed a mutual defense pact. Egyptian MiGs made reconnaissance flights over Israel's nuclear facility in the Negev. Tensions continued to build amid the bluster of mutual threats. It has since been argued that Nasser's bellicose speeches were nothing more than part of an Arab tradition of grandiloquence—and that words were the only weapons intended.

Israel took the words seriously, though, and in an early dawn preemptive strike on June 5 destroyed 90% of the Egyptian air force on the ground. The next six days of fighting were essentially a mopping-up exercise, at the end of which Israel occupied the Sinai Peninsula, the Gaza Strip, the Golan Heights, East Jerusalem, and the West Bank. Jordan offered only token resistance—and that to honor their commitment to Egypt—and Jordanian troops quickly retreated across the Jordan River.

As increasing tension signaled the coming war, in late May the Friends Schools closed, and final exams and graduation exercises were canceled. A day after war broke out, Israeli troops occupied the cities of the West Bank, including Ramallah. Jordanian forces had fled, even as King Hussein's radio addresses urged Palestinians to resist. As Ramallah Quaker Sina Mansur commented about the King's entreaty, "We had no weapons! What were we supposed to attack Israeli tanks with—our fingernails and teeth?"

Damage from the war was not as extensive in Ramallah and El-Bireh as elsewhere, but the impact of artillery shells was felt at the Boys School, where the School's station wagon was heavily damaged, hundreds of windows were broken, and many trees affected. Across the road at Swift House, the cistern was cracked, and two neighborhood girls were killed when their house was hit by shells. (When Annice's grand-nephew Max Carter was living in Swift House in 1970, at the beginning of his teaching at the Boys School, he found shrapnel on the roof as he cleaned it in preparation for the rainy season and filling the repaired cistern.)

The meetinghouse roof was damaged and one of the rooms in the annex destroyed. Worship continued in the building, however, until June 11 when a curfew was imposed.

Back in the U.S., Annice received a June 5 letter from Harold Smuck, who wrote, "The news from the Middle East is certainly not good. I expect that you are as keenly aware as anybody!"[146] That letter precipitated a conversation that resulted in Annice's agreeing to undertake a short period of emergency service in Ramallah to assist the new principal at the Girls School and "take considerable initiative in deciding what can and ought to be done."[147] Salary arrangements were agreed upon, and July 25 was set as her departure date. There were reports from Ramallah that the Israeli Military Governor had declared that schools would reopen and be conducted as they had been in the previous year.

Annice fulfilled her commitment to the Quivering Arrow Camp but canceled all other appointments, including her registration for the Third Friends World Conference, to be held that summer at Guilford College in North Carolina. Evidently not all were in agreement about the wisdom of Annice's returning to Ramallah. She shared with Harold that when she told her brother Oakley, he responded that she had no business going over there at her age! She quipped that her (older) brother must think her old and decrepit.

On July 25, three days after returning from her service as a camp counselor in Oklahoma, she left for Ramallah. She carried with her a letter from FUM staff member David Stanfield which stated, "This is to inform you that the holder of this letter, Annice Carter, is under the special appointment of our Board of Missions to aid the Ramallah Monthly Meeting of Friends in the administration of Friends emergency relief services in Ramallah."[148] The letter could have stated "and other services in Ramallah

---

146 Friends United Meeting Wider Ministries Records.

147 Letter from Harold Smuck, July 7, 1967. Friends United Meeting Wider Ministries Records.

148 Letter written by David Stanfield as requested by Harold Smuck, July 25, 1967. Friends United Meeting Wider Ministries Records.

as required," as work under the auspices of the Friends Meeting was minimal, but other tasks were plentiful!

Paull's report after that first year included her remarks on the difficult situation. A military governor had taken up residence in the former compound of the British Mandate Authority in Ramallah, which had later housed the Jordanian authorities. Israelis replaced Jordanians in the police station next to the Boys School. Army patrols circulated around the city. Travel was restricted, funds in Jordanian banks were inaccessible, and the economy was severely impacted by the closing of borders. Those same closures also meant the loss of students from elsewhere in the region.

Annice's travel to Ramallah was not easy. El Al, the Israeli airline she was booked on, bumped her in Athens, and while she was seething in anger from the treatment, she heard a voice, "Why, Miss Carter, what are you doing here?" It was Joyce Herman from the U.S. Consulate in Jerusalem. He was in the Athens airport on his way back to his post and remembered Annice from her previous stint in Ramallah. He managed to find her a seat on the British airline BEA, met her in Tel Aviv to drive her to Jerusalem, and had another Consulate staff person drive her on to Ramallah.

"He's a constant drinker and sometimes quite high, but I was very grateful for his assistance," she wrote in a July 29 letter to her friend Mina Emily Seidler.

In that same letter, Annice wrote that she was already hard at work on class schedules, finding teachers, and preparing the School buildings for classes after 100 refugees had been housed there before moving on. She helped in the FGS office and tried to stay behind the scenes, as she was not the acting principal. Interestingly, Annice wrote her return address as "Ramallah, Israel." She learned quickly, however, that nobody in Ramallah considered the city part of Israel. All subsequent letters had a return address of "Ramallah via Israel"!

In letters home, Annice described the changing scene in Ramallah. The city was crowded, not only with refugees but also with Israeli tourists. The Israelis were buying up so many things, she reported, that there was little produce left for the locals. Israeli soldiers patrolled the streets, many of them Yemeni and Iraqi Jews who could speak Arabic.[149] She noted that

[149] Annice expressed surprise that there were such Jews—as well as finding that among the Israeli soldiers were Arabic-speaking Druze.

the meetinghouse roof had been damaged by rocket fire and that wrecked and burned cars and buses still littered the highway to Jerusalem.

In spite of the Palestinians' discouragement and lost hope following the recent war, continued deep bitterness about 1948, and hatred of the United States for its support of Israel, Annice found people in Ramallah to be friendly, courteous, and generally happy. She experienced no difficulties as an American, as Friends workers were trusted. She commented that "my return brought a ray of hope for the parents and teachers who were fearful that the Schools would not open this year."[150]

Annice observed that, unlike the 750,000 Palestinian Arabs who had fled their homes during the 1948 war that created the state of Israel, Palestinians did not abandon their property during this war. They were aware of the fact that Israel had instituted laws barring Arabs from returning to their homes and did not compensate them for the property taken over by the state. "This seemed to disappoint Israel," Annice wrote, "because they voiced the problem of having to rule an area with about one million unfriendly Arabs living in it. They would evidently like to have the area for Jewish occupation but hardly know what to do with so many Arabs. Various methods have been devised to encourage Arabs to leave. Time will tell how effective they will be."[151] Annice found that the Arabs living in the occupied areas were tired of war and simply wanted a real peace that would give them the opportunity for a normal life, even though they realized that—as in Israel—Arabs would be second-class citizens if they remained militarily occupied.

She also shared an interesting incident that took place at the home of Friends Meeting member Najla Shahla. Soldiers had come to her house, searching for a refugee reported to be living there who was suspected of having a revolver. They made another man residing at the compound rake out the pit under the outhouse. He found a rifle in two pieces but no revolver. Later, he did find the revolver, and when he reported it to one of the Iraqi soldiers, he was advised to go to Jerusalem and buy an old one to turn in—and keep the newer one!

Annice's August 9 letter to Harold Smuck discussed her difficulty working with Jirius Mansur, the clerk of the Friends Meeting. She felt that he

---

150 1967 Christmas letter. Private collection of Betsy Alexander.
151 1967 Christmas letter. Private collection of Betsy Alexander.

had outsized plans for the $5,000 that FUM had sent with her. He not only wanted to repair the roof and annex, which had sustained considerable damage from Israeli rocket fire, but he also wanted to repair the stone wall around the meetinghouse and affix a decorative metal railing on top. Annice was of the opinion that the grounds didn't deserve such a fancy fence! Jirius was critical of the women who arranged to have the windows repaired, saying it cost too much—even though the total of all the repairs came to only a few hundred dollars. Jirius clearly wanted money left over for his wall.

Fortunately for Annice, the Meeting committee that was coordinating response to the damage refused most of Jirius's ideas, including his suggestion that the Schools lower their fees by 25%. Fuad Zaru, a pharmacist who would later be named the new principal of the Boys School, pointed out that most people in Ramallah and El-Bireh still had jobs and that the shopkeepers were doing okay. The main issue, he said, was that there were still delinquent fees to be collected after the Schools had closed so abruptly in May.

Annice was concerned about prospects for the Boys and Girls Schools. They were scheduled to open on September 5, but no other schools had yet announced intention to open. She was looking forward to the arrival of new FGS principal Peggy Paull but admitted that she was rather dreading it, too: "I feel so helpless in a position of being supposed to give her aid and counsel. We really do not know what is possible. I have never felt so hopeless."[152]

There were to be no boarders at the FBS and only a handful at the FGS. She found it "queer" that, while she had previously advocated for the Girls School to stop receiving boarders and the Boys School had long been asking to increase their boarding capacity, now the Boys School would have none while the Girls School would have a few. Of further concern was a rumor that Israel would be forcing their own curriculum on the Schools, including their version of history and geography.

Knowing these difficulties, it is surprising to read what followed the opening lines of a letter Annice sent to Harold Smuck on August 15: "I am heart-sick, discouraged, and disillusioned," she wrote. But the cause of her distress was not the military occupation, the difficulties of preparing for the opening of school, or the issues at the Friends Meeting. No, Annice was

152 Letter, August 13, 1967. Private collection of Sarabeth Marcinko.

appalled that a young American teacher at the Girls School was wearing a mini-skirt and not observing local customs! Not only that, $700 had been spent on a hi-fi set for the principal's residence at the Boys School and other funds had been used by the principal to buy liquor! Moreover, the Boys School principal preferred socializing in Jerusalem rather than in Ramallah. Annice was very worried about the Schools' reputation. She did quip, though, that she was probably born 50 years too soon!

The good news in the letter was that Jirius Mansur had paid for the meetinghouse roof repair out of his own pocket.[153]

In spite of her concerns, Annice settled into a routine that was difficult in another way. Even with Peggy Paull's arrival, Annice was having trouble holding back from taking over her former responsibilities as principal. She tried to be patient and explained to people that there was a new person in that role. But she found simple pleasures, too. She enjoyed breakfast with fellow early riser Donn Hutchison and quipped that Peggy sometimes didn't rise until after 9:00 A.M.

While continuing to assist in the office, Annice also spent a great deal of time at the Military Governor's Office obtaining the proper permits for the School and travel permits for an FGS graduate who had been accepted for enrollment at Aurora College in Illinois. She advised Peggy Paull on the work to be done, and even washed Peggy's dirty clothes that had been thrown unwashed into her luggage as she rushed from the World Conference at Guilford College to catch her flight to Ramallah! As Annice explained in one of her letters, the clothes were drip-dry, and she didn't think the women doing cleaning at the School knew how to do clothes like that.

Annice also "ran interference" with some of the teachers. Five of the Girls School faculty had told Peggy Paull that there were rumors the School would be blown up if they opened in September. "I really gave them a lecture," she wrote, and apologized to Peggy later. "We may not like the idea of [the Israeli] occupation or occupiers, but they have the power and authority now, and we will get along better to go ahead and do what is right than spend our time trying to oppose them."[154]

153 Friends United Meeting Wider Ministries Records.
154 Letter to the FUM Central Office, August 27, 1967. Friends United Meeting Wider Ministries Records.

In a September 3 letter, Annice commented about a "radical" lecture from Fuad Zaru's brother about the Schools' re-opening. He believed it was inappropriate to do so. The occupation should be resisted in all ways. She was of a different opinion, even while admitting that many families would be hesitant to send their children the first week and that schedules and staffing would be a work in progress for the first several weeks. Teachers already committed for the year were being loaded with extra classes until it was certain what faculty would be returning, some being assigned 31 class periods a week. It should be noted that in Kenya and at Pacific College, Annice had even more!

School did open in September with 217 registered students, but attendance was irregular as there continued to be rumors of threats, and parents were afraid. Amman radio urged non-attendance as a protest against Israel's occupation of the formerly Jordanian West Bank. The Friends Schools were the only schools open. There were, of course, other difficulties. Israel wanted to determine textbooks and curriculum, but the Schools were following the former Jordanian system. The biology teacher at the Girls School didn't return, making it necessary for Annice to fill in. Only one-third of delinquent fees had been collected; there was a shortage of books; and with borders closed, the Girls School had only three boarders.

"Money is a real problem," Annice wrote in a September 15 letter. "We can't pay staff their compensation yet. I tell Peggy not to worry. Something will happen. I know not what."[155]

Not all the news she shared in letters was of difficulties with the occupation, the Meeting, or the staff. Annice commented that she was eating too much at social teas, which "does not help one to lose pounds." She noted that her form-fitting dresses were showing off her "round belly." Also in the "eating" department, Annice complained that ants had gotten into her closet and eaten holes in three of her good dresses! She noted that an American teacher, Donn Hutchison, would be housed at the Girls School so as to have a male presence on the campus. In non-School news, she told about how Orthodox Jews in Jerusalem were stoning cars that violated the Sabbath.

In a lengthy September letter to the FUM Central Office, Annice shared what she did know about the political situation and the nature

155 Friends United Meeting Wider Ministries Records.

of Israel's occupation. She believed that the Arabs had been "taken in" by their leaders' bellicose talk, while it should have been obvious to all that Israel would win in the '67 war. She noted that Egypt had done nothing for the Arabs in '48 or '56, and they should have known by now that "big talk" ought not to be believed.

Annice also knew that Israel had a detailed plan to take all the land from the Jordan to the sea, and she was aware of Israel's violations of the Armistice agreement in '49, including making Jerusalem the Capital and keeping heavy weaponry there. She had learned that, when the Israelis came into Ramallah during the June war, they found no Jordanian soldiers there since they had been withdrawn without fighting. No Arabs fired a shot. Yet two girls, one a student at the FGS, were killed near the Boys School by Israeli rockets launched from the outskirts of Jerusalem.

"Three and a half months after the war," she wrote, "people are still wondering, are we pawns for greater powers?"[156] Israel had bulldozed several villages on the border, but they were letting people carry on in their own jobs. Israel was surprised by the cooperation of the Arabs, but Annice also noted that Arabs are very courteous people.

In further commentary, Annice acknowledged the injustice of the British (with the Balfour Declaration) letting Jews set up a national home in Arab lands. In the '48 war, Arabs had fled in fear but hadn't been allowed back. She did recognize that after the '67 war refugees were allowed to return to their homes in the occupied territories, and noted that two Ramallah sisters were in a *Time* magazine photo of Arabs returning to the West Bank. She believed world opinion had helped the situation.

Annice went on to say that Israel was afraid of having a large population of Arabs in a Jewish state, so she believed that they would be willing to negotiate over a return of the West Bank.

In other observations, Annice described how Israel demolished homes in places where Israeli soldiers had been shot at. In Jerusalem, more than 135 Arab homes had been destroyed to build a plaza in front of the Western Wall, holy to Judaism. Arab shop owners in East Jerusalem were being told by Jewish visitors that they should stop selling Christian souvenir items and switch to Jewish ones.

---

[156] Friends United Meeting Wider Ministries Records.

She said building in Ramallah had stopped; banks were closed; people were out of work; and a permit system was in place for travel to Jerusalem, nine miles away. No solution was in sight; all was in flux. When there were strikes, Israeli troops forced merchants to re-open their shops. Israel imposed a curfew so they could take a census, which Annice likened to the Roman census in New Testament times. When shops were open, Israeli tourists would come again and buy up items, especially, she commented, the figs!

There continued to be rumors of strikes, causing classes to be canceled on occasion. School attendance was irregular into late September. Of the 285 students registered, only 223 were attending. Families were nervous. Teachers were afraid to raise controversial subjects in the classroom. If Jordan returned, would there be a return to the law that had required teaching Islam to Muslim students? The students liked the combined "Ethics" class as it didn't foster division among them.

With all that, Annice remarked that things were beginning to return to normal. Enough fees had been collected to pay salaries, and Peggy was feeling better about things. Annice had even been able finally to take her to Jerusalem for sightseeing, and she commented on Peggy's fancy camera that she fiddled with to get the right settings and exposures. Annice noted that this took too much time; her own camera was a basic one with which she could just "snap and go." With the occupation and changes in Jerusalem, however, Annice indicated that she took no pleasure in going there anymore. "Tie me up and keep me in Ramallah if ever I express an intent to go there on a Saturday again," she wrote.[157]

Annice was delighted to be able to get away for a visit to the Galilee, enjoying seeing sites that had been "off limits" to those in the West Bank between 1948 and 1967. She visited Tiberias and Capernaum as well as the site of Jesus' feeding of the 5,000. She relished a stay at the Scottish Hospice by the Sea of Galilee. This was refreshing for her after the hard work of the first few weeks of opening school. She expressed that she had been at a "low ebb" from all the effort.

In an October 21 letter,[158] Annice reported an incident that has become an embellished legend. Around 9:00 P.M. one night, she was in bed

---

157 Letter, November 12, 1967. Private collection of Sarabeth Marcinko.
158 Letter, October 21, 1967. Private collection of Sarabeth Marcinko.

at the Girls School when she heard two explosions. The frightened FGS boarders came to her third-floor apartment. She got out of bed, put on a robe, and was met by some of the FGS staff, too. Then she heard shooting on the circular drive inside the front gate. Peggy Paull, too, had come to Annice's apartment and was so frightened by the shooting that she simply sat on the stairs.

There were three or four rounds of machine gun fire from two Israeli jeeps, which then drove away. "The business made me angry," Annice wrote, "so I went downstairs and called the Israeli Police Post." She spoke with six people before she found someone who knew English. Meanwhile, another jeep entered through the open gate.

By then, the Military Governor's Office had called, and she was asked to go to their compound (the former British Mandate and Jordanian Governance buildings): "I asked them if they knew it was night and that there was shooting." She told them she'd go in the morning, then put on a coat and went out to close the gate.

Annice returned to bed, but at midnight heard the gate open again. The soldiers had returned, this time shining their spotlights around and knocking on doors. She turned her light on and went outside to ask them what they wanted. They said they were trying to scare away saboteurs. She confronted them about the earlier shooting, chastised them for scaring her, the girls, and the staff, and told them to leave and close the gate behind them. Which they did.

When Annice did go to the Military Governor's Office, she "told the Military Governor that the next time they wanted to frighten saboteurs in our school to let us know before they started shooting."

Donn Hutchison, asked about the incident and whether Annice had, in fact, confronted the soldiers, confirmed that it happened, but that Annice admitted her knees were knocking under her bathrobe!

By late October, there had been seven weeks of school without the rumored difficulties coming to pass. Attendance was increasing and finances were becoming settled, but government schools were still not open; they wouldn't open until mid-November, when their classes also began with no difficulty. Annice's letters reported mundane matters such as dress-making for staff and students; helping in the kitchen with meal preparation; and the visits of Friends from the States, Korea, and India, as well as other guests who tried to "straighten me out" on the politics of the situation. She reported that she had remained calm until they were leaving, and "then I gave a rather pointed statement."

Annice reported that the Schools had decided to observe the Muslim holidays, but not the national ones, and commented on the recent feast of Eid ul-Mi'raj. Confessing that she had not known the significance of the holiday before, she now described it as similar to the Christian Ascension Day.[159]

The political situation, however, continued to be far more unsettled than conditions at the Schools. Annice was upset with the UN for taking so long to address the matter. "The longer they take, the more firmly entrenched are the victors," she wrote in a November letter.[160] She worried about the reports that pressure was building in Israel to move Israeli families into the West Bank.

In late November, Annice was happy to welcome the visiting president of George Fox College, Milo Ross, and his wife. She accompanied them to a variety of sites, including Jericho, where they visited the archeological digs and Hisham's Palace, the Dead Sea, and the Jordan River.

Her letters resumed reporting on the day-to-day: concerns about a male staff member whose "gallantry" was attracting too much female attention; preparations for a big Thanksgiving dinner; more sewing; and the start of the Ramadan fast, with cannons going off to announce the beginning—which she initially thought were another kind of explosion.

Annice commented on Israel's new regulations at holy sites, especially at the Western Wall. In typical Annice fashion, she noted that women were to cover their arms at the Wall, but elsewhere they were hardly covered at all! She also critiqued the Israeli coffee that was all she could find in the stores, lamenting the absence of Maxwell House. She was glad she hadn't heard any staff complaints yet but noted that they typically preferred tea, anyway.

Although finances were stabilizing at the FGS through the collection of fees, Annice mentioned that the Boys School was running short, and

---

[159] The observance commemorates the Prophet Mohammed's miraculous flight on his steed Barak to "the farther mosque," assumed to be in Jerusalem. From there, he ascended into the heavens, where he communed with the prophets and Allah.

[160] Letter, November 5, 1967. Private collection of Sarabeth Marcinko.

the principal might have to make an emergency trip to Jordan to get funds out of the bank there. However, she feared that the Girls School would be running a deficit of 3,000 Jordanian dinar (nearly $5,000 U.S. dollars) in the summer to pay for salaries. She recalled the time in 1957 when she had arrived as principal and the Girls School had only JD 72—and then came a bill for wood amounting to JD 110: "It wasn't too pleasant."

"FUM will probably have to do fund-raising to keep the School from going in the red," she wrote. "I still think the right thing to do is to phase out the work here and close up."[161]

Finally in late November, just before she began making plans to return to the U.S., Annice was relieved of teaching her biology class. She had not known, when she accepted the task of helping the Girls School in its new post-war situation, how long she would be needed. In one early letter, Annice had said that she supposed she'd stay until "I step on someone's toes." She evidently hadn't done that, as she was needed for half of the academic year.

Wanting to experience one more Christmas in the Holy Land, she scheduled her departure for December 28 and went with the Rosses to Christmas Eve observances in Bethlehem. She also participated in the Christmas programs at the School, held even though some protested that it was inappropriate to celebrate during the time of mourning under military occupation.

"I want to stay to see how things progress," she wrote in a letter. "I know all the problems have not yet been met. On the other hand, I am always eager to get back home."[162]

Ready for the next chapter in her life, Annice returned to Russiaville—after teaching the FGS cook, Jalileh, how to prepare American foods!

---

[161] Letter, December 10, 1967. Private collection of Sarabeth Marcinko.

[162] Letter to family, November 26, 1967. Friends United Meeting Board of Missions Records.

CHAPTER 11

Annice and USFW

During the times Annice was not directly serving on the mission field, she devoted much of her time and energies to activities that supported mission work and other missionaries. One of the greatest beneficiaries of her efforts was the group now called the United Society of Friends Women International (USFWI). Her involvement and interest in this organization, like her interest and work in Palestine, is known to have extended at least from her first time of service on the mission field in 1929 to her death in 1988—more than 60 years. Over the time of her involvement, USFWI, like Palestine, experienced many changes in its organization, names, and members. Like family, church, and service on the mission field, the organization was a major part of her life and, because it had originated in Western Yearly Meeting where she grew up, may have been an influence on her life choices from her early childhood.

ORIGINS OF USFWI

Eliza (Clark) Armstrong Cox is known as the first leader and organizer of the woman's missionary society movement among Friends. Born in North Carolina, she grew up in Monrovia, Indiana, as a member of West Union Friends Meeting and settled with her first husband in Sand Creek Quarter, where they were members of Hopewell Monthly Meeting. An article in the March 1941 *Friends Missionary Advocate* says that she "…became more active in the church, and was deeply interested in missions."

> In the late winter of [1880], Eliza visited her parents at Monrovia. There she heard of the organization of a woman's foreign missionary society by Methodist women in the community. Being the only organization in that village for the study of missions, women of other denominations were join- ing the new missionary society, including some Friends. The thought was impressed on Eliza's mind that if our women were joining other denomi- national groups to study missions, it showed a desire on their part to work

160

for missions and that there were no opportunities among Friends for them to develop along missionary activities in our own denomination. . . .

Eliza says she "suddenly found herself in the grip of a beautiful vision." Here was a new field of opportunity for Friends.

She went home and organized a group for mission study. In March of 1881, corresponding with a close friend and former teacher from Mooresville, Indiana, she found that the women of White Lick (now Mooresville) Meeting had already formed a woman's foreign missionary society. So she began the work of planning a course of study on missions for Friends women. The article continues:

Letters were sent to influential women in other parts of Western Yearly Meeting. . . . By the time of Western Yearly Meeting [annual sessions] (which in those years convened in September) there were eight missionary auxiliaries in active operation within the yearly meeting.

In September, 1881, one day during yearly meeting week, ten or twelve women, all vitally interested in the new missionary move [sic], met at noon under a tree on the campus and were united in thought of presenting the whole plan to the women's meeting that afternoon, which was done, and all were encouraged by the hearty approval. Steps were taken to organize the scattered auxiliaries into a yearly meeting missionary society. . . .[163]

The 1940 May, June, and July-August issues of *Friends Missionary Advocate* told how, after a few years, the Western Yearly Meeting Missionary Society reached out to begin working with other yearly meeting societies:

At Western Yearly Meeting held in September, 1887, the Woman's Missionary Society, being the first organized, felt it to be its duty to invite all the other yearly meeting missionary societies to meet with delegates from Western in Indianapolis in the spring of 1888. The invitation was cordially accepted and representatives appointed by the other yearly meetings. The months intervening were spent in shaping the framework for the new organization and in preparing a program for the first representative gathering of Quaker women on the American continent.[164]

This five-day conference with delegates from ten yearly meetings was so inspiring that the group determined to meet again in two years.[165]

163 "Early Years of Eliza Armstrong Cox," *Friends Missionary Advocate*, March 1941.

164 *Friends Missionary Advocate*, May 1940.

165 *Friends Missionary Advocate*, June 1940.

The second conference held in the interest of missions by Friends women gathered in Glens Falls, New York, in May, 1890. This, too, was a time of great blessing and inspiration as had been that first assembly in Indianapolis, two years previous. In Glens Falls an official name, "The Woman's Foreign Missionary Union of Friends in America," was adopted, and this continued to be the title until 1917. At that time, leaders felt one organization should direct all the work for missions sponsored by Friends women, including mission activities in the home field as well as those in foreign lands. The name thus became the "Woman's Missionary Union of Friends in America" [W.M.U.F.A.], simply by omitting the word "foreign" from the title. About the same time, there was a change in when conferences were held. They had convened once every three years and were called "Triennial Conferences." Our women were united in feeling that we could best promote the cause of missions by meeting twice in five years, one conference convening in the week just preceding the sessions of the Five Years Meeting [now Friends United Meeting], and the other coming together in two and one-half years, or half way between the dates of the Five Years Meeting.[166]

ANNICE'S EARLY CONTACT WITH USFW

By the time Annice was born in 1902, the Woman's Foreign Missionary Union conference had also met in Blue Island, Illinois; Wilmington, Ohio; and Marion, Indiana. It was scheduled to meet in Westfield, Indiana, that year. Of the next nine conferences through 1927, five were held in Indiana. It is very likely that Annice's home meeting, Russiaville, had a Woman's Foreign Missionary Society during the time she was growing up. At yearly meeting in September of 1882, New London Quarterly Meeting reported that only Honey Creek Monthly Meeting had an organized society, but that there was much demand for more literature pertaining to the work of missions. Did the influence of the woman's missionary societies in Western Yearly Meeting fuel Annice's early interest in becoming a nurse so that she could serve on the mission field? Was that also why her older sister,

[166] *Friends Missionary Advocate*, July-August 1940. Ironically, USFWI and Quaker Men International met in July of 2023 for the first joint triennial conference with FUM after more than fifty years of meeting in separate years. One of the main reasons now for having the triennial conferences jointly in the same year is the same as in the past—to best promote the cause of missions.

Achsa, felt the impetus to teach at Southland Institute, a school for blacks in Arkansas that was a mission supported by Indiana Yearly Meeting? Annice was 16 and still in high school when Achsa went to Southland with Mildred White (who later worked with Annice in Ramallah) after their graduation from Earlham College in 1918. At that time the only options for women on the mission field were teaching or nursing.

There was a Friends meeting and Woman's Missionary Society in Muncie, Indiana, where Annice attended Ball State in the 1920s. (The 1914 national conference had been held in Muncie.) Her plans to become a nurse having been thwarted by her parents, she became a teacher instead. After graduation she went to Bloomingdale, Indiana, to teach at the high school. She was the third Carter sister to go to Bloomingdale. Her sister Achsa had gone there to teach in the Penn Township high school after her time at Southland Institute. She married a local farmer in 1922 and, by the time Annice moved there in 1927 to teach, had three children. Annice lived with the family of her oldest sister, Nora, whose husband, Lyman Cosand, was the pastor of the Bloomingdale Friends Meeting. Besides teaching, she surely spent time with her four young nieces and one nephew who lived there.

Annice certainly encountered the Woman's Missionary Union at Bloomingdale, as it had been among the earliest meetings in Western Yearly Meeting to form a woman's missionary society. While Annice was living in Bloomingdale, the editor of the *Friends Missionary Advocate*, the "Official Organ of the Woman's Missionary Union of Friends in America," was Lenora N. Hobbs, a member at Bloomingdale Friends and a teacher at the school. Lenora wrote one of the letters recommending Annice to the Candidates Committee of the American Friends Board of Missions when she applied to go to Ramallah the first time.

ORIGINS OF THE *FRIENDS MISSIONARY ADVOCATE*

According to the *Friends Missionary Advocate* of January 1960:

> Soon after the first Missionary Societies were started in Western Yearly Meeting, 1881, women sought [publicity] for their aims and activities. At that time, the Friends church paper was *The Christian Worker*, published in Chicago by the Association of Friends and edited by Calvin W. Pritchard. In

response to the women's concern for a medium of publicity, he gave them a column in each issue. This was prepared by Ella J. Davis of Vermillion Quarter, (Western Yearly Meeting), and carried news of what mission minded women were doing. This continued until 1885, when women felt the time had come for them to start a separate publication. The *Missionary Advocate* then made its first appearance, with Esther Tuttle Pritchard as editor. She retained this position until 1890, when the Advocate [sic] became the official organ of the Women's Missionary Society and Eliza Armstrong Cox accepted the Editorship.[167]

When Eliza resigned after many years of loyal service, Lenora N. Hobbs took up the work as editor and served from 1916 to 1940.

ANNICE'S EARLY CONNECTIONS WITH THE *FRIENDS MISSIONARY ADVOCATE*

Annice most likely had heard of the *Friends Missionary Advocate* before she moved to Bloomingdale and worked with Lenora Hobbs. From the time of their beginnings, the Woman's Missionary Societies wanted information about missions—communications from mission workers, needs of the missions work, methods of mission service, new fields of service, news of what other groups were doing in the name of missions, and studies of mission areas. The *Friends Missionary Advocate* quickly became a unifying "organ" for providing this information to the local and yearly meeting groups. Over the years, secretaries of Friends Missionary Union departments such as Missionary Education, Literature, Stewardship, Peace and Public Morals, Young Woman's Work, and Junior and Primary Missionary Education wrote articles and developed programs of study. Reading lists were compiled and study books were sold and promoted. Columns such as "From Friends Fields" published excerpts of letters from Friends missionaries around the world. Another feature, "Interest and Organization," published information about what local and yearly meeting societies were doing. For instance, the September 1940 issue reported that Annice's sister Achsa Chapman would be vice-president of the Bloomingdale Missionary Society for the next year. And the October 1940 issue noted that Achsa was installed as

---

[167] *Friends Missionary Advocate*, January 1960.

Western Yearly Meeting Missionary Union's second vice-president during yearly meeting week that past summer.

Annice herself contributed to the *Friends Missionary Advocate* during her times of service in Ramallah and Kenya. During her two earliest times, from 1929 to 1941, she may not have sent as many letters as in later years, when she was either the principal or the administrator of the School. The March 1941 issue included this excerpt:

> In a letter that has just arrived from Ram Allah, written December 30th, Annice Carter writes: "Our relief work is still being held up by the Government. We have made our proposal to pay the salary of a nurse if the Government will do the rest. They have seemed so hesitant that I am wondering if we will ever get it done. Some of the Government people seem quite eager to cooperate and others seem afraid of us. I suppose they are afraid of getting involved in something, perhaps religious.
>
> The health side of things is by far the most needed this year; it has been neglected in all sections of the country during disturbances. Crops were good this year in most places so people are not suffering from lack of food as in previous years.
>
> Both schools are having a good year. The Boys' School has a total enrollment of 243 and the Girls' School 219. We are both full up with boarders, and are thankful for a good enrollment as expenses are greater. The Girls have a quantity of supplies left from last year, so we expect to get by all right.[168]

Annice's name continued to appear in the magazine even after she came home in 1941. The editorial in the March 1942 issue noted:

> Now that Annice Carter is home on furlough and is free for deputation work, those of you who are fortunate to be able to hear her speak, will learn interesting details of the whole situation [in Palestine]. Word has come that her schedule will probably include being in Western Yearly Meeting limits the last half of March, in Indiana Y.M. the first half of April and in Wilmington Y.M. after the [W.M.U.F.A.] Board meeting—that is the last half of April. Be on the lookout for local arrangements for her coming this spring, Friends of these sections.[169]

---

168 *Friends Missionary Advocate*, March 1941.

169 *Friends Missionary Advocate*, March 1942.

In the October 1942 issue, Annice wrote an article about the clinic that the government had agreed to open in Beit Ur el Tahta in March 1941, if the Friends in Ramallah, who had been doing relief work, would pay the salary of a nurse for two years. She explained that a nurse at one of the other four clinics had retired, and the government felt that "because of present conditions" they must close that clinic ". . . unless Friends will guarantee salary for their nurse for two more years, or until 1945."[170]

ANNICE JOINS THE EXECUTIVE COMMITTEE OF WMUFA

The 1943 General Conference of the WMUFA was held June 2–7 at Guilford College in Greensboro, North Carolina, in spite of concerns about wartime gas rationing. In an article, "Why? What? How?," Amy J. Marvel, then president, explained that when

> . . . the subject was being discussed as to whether it should be held this year, Ward Applegate said he lived on the three C Highway between Cincinnati, Columbus and Cleveland, and that more than fifty percent of the big trucks that passed his place were filled with beer and hard liquor. So long as that condition exists and so much gasoline is being used in this way, he thinks religious conferences should go on. (We agree with him!)

She went on to explain:

> Pastors who have C ration books can get gasoline enough to go and take a carful (if the distance isn't too great) and others can apply to their ration boards explaining the situation, and try to get extra gas. Some boards are more considerate than others, but in any case, cars must be filled, which will divide the expense and help the cause.[171]

In the same issue under "Highlights of the Conference in Prospect," Annice was mentioned as being one of the Friends missionaries, past and present, expected to be at the conference. Then in the July-August issue following the conference, this announcement appeared: ". . . Annice Carter has proven her real interest in the young people by agreeing to be Secretary of Young Woman's Work."[172]

---

170 *Friends Missionary Advocate*, October 1942.

171 *Friends Missionary Advocate*, May 1943.

172 *Friends Missionary Advocate*, July-August 1943.

Helen L. Woodard of Georgetown, Illinois, was serving on the Executive Committee at this time, as Literature Secretary. Since she was also from Western Yearly Meeting, Annice may have already known her. They were the same age, 41, and would become good friends. Helen was one of the "gals" to whom Annice would write her group letters in later years. And in 1960, after Helen was widowed and after Annice's sister Achsa had died, Helen would marry Achsa's widower, Leland Chapman.[173]

YOUNG WOMAN'S WORK (MARGARET FELL GIRLS) 1943–1948

As a department secretary, Annice wrote a monthly column for the *Friends Missionary Advocate* and attended Executive Committee meetings twice a year. Her columns offered program ideas to encourage groups of young teen girls to take an interest in missions and to promote giving to a special youth project for missions. The groups were often called "Margaret Fell Girls" after the wife of Quakerism's founder, George Fox. The motto of the department was "Every girl a spiritual center, radiating the Master's purpose in her home, daily life and church." From her first article, Annice struck out on her own path. The special project for 1943–1944 was to be contributions to the Lyndale Girls Home and the Swift-Purscell Boys School and Home in Jamaica. Annice suggested that "since we have included a contribution to the Swift-Purscell Boys School and Home in our project for the coming year, it should help us to encourage young men and boys to join in our Young Peoples Missionary Departmental activities."[174] By the December 1943 issue of the *Friends Missionary Advocate*, the title of her column was "Young People's Department," although the motto and title of the Department Secretary were not changed officially until after the 1946 General Conference in Muncie.

But Annice didn't insist on "my way or the highway." In the same first article, she also asked for help and feedback from her readers:

NOTE: Realizing how new and inexperienced I am for the work required of a Young Peoples Secretary, I shall depend upon group leaders and

---

[173] Helen's collection of bound copies of the *Friends Missionary Advocate*, 1938–78, provided many research materials for this book, especially for this chapter.

[174] *Friends Missionary Advocate*, September 1943.

supervisors to give aid and suggestions for carrying on the work. One of the ways you can be of great help is to write to me suggesting things that you would like included in our Advocate column. Do you want program suggestions and materials? Would it be helpful to review chapters in our study books? What methods have you used successfully to make your meetings interesting? If you would like to know what other young peoples groups are doing write and tell us about yours so we can have an exchange of ideas.[175]

The lack of response to this inquiry led to 12 more questions, in her December article, which she asked local group leaders or secretaries to answer.

The program suggestions for youth groups followed the same themes of study as those for the adults. However, different study books and other materials were often used. Annice must have spent a great deal of time in study and reading, as she would often quote excerpts and then pose questions for thought. An example is in the first article:

The study books for the young peoples groups this year are: 1. "The Trumphet [sic] of a Prophecy" by Richard Terrill Baker. This book shows that real missionary work starts at home with building up a cooperative spirit in the local group and making it cover all local projects as well as widening out to cover foreign projects. If your group can learn to see and meet the needs at home with a spirit of cooperation they are sure to cooperate in meeting the needs of the world. Think of your own community, your own church. Does anything happen there because you have a young peoples group?[176]

Annice also drew inspiration for the columns from other reading materials and from her past and present experiences. She described the Christmas evening service at Shepherds' Field near Bethlehem in a January 1944 issue (see Appendix C). And several times she referenced the welfare work she was doing in Howard County, her home county in Indiana.

My experiences as a Child Welfare Worker have brought a new realization for the all important business of living. The children who come into our care

175 *Friends Missionary Advocate*, September 1943.
176 *Friends Missionary Advocate*, September 1943.

are from non-Christian homes and most of them have had parents whose selfishness and lack of discipline have made them unfit for parenthood. . . . One of the ways Christian people are helping to minister to the least of these is by opening their homes to these unfortunate children and giving them training that will help them to adjust to society and to take their places as useful citizens. . . . It is our responsibility to help young people, who are looking forward to setting up a home, to start that home on Christian principles.[177]

Maybe because she felt that action and involvement are important parts of mission service, she often suggested projects such as collecting gifts for AFSC to give to Japanese-Americans in relocation camps. "To get to know all of our brothers and sisters in Christ," she suggested helping to put on a Vacation Bible School or some other activity at a Native American center. Annice also wanted the young people to be aware of and act on all of the needs around them:

With the crying needs of humanity in all parts of our world during this Christmas Season of 1945, let us remember that Jesus said, "Inasmuch as ye have done it unto one of these my brethren, ye have done it unto me," and let us celebrate His birthday this year by giving unto Him. Put prayerful thought on your Christmas plans this year and let your celebrations be, not so much for your families and friends, but for the sake of the Master.[178]

Annice also shared in these articles what mission service meant to her:

Do not get the idea that missionary work or Christian service is done only on some special designated field. In fact it can begin quite close home. Do we talk to our friends about spiritual experiences, or about the weather? In a recent Sunday School lesson we had the verse, "And many Samaritans of that city believed on him for the saying of the woman, which testified, He told me all that ever I did." A good word for our Master to a friend or acquaintance may mean a new disciple. Begin now, at home, to prepare for that broader service when you go to some special field as God's ambassador. "Christ has no hands but our hands to do His work today; He has no feet but our feet to lead men in His way."[179]

177 *Friends Missionary Advocate*, May 1946.

178 *Friends Missionary Advocate*, December 1945.

179 *Friends Missionary Advocate*, March 1947.

and

Jesus has set a standard for us: Preaching, teaching, healing, loving, serving. The choice is ours, for He cannot force us to follow. But any young person who will accept the challenge and give a life of consecrated service in any type of Mission work will be rewarded with a life full of pleasures and thrills, capped by a feeling of joy and satisfaction in having given all in the service of the Master and in helping to create a brotherhood of all His children. There is an increased need for Christian workers, both at home and abroad.[180]

Perhaps she was speaking also to herself—preparing, and yearning, for more time on the foreign mission field.

CHANGES PROPOSED FOR WMUFA

Maybe Annice's knack for bringing about change influenced the whole Executive Committee of WMUFA. The period of time from 1943 to 1948 brought about significant change for that organization. In advance of the 1946 General Conference in Muncie, Indiana, the March issue of the *Friends Missionary Advocate* published "Substitute By-Laws." These by-laws proposed both a new name, "The United Society of Friends Women," and an affiliation with FYM. Like the earlier enlargement of focus in 1917, which combined interest in foreign and home missions into one group, this change would enlarge the focus of the organization to include all the work of the Church at home and abroad. In many local meetings, there were two or more women's groups such as Ladies Aid, Missionary Societies, and Christian Endeavor, which sometimes were working on the same types of projects. If these could be combined into one group or society, their work might be more efficient and productive.

The WMUFA president at the time, Helen E. Walker, put forth this argument in her monthly letter: "There is a definite place for a Woman's Society in every Meeting . . . Christian women should be informed and concerned about the issues at our own door, as well as those in distant places. . . . It is our feeling that the Woman's Society should be an integral

---

[180] *Friends Missionary Advocate*, March 1945.

part of the Meeting and that this close relationship should prevail on other levels for our united work."[181]

The Executive Committee had already expanded the suggested programs for the year to include other topics in addition to the usual information on mission concerns. "The Seven Pillars of Purpose, 1944–45" were ". . . suggested as an aid for more efficient work in the Society." In addition to knowledge of the "Missionary situation," they included purposes such as developing and strengthening "Christian attitudes toward our fellow man," deepening prayer life, and aiding in the "cultivation of the Christian Home."[182] They also developed a "list of Monthly Program Emphasis" and published a new program handbook, *Blueprints*. The foreword of the first volume gives the purpose of this new publication: "This year, Suggested Program Outlines or BLUEPRINTS have been prepared which follow the recommended Monthly Emphasis. These are suggestions, and it is hoped that they will be suggestive; and that no one will be satisfied to use just what is in the outline. These are in no way to preclude the originality of persons planning and presenting a program. However, greater strength will come to us as a Union, as we think together on these things each month."[183] Annice prepared the section in *Blueprints* with "Suggestions for Young People's Groups." She continued to do this in four more editions through the end of her term as secretary of the Young People's Work Department.

The new by-laws were not adopted in full at the May 1946 conference, but the report was positive: "There was unity in the suggestion that the new By-Laws be studied for the next two years, tried out in societies and Yearly Meetings which want to test them, and that we bring our findings to our next conference. Many groups or meetings are already trying the plan of a United Woman's organization and are enthusiastic about it."[184] And the conference did approve of a "Program Editor" for *Blueprints* and a "Christian Service Secretary" being added to the Executive Committee to work towards the new plan.

[181] *Friends Missionary Advocate*, May 1946.

[182] *Friends Missionary Advocate*, June 1944.

[183] *Blueprints: Suggested Program Outlines for Woman's Missionary Societies of Friends in America*, 1944–1945.

[184] *Friends Missionary Advocate*, June 1946.

AN END AND A BEGINNING: 1948

Annice finished her time of service on the WMUFA Executive Committee with her usual "strictly business" attitude. She was very involved in the preparations and activities for the 1948 General Conference held at Poughkeepsie, New York. She chaired the Nominating Committee and had spent "long months of letter writing and several meetings" to find the group of women who would lead the society for the next term. New by-laws were again presented for approval, with much of the reasoning for change stated in the Preamble:

> Whereas, with the ever-broadening responsibilities evolving upon Christian women, and the need of enlisting all the women of Friends Meetings to share in the mission of the Church at home and abroad, and in order that a more unified organization might be consummated through which all the interests of Friends women might be channeled, it was voted at the conference held in Poughkeepsie, New York, May 1-5, 1948 to be known as The United Society of Friends Women.[185]

This time, the changes in name and expansion of purposes were approved and several positions of department secretaries were reorganized. As the outgoing, and last, Secretary of Young People's (previously Woman's) Work (the person replacing her was now the Secretary of Youth), Annice led a workshop on "Missionary Education for Youth." The report noted that "indifference on the part of adult leaders to the interests and needs of young people is disastrous to the future as well as to the present of our meetings. Losses in the ranks of our young people are irreparable. Consecrated, intelligent, efficient, sacrificial effort is a requirement in successful leadership for young people and it yields rich rewards."[186]

Even though her term had ended, Annice was not finished with her work with the organization now called the United Society of Friends Women (USFW). The same issue of the magazine that reported on the General Conference activities also reported that Western Yearly Meeting's Society had nominated Annice to be its president. There is a mystery, though, as to why, less than six months later, the November 1948 issue listed

185 *Friends Missionary Advocate*, February 1948.
186 *Friends Missionary Advocate*, June 1948.

a different name as president than Annice's. However, she did continue to aid USFW by writing a program outline on "The Near East" for the 1950–1951 issue of *Blueprints*. Her program discussed "interesting customs and activities of the people in various Near East countries." Perhaps closest to her heart would be the example from Palestine:

> I would like for you to know some of our Palestinians today. The majority are Moslems and Jews. Before World War I they lived together in peace and harmony, and had friendly business dealings with each other. As time went on great numbers of Jewish immigrants poured into Palestine and tensions developed that tended to separate friends. A spirit of nationalism developed in each group. Sometimes riots were instigated by the Jews, at other times by the Arabs. At last Jews and Arabs had no dealings together in the land that is dear to the heart of every Jew, Christian, and Moslem. Palestine has been torn asunder and we Christians have understood so little of the problems of its peoples that we have allowed it to become a victim of political maneuvering. It is costly not to know our neighbors today.[187]

MISSIONARY EDUCATION SECRETARY—1951-52

Annice was back on the Executive Committee in three years. After the Marshalltown, Iowa, General Conference, the *Friends Missionary Advocate* reported:

> Annice Carter needs no introduction to the United Society of Friends Women for she served as Youth Secretary from 1943 to 1948. She has also served for nine years as a teacher in our Girls School at Ramallah. She is particularly well fitted for her new task as our Secretary of Missionary Education.
>
> She is also Chairman of the Education Committee of the American Friends Board of Missions. She lives with her mother at Russiaville, Indiana. She has been doing welfare work in her home County since her return from Ramallah and serving Friends capably in various capacities.[188]

Annice's work with the American Friends Board of Missions, and other experiences, did make her very well suited for this new responsibility. Her articles were long and detailed, with much information about Friends

187 *Blueprints: Suggested Program Outlines for Friends Women*, Volume 7, 1950–1951.
188 *Friends Missionary Advocate*, September 1951.

missions and the individual's obligations and responsibilities for supporting mission work. She started "preaching" in her first column:

In thinking about the importance of Missionary Education for those who claim an interest in mission work we have been reminded of the verses in II Peter 1:5-7. [*For this very reason, make every effort to add to your faith goodness; and to goodness, knowledge; and to knowledge, self-control; and to self-control, perseverance; and to perseverance, godliness; and to godliness, mutual affection; and to mutual affection, love.*] We have often stressed the need for Faith in our Christian lives. It is important. It is basic. Yet it is only a beginning. Peter urges that followers of Jesus Christ must diligently seek to "add to our faith virtue; and to virtue knowledge"; Many of us have been content to stop with faith.

Friends groups have built up missionary work that is world wide. In early days members of Friends felt concerns for spreading the gospel in certain areas. Their families and fellow-Christians co-operated to send these missionaries to their chosen fields. The work has grown so that greater interest and co-operation have become necessary. The members of the [USFW] are now interested in and contributing to missions work in [many places around the world.] It is our duty, during the coming months, to "add knowledge" of our mission work and its needs so that our interest may be increased.

She also emphasized what she felt were the importance and benefits of attending conferences and reading the USFW magazine:

If you did not attend the Marshalltown conference you have had opportunity to read about it in the Advocate or perhaps you have heard a report from some one who was fortunate enough to attend. The experience of attending a conference, of seeing the people you have read about and getting interesting new items regarding new projects is a stimulating experience and increases the interest in all missionary projects. As we enter into our work this fall let us be mindful of the obligations we have assumed. We will remind you of a few this month and plan to mention others in the months to come.... You will be glad to know what your representatives are doing in your mission fields. Seek out sources of information. Be alert to the interesting stories from your mission area. The better informed you are the greater your interest will be and, through co-operation, our work will grow.[189]

---

[189] *Friends Missionary Advocate*, September 1951.

Even though each column was focused on a different monthly emphasis, she continually stressed the need to learn more about, and give to, Friends missions:

> Because we desire to show forth the love of God and minister to all mankind in need, we sometimes start new work or support work of other groups in needy areas. A consecrated individual, bearing a burden for needy people, can always present an appealing plea that touches our hearts and makes us want to help. All philanthropic organizations depend upon the appeal of human suffering to promote the financial giving that makes possible a ministry to that suffering. If we do not give our money wisely and prayerfully we may find that the work dearest to our hearts has suffered because we yielded to too many other calls of need. We are familiar with the old saying "the cobbler's children have no shoes." We, as missionary minded Friends, should look carefully at the needs of our own work.[190]

She was also not afraid to point out where she thought mission work had failed to reach the mark:

> Although we do not have American workers in Cuba and Mexico, we do have Friends work in these areas. It would be quite helpful to have some American workers in Cuba again because the Cuban Friends feel the need of spiritual guidance. Sometimes, for various reasons, we cut our mission endeavors too soon and leave to the Nationals too much responsibility before they are ready to assume it with courage and zeal. Such was the case in both Cuba and Mexico.[191]

EDITOR OF *FRIENDS MISSIONARY ADVOCATE*—1952-57

Annice's last column as Secretary of Missionary Education appeared in the same issue as this notice by the current editor:

> With Spring comes new life and change. Thus with the forth-coming June Advocate a new, yet old friend will greet you from the Editorial page. I am sure you will enjoy Annice's fresh wit as well as deep thoughts, as she brings to us, through the coming months, assistance and inspiration for our work and Society meetings.

[190] *Friends Missionary Advocate*, March 1952.
[191] *Friends Missionary Advocate*, October 1951.

Annice lives with her aged mother, having resigned recently from the Social Service work in which she had been engaged for several years. . . . We welcome you, Annice, as our new Editor and pray God's richest blessing may be yours.[192]

Annice titled her editorial page "Gleanings," and it was often a collection of poems and quotes from sources she had "gleaned" from her reading. But she still wrote her "sermons" and even did some creative writing. Before the 1954 conference in Whittier, California, her April editorial was a poem, "The Call to Whittier." The June issue credited the words of the conference hymn to Annice and another USFW member from Russiaville, Dorothy Stratton. The theme of the conference was "The Upward Call," and the tune was the hymn, "Jesus Calls Us O'er the Tumult." She again used her creative talents for an editorial poem, "Pray for the Conference," in the September 1956 issue before the Wilmington, Ohio, gathering. (Some excerpts from her editorials and other articles can be found in Appendix C.)

The position of editor did not have terms, as editors were appointed by the Executive Committee rather than being nominated and approved at the conferences. Annice might have served longer as editor if not for the opportunity to return to Ramallah after the death of her mother. Her final editorial expressed her regret and thanks to USFW.

I wish to take this opportunity to thank Friends Women for the fine cooperation they have extended to me during the years I have served on the Executive Committee, but especially since June of 1952 when I accepted the editorship of FRIENDS MISSIONARY ADVOCATE. There have been many interesting and pleasant experiences mixed with the rush and struggle of meeting printer's deadlines.

It is with real regret that I have resigned from editing our magazine. I really feel I could not have done it, had it not been for the longed for opportunity to return to the work in our Friends Girls School in Ramallah. When opportunity came to substitute for Anna Langston while she has a much needed furlough, I felt that God had answered prayer. It is a very big assignment as I can never hope to fill Anna's place, but I am hoping, with His help, to be able to do some small service in Ramallah. . . .

I have very much appreciated the friendships and contacts with Friends Women as we have met together in Conferences, and with those who met in Executive Committee sessions. One always gains inspiration and enthusiasm through these experiences of working and worshiping together. I realize that I shall sorely miss these contacts as I separate myself from you physically, but I am trusting that your interest and prayers will enable me to feel close to you spiritually, and I shall greatly need that if I am not to feel lonely and discouraged when faced with the heavy problems which so frequently confront one in Ramallah.

Many times I have received notes from you with such kindly messages of appreciation and encouragement. These always bring surprise as well as pleasure because they seemed so undeserved. And now, as various groups learn of my opportunity to return to Ramallah, the offer of gifts for our work there seems so generous and bring additional surprises. . . . May God's richest blessings attend you in your study and activity next year.[193]

USFW expressed its appreciation by making Annice the recipient of their Love Fund, one of four funds (the others were Faith, Hope, and Joy) designated for support of missionaries, especially women missionaries. Established in 1914 for the support of Esther Baird in India, the Love Fund had also provided support for Mildred White and Julia Reynolds in Ramallah. As the new editor explained, "Friends women may claim Annice Carter as a personal representative to Ramallah. . . . We shall follow the activities in Ramallah with renewed interest because of our associations with Annice through the past 15 years."

The editor also listed other tangible gifts that would go with Annice when she sailed: "Among the pieces of baggage accompanying her will be boxes of comforters and warm clothing contributed by many Women's Societies, drinking glasses and stainless steel ware for the girl's dining room, books for the library and other gifts being made to the school."[194]

Because of this "honor," as she called it, Annice would regularly write letters to be shared in the periodical, expressing her thanks and letting USFW members know about the work they were supporting. In one of her first letters after she arrived in Ramallah, she cited the differences she saw after 16 years away. She also reminded members of the differences their support had made in the past:

[193] *Friends Missionary Advocate*, July-August 1957.
[194] *Friends Missionary Advocate*, July-August 1957.

There are only two places in the Girls School that have changed much in the sixteen years I have been away. One of those is the office. I do not know how many of you know that the Friends Women of New England gave a sum of money, in memory of Frances E. Wheeler, to be used to refurnish the FGS Office. A large desk, cupboard, and four office chairs built of pretty maple have been provided. Also the office door is of maple. It makes the office so attractive and is a most welcome improvement. The other change is also a great improvement. That is the enlarged kitchen and storage space provided by the [USFW] Thank-Offering Fund a few years ago. I will say more about that at a later time, but now, many, many thanks.[195]

Annice continued to receive salary support from the Love Fund through 1959 when she went to Kenya. In an article about the recipients of the Four Funds in the December 1957 issue of *The Advocate*, her salary and that of Edith Ratcliff in Kenya from the Faith Fund were both said to be "$1320.00 per year or $110.00 per month." When contributions were more than enough to pay the salaries, the excess funds were used to do something extra for the recipients and their work.

Annice may also have been responsible for USFW adding scholarship funds for FGS students to their special projects list. An article/letter titled "Jesus Needs Loaves and Fishes" was printed in the December 1957 issue:

Before I returned to Ramallah, I was warned that one of the most difficult experiences I would face, would be that of refusing aid to the vast number of parents who are faced with the economic struggle so prevalent in Jordan. Yes, I admitted that it would be hard, but how really difficult it is no one can know until they are faced with the actual circumstances.... When I think of the help we could give these people [who are wanting to attend the Friends schools] if each concerned Friend in USA would give just a few dollars, I wish that each of you might see the circumstances of some of these fine people.... Only a small number can be admitted into this [one Secondary IV and V] school and the others are left without any school. Many people have sacrificed much to send them to school and it is of little help as far as employment is concerned unless they can finish Secondary V. There are many, many problems in this weary land. Let us ask ourselves, "What could Jesus do with my five loaves and two fishes!"

BRIEF RETURN TO THE U.S.—NOT ONCE, BUT TWICE

Since Annice went directly from her work in Ramallah to work in Kenya, she was not home for several years (1957 to 1962). Among her opportunities after her arrival back in the States in the late spring of 1962, she was able to speak to the Western Yearly Meeting USFW women in August. The October 1962 *Friends Missionary Advocate* reported:

> "Ye are My Witnesses" was the theme chosen by Annice Carter when she spoke to the women of Western Yearly Meeting during the 1962 annual sessions. She told of her years of service in both Africa and Ramallah with the kind of enthusiasm that made those listening feel she had had many rewarding experiences. In keeping with the needs in Ramallah mentioned by the speaker, $395 was received in a free-will offering to be used for the Ramallah Girl's School Project of $6000*.[196]

Also mentioned in the same news item was that the incoming president of the Western Yearly Meeting Society was Annice's friend, Helen (Woodard) Chapman. Annice returned to Ramallah just over a year later. Before she left her home, in a letter dated July 26, 1963, she pleaded the case for more funds from USFW members for scholarships for the School:

> On the eve of my departure to Ramallah for a short period of service I feel compelled to remind you of the continuing need for scholarship funds to permit a limited number of refugees to attend Friends Girls' School. Because of my experiences at F.G.S. a few years ago, I have a vivid recollection of the problem of trying to coordinate the pleas of refugee girls for admission to F.G.S. and stretching the limited funds to cover the necessary aid for their admission....
>
> It is important that Friends continue to demonstrate our belief in the teaching of Jesus that we must be our brothers' keepers. . . . The fact that our main Christian witness is in action rather than work makes it doubly important that we demonstrate our belief in ministering to the "least of these."
>
> It is our desire to have in our schools a cross-section of the economic and social groups of Jordan. We would be missing our mark if we failed

---

[196] *Friends Missionary Advocate*, October 1962. (*United Thank Offering/75th Anniversary of Ramallah--$3000 for Second story for Girls School and $3000 for Sanitary Unit for Whittier Hall).

to have a representative number of those who are underprivileged and in the refugee economic group. We are hoping that many groups, Sunday School classes and U.S.F.W. societies will send gifts of money for our scholarship fund.

The thing we are trying to get across is that we are happy to have any and all gifts, large or small, for this important project. Please do not forget this area of Friends witness in Jordan.[197]

When Annice returned to Ramallah in 1963 she was again the recipient of the USFW Love Fund. Her appreciation was apparent in her comments published in the November 1965 issue of the *Friends Missionary Advocate*.

One of the blessings of being the LOVE FUND recipient is the constant assurance that hundreds of women are expressing their love of God and interest in His work by contributing to this Fund. We work along, doing what has to be done, and hoping that our heavenly Father can bless and increase it for His glory.

I hope and pray that I may, in some measure, pass on to those with whom we work, a knowledge of God's love for us all. May Friends women be blessed as they labor, serve, and share in God's great program of outreach.

Annice retired after the 1965–1966 school year, but she wasn't able to return home until early October 1966. Her retirement was short, owing to the June Six-Day War in 1967. She returned to Ramallah in an emergency capacity at the end of July to help the new principal repair and prepare the school to reopen. Wanting to have the chance to go to Bethlehem again on Christmas Eve, she delayed her departure until late December. Her annual letter sent after her return home, "Greetings for 1968," detailed the Bethlehem trip and showed some of the hardships of daily life resulting from Israel's military occupation: "Five of us went from Ramallah, and we had to have permits for each person and one for the car and driver. We were stopped for checking 15 times between Ramallah and Bethlehem. At some checkpoints they did not want to honor the permit for the car. A trip that should have taken 30 to 40 minutes took us one hour and fifteen minutes. We were late for the Vesper Service at Shepherd's Field."[198]

---

197 *Friends Missionary Advocate*, October 1963.

198 *Friends Missionary Advocate*, March 1968.

(Her description of an earlier visit to Shepherds' Field can be found in Appendix C.)

Both times she came home, Annice was a speaker at the Western Yearly Meeting USFW Mid-Year Conferences in April. In 1967 she used the theme of "Let Your Lives Speak" to tell of life in Ramallah. In 1968, when the offering was designated for scholarships for Friends schools in Ramallah, she spoke about the urgent need due to the recent war—the same needs she had mentioned in her annual letter:

> Our schools are open and going along. Our enrollment is about 60% of last year's number. Many students did not return because parents could not find money for fees. Some students dropped out because we could not offer enough scholarship help. Many students are outside the area and cannot come to our school because of border restrictions. The Arabs on the West Bank are cut off from family and friends in all other Arab countries. West Bank students cannot legally attend Arab colleges and universities. There are no boarders at F.B.S. and only five at F.G.S. Problems! Problems! Problems!—political, social, economic. Financial problems are in top place now for Friends Schools.[199]

CHRISTIAN SERVICE SECRETARY AND WESTERN YEARLY MEETING USFW PRESIDENT 1968–1974

Annice didn't take much time off before assuming more duties for USFW. After returning from Ramallah she wrote a program lesson, "Friends in Bible Lands," about the history of the Friends Schools in Ramallah, for the 1968–69 *Blueprints* program outline. Then, following Helen Chapman's six years of service, she took up the presidency of the Western Yearly Meeting USFW. This time her term of service lasted six years and not a few months. At the 1968 Oskaloosa, Iowa, National Conference, she was also approved as the Christian Service Secretary, a position that had been added to the Executive Committee in 1946. Her picture on the cover with the 1968–1971 Executive Committee, her first article for Christian Service, and her first listing as the Western Yearly Meeting USFW president all appeared in the October 1968 issue of the Advocate.

---

[199] *Friends Missionary Advocate*, March 1968.

Many of her columns promoted the Christian Service Projects. She gave detailed information about the needs the funds would address, as well as what was eventually accomplished with the funds. During the years she served as secretary, the projects included maintenance and repairs at Ramallah Friends Schools; an East Africa Yearly Meeting Literature Program; a social worker and social work program at Kaimosi Hospital; a Friends Centre in Kingston, Jamaica; and the Rural Service Programme in Kenya.

When she wasn't promoting the projects, she shared her views of what "Christian Service" was. Here are examples spanning the years 1969 to 1973:

> If we think of service we probably have as many ideas as we have people.... A desk dictionary at hand says, "conduct that is useful to others." Don't we all want to be useful! If we think of Christian we have a simple forthright definition: "believing in Christ and following His example and teachings." When we put these two words together we have a beautiful expression and a goal for which to strive.[200]
>
> The U.S.A. is usually labeled an affluent society. Have you ever noticed that the more affluence we have, the more we spend on ourselves? May we consider Christian service to our brethren our privilege in 1969?[201]
>
> Christian service is the task of showing Christian concern for our neighbors, near and far. It requires Christian courage to learn of those needs and Christian love to minister to the needs. It may be easy for some and difficult for others. But it is a simple matter of doing the job that God has for us to do.[202]
>
> How much more effective our lives would be if we served with gladness instead of complaining about the lack of time. Christian service should be done with gladness.[203]
>
> Our efforts in Christian Service are attempts to show our love and to share our blessings with others. The stimulus which prompts our sharing is the love of God to us and the desire we have to witness for Him. Our lives would be so different if we would keep the Christmas spirit throughout the whole year. Let us make this a part of our Christian Service.[204]

[200] *Friends Missionary Advocate*, November 1968.
[201] *Friends Missionary Advocate*, February 1969.
[202] *Friends Missionary Advocate*, November 1969.
[203] *Friends Missionary Advocate*, September 1970.
[204] *Friends Missionary Advocate*, December 1971.

A needed goal in Christian Service is to try to help parents realize their responsibilities and desire to give training to their children that will help develop integrity of character.[205]

How much good (Christian service) we could accomplish, near and far, if all of Christ's followers would count blessings and give praise instead of complaints. In our affluence, we have much for which to be thankful and much to share. Let us be thankful we are able to share instead of needing what others are willing to share.[206]

Some other excerpts from her Christian Service columns may be found in Appendix C.

In earlier times of the missionary societies, women had given money for salaries and donated "things" for the mission work. Christian Service work had mainly been thought of as sewing baby layettes, donating books and clothing, knitting and rolling bandages, saving medicine bottles, etc. Gradually, as the supplies needed for the mission work became more available locally and as shipping costs rose, USFW began asking more for money for the projects rather than donations of materials. Annice promoted both forms of giving as well as encouraging conference attendees to donate books of trading stamps, redeemable for cash to buy a vehicle for a mission area.

Annice's 17 years of Executive Committee service concluded at the USFW Triennial Conference in June of 1974 at Guilford College. She did, however, continue to work for and support USFW. For instance, in 1977 at the Triennial Conference in Richmond, Indiana, she placed over the shoulders of the newest editor of *The Advocate*[207] the same shawl that the first editor, Eliza Armstrong Cox, had received from Esther Tuttle Pritchard.

In that summer of 1974, Annice also turned over the duties of the president of Western Yearly Meeting USFW to Leanna Roberts, who would later be president of USFW. Again, this did not end her work and support for Western Yearly Meeting USFW. During the many years she lived at Friends Apartment Homes in Plainfield, Indiana, she served as the Publications Secretary, composing, copying, and mailing the organization's newsletter.

---

[205] *Friends Missionary Advocate*, October 1972.

[206] *Friends Missionary Advocate*, June 1973.

[207] The name of the official publication had been changed by the USFW Executive Committee to *The Advocate* in January of 1977. A change to *The Friend's Advocate* had been suggested in 1946 but not adopted.

Why did Annice spend 17 years working on the Woman's Missionary Union/USFW Executive Committee? Why did she faithfully contribute articles to *The Advocate* promoting projects and encouraging the giving of time and money? In her Western Yearly Meeting USFW President's report for 1971, she wrote, "We need to inspire our members to read the *Advocate*, be aware of the work being done and make personal contributions. Without information we cannot have interest. Without interest we do not have participation."[208] Her faithful work shows how important she felt "missionary education" was to building God's Kingdom, and it echoes her statement as Secretary in the September 1951 issue of the *Friends Missionary Advocate*: "The better informed you are the greater your interest will be and, through co-operation, our work will grow."

A quote from one of the earliest issues of *The Advocate* in 1898 may give another insight into Annice's motivations: "Don't pray, 'Lord Use me.' He is already using you to the utmost of his power. Pray, rather, 'Lord make me usable.'"[209] Wherever she was—on the mission field, at work, or at home—Annice endeavored to be "usable" in service for Christ.

[208] *Friends Missionary Advocate*, February 1972.
[209] *Friends Missionary Advocate*, March 1974.

CHAPTER 12

Annice in retirement

Home again, Annice contemplated where she would live and whether she should retire or get a job. The house in Russiaville that Annice's father had built was sold following her mother's death in 1955. She was always welcome at the home of her friend Mina Emily Seidler in New London, and when her brother Walter retired from farming and built a house in Russiaville, it included an apartment upstairs for her use.

But Annice was looking long term, even as she commented that her life of service had left her with little in life savings or payments into Social Security. She thought for a while about being a "house mother" in some small college dormitory, although she admitted that some of her friends wondered whether she could take the behavior of modern youth. Annice reasoned, though, that youth were much the same the world over—and they all needed supervision and guidance!

Instead, as Annice settled back into the routine of speaking, committee work, family visiting, and sewing, she took a part-time job in the FUM Central Office in Richmond. That, however, soon ended as another opportunity presented itself.

In 1958 in the middle of Annice's service as principal of the Friends Girls School, with work in Kenya, a second term as principal of the FGS, and her 1967 return to Ramallah yet to come, she was already contemplating life after her missionary work was done. Learning about plans for a home for "aged Friends" in Plainfield, Indiana, she wrote, "By the time I get home, I will be ready for such a place, especially since I have no other home now."[210] Quaker Village—later Friends Apartment Homes—finally opened in 1969, and Annice became the director, remaining in that position until 1976.

Perhaps her notion about being a "house mother" was partially fulfilled—and with less-rowdy "residents" to supervise and guide!

---

[210] Letter, January 19, 1958. Private collection of Sarabeth Marcinko.

As director, Annice had fewer responsibilities than as a principal. There would be no working on class schedules with teachers coming and going; no riding herd on adolescent girls; no worrying about feeding boarding students with food costs rising; no keeping boys and girls apart! She was able to pursue some of her interests, though. There would be flowers on the grounds, bird feeders, and programming that offered opportunities for spiritual and intellectual growth. She enjoyed visiting with other residents and attending monthly meetings of USFW that were held at the Apartments. In appreciation of her service, the library there was named in her honor.

But work at Quaker Village/Friends Apartments was not her only activity, especially after she left the position of director. Annice traveled widely, not only attending Quaker gatherings and speaking often at missionary conferences but also taking trips for pleasure and opportunities for family time. As the last surviving member of her generation, she was a treasured attendee at Carter family reunions. Whenever she could, she spent time with her longtime friends, the "gals" she wrote to weekly from the mission field.

Annice also maintained her connections with Quaker work abroad. She visited the new Friends work in Belize established by a fellow missionary, Sadie Vernon. There were also further visits to the Middle East. In March of 1974 Annice participated in a Holy Land tour led by her nephew Wayne Carter. While she was delighted to return and see old friends, especially without responsibilities, Annice was not always pleased with how the tour was going. The guide was Israeli and had his own ideas of what should be seen—and how it should be described. His ideas didn't always meet Annice's approval.

Writing to Mina Emily Seidler during the trip, Annice detailed sites she wanted to see but that were cut out of the itinerary. The guide was interested mainly in history, but Annice felt there were other cultural and religious locations the group ought to experience, and sometimes she intervened to be sure they did! It wasn't just that, either. Annice went on to write, "We have a Jewish guide and are staying at a Jewish hotel in Israel. Some in the group take everything they hear as fact. We're having a very good course of Jewish history and accomplishments. I assure you I am keeping very still."[211]

211 Letters, March 4 and 7, 1974. Private collection of Sarabeth Marcinko.

Evidently, though, Annice wasn't always still! In a conversation with Max Carter in January of 2022, Wayne Carter recounted just how displeased Annice was with the Israeli guide—and how she handled him. She would engage the guide in conversation about events of the 20th century related to the Israeli/Arab conflict and ask him if he agreed with her understanding of the facts. Bit by bit, she got the guide to agree to her understanding of events until, in the end, she had woven a picture that coincided with her position regarding the legitimacy of the Palestinian complaint against Israel. "It was brilliant," Wayne said. "The guide hardly knew what hit him."

Annice stayed behind in Ramallah for two weeks after the trip to spend time visiting friends. She was happy to be in Ramallah again, even though she once more experienced the shock of seeing how much had changed. One thing that had not, however, was the cold! Staying in her old room at the Girls School, she commented that when she slept in her old bed, all the cold of the past six years of its not being slept in must have accumulated! She quickly applied a hot water bottle.

Among the changes, though, Annice was particularly pleased to see so many birds on the campus of the Girls School, some of which she had never seen before. She credited the proliferation of birds to Israel's ban on Palestinians' owning guns. Before, it had not been uncommon for boys to come onto campus to shoot birds.

In Ramallah Annice was able to introduce the group to some of her favorite Arabic foods as well as to her friends. Ellen Mansur opened the women's co-op cross stitch shop for browsing, and Annice was shocked that the prices were four times higher than when she had been there before. There was tea with Fuad and Jean Zaru at the principal's home at the Boys School and a meal at Na'oum's, one of only two restaurants in Ramallah. Annice even fit in a trip to the shop of a hairdresser friend and commented that everyone in Palestine dyed their hair when it began to turn gray—but hers remained white.

In the summer of 1979, Annice was back in Ramallah with an FUM service-learning trip led by her grand-nephew Max Carter. As she described it, she was "drafted" by the Wider Ministries Commission of FUM to supervise food preparation and again to introduce a group to local fare. The kitchen facilities she was used to as principal were no longer in service, as there was no longer a boarding section. A small kitchen had been set up in the former lounge for the resident teachers, and Annice displayed all her home economics skills in feeding everyone.

Annice did share many of her favorite Arabic recipes, but she also came equipped with homemade egg noodles, knowing that some might experience stomach upset with the water and the work—and she wasn't wrong. When several did come down sick with tummy distress, Annice made chicken and noodles on mashed potatoes and nursed folks back to health.

On outings from Ramallah to Jerusalem and Bethlehem, Annice introduced the group to her favorite shops and vendors. When they went to the Galilee, she had them stay at her favorite getaway place in Tiberias, the Scottish Hospice.

While not assuming leadership in planning the political and cultural programming of the trip, Annice did speak up on occasion when she felt participants were getting "off script." During a visit with the mayor of Ramallah, she became disturbed when a Jewish member of the group expressed disagreement with the way the mayor described elements of Israel's behavior as an occupying power. Annice curtly shut her down. Later, though, when that person became ill, Annice sat by her bedside and took care of her.

Annice described the 14 adults and two children on the trip as hard working and "cooperative in the matter of strange foods." Comparing the '79 trip to the '74 visit she had been on, she noted that she preferred the "work-study" kind, but acknowledged that it did keep her too busy to see friends.

The three weeks in Ramallah that summer of 1979 would be her last time in her beloved Palestine, but it was not her last travel abroad. The next year she visited Hungary, Austria, Czechoslovakia, and Germany on the way to experience the Passion Play in Oberammergau.

Annice continued her Friends work through activity at Plainfield Friends Meeting and service with USFW. She was a frequent visitor at the FUM Central Office in Richmond, typically combined with dropping in on her longtime friend and colleague Mildred White, who was living at Friends Fellowship Community in Richmond. Annice did a great deal of sewing for missions, and served on the board of Plainfield's Meals on Wheels and on the Administrative Council of Western Yearly Meeting. She was active with the Church Federation and became an associate member of the missions committee of a Black church, Plainfield's Bethel A.M.E.

She undertook extensive travel within the U.S. to the triennial gatherings of USFW and FUM that took her as far away as California and as nearby as Indiana and Ohio. With her nephew Orville Carter, she became active in the work of the Associated Friends Committee on Indian Affairs (AFCIA), and in 1983 traveled to the four Oklahoma Indian centers under AFCIA care to deliver supplies and attend committee meetings. Another AFCIA meeting in 1984 took her to White Plains Friends Meeting in North Carolina, where she was touched by the young pastor's enthusiastic greeting. As a ten-year-old boy, David Hobson had heard her in conversation with his parents when they hosted Annice in their home during one of her deputation visits to North Carolina. He had been so intrigued that he followed her work.

A 1985 trip took Annice to Moorestown, New Jersey, to spend time with her niece Miriam Ward and her family. While there, she made a familiar Palestinian dish, *mahtloubeh*, for a talk at Moorestown Friends Meeting given by a young couple that had just returned from teaching at the Friends Girls School in Ramallah. In a letter describing the trip, she wrote, "I was glad to talk with this young couple, but I could not understand why they had different last names when they claimed to be husband and wife."[212]

In the same letter, Annice noted that her nephew Max Carter had come to Moorestown Friends from his family's home in Philadelphia to lead a Sunday School class while she was there: "He lectured on Old Testament history. I think he did a good job, but he could have done something more helpful, as I do not care for Old Testament history. He did not treat it too seriously, though."

Annice maintained a keen interest in the situation in the Middle East, commenting in 1982 about an American Jew who forced his way into the Dome of the Rock in Jerusalem and started shooting. She criticized Israel's prime minister, Menachem Begin, for the invasion of Lebanon that same year and lamented that, even if it caused him trouble, the U.S. would keep bailing him out. In 1983 she expressed concern about the expanding Israeli settlements in the occupied territories and confiscation of Palestinian land.

---

212 Letter, January 22, 1985. Private collection of Betsy Alexander.

"Begin is dead-set on doing away with Arabs and gaining new territory," she wrote to friends.[213]

"Things do not seem to get better in the Middle East," she wrote in another letter in 1983. "I sure wonder just what will happen. It is thought that this Lebanon business is to keep attention off the West Bank settlements."[214]

After watching a *60 Minutes* piece about Israeli Arabs, Annice registered her surprise at the frank statements of Israelis about their dislike for and disregard for Arabs. *So little has changed*

In a letter to family in February of 1988, she noted that she was still going places and doing things. She had just finished mailing out the USFW newsletter, and recounted enjoying a drive to a program on the Indiana Friends Committee on Legislation, a Quaker lobbying organization. She added that she really didn't need more meetings to attend, but that "we keep on doing what needs to be done, if possible." She did keep busy, indeed. By all accounts, her time of service for Friends interests while in the U.S. was equivalent to her time working abroad. In that same letter, Annice noted that she needed new glasses but would wait until May to get them.

In early April, Annice attended the memorial worship for her longtime friend Mildred White, who had died at Friends Fellowship Community in Richmond. "She was 94. A long and useful life," she wrote. "I am glad I had the privilege of knowing and working with her."[215] Annice went on to note how Mildred had been a close friend of her sister Achsa, had been in the Carter home in Russiaville a few times, and was in Ramallah when Annice first taught at the Girls School in 1929.

A little over a week later, on April 13, 1988, Annice died after suffering a stroke in her Plainfield apartment. Already in 1982, to address the headaches she was suffering, she had begun taking medication to expand the blood vessels in her brain. Her obituary noted that her death was confirmed in the Hendricks County Hospital and that her body was donated to medical science. Two memorial services were held on April 18, one in the morning at Plainfield Friends Meeting, led by Western Yearly Meeting Superintendent Robert Garris and Plainfield Friends pastor Keith

213 Letter, February 7, 1983. Private collection of Betsy Alexander.
214 Letter, February 14, 1983. Private collection of Betsy Alexander.
215 Letter, April 4, 1988. Private collection of Betsy Alexander.

Kirk. An afternoon service took place at Russiaville Friends, her home meeting, led by pastor Morris Jones. Later her body was buried in the New London Friends Cemetery in a Carter family plot.

Memorial contributions to FUM for the Ramallah Emergency Fund were encouraged. The spring of 1988 was seeing the Friends Schools in yet another challenging situation, as the Palestinian Intifada[216]—an uprising against the continuing Israeli occupation—had brought severe reprisals from the Israeli military administration. The Schools were forced to be closed, many families were without employment, and the financial exigencies that Annice so often faced as principal were multiplied by the situation. Even in death, Annice sought to address the needs of the mission that had been the focus of so much of her life's service.

Already in 1977, as she recounted in a June letter to her nephews and nieces, Annice was contemplating the end of her time on earth and explained her thinking about the disposal of whatever of hers might remain after her death. Noting how pleased she was with their accomplishments and interests—and with their comfortable homes—Annice went on to express that she had never had a very high income, owing to her 17 years as a missionary. She would share the souvenirs she had accumulated, but since her nephews and nieces were all doing well, her limited money would go to various organizations.

A May 25 letter to Annice's relatives following her death, written by her nephew Orville Carter, listed her earthly possessions. It covered only a page and a half, mostly describing pieces of furniture, household appliances, many New Testaments, slides, and Ramallah dresses. When her estate was settled, $30,703.36 was given to Friends Apartment Homes; $61,406.76 went to Western Yearly Meeting; $61,406.76 was distributed to FUM; and $2,495.42 was spent on cleaning her apartment and disposing of her belongings.[217]

---

[216] The Intifada (in Arabic, shaking off) began in December of 1987 when an Israeli truck in the Gaza Strip struck a Palestinian vehicle, killing four and wounding ten. Lasting until 1993, the uprising brought severe repercussions from Israel but a sense of solidarity and pride among Palestinians. The Friends Schools were closed for 17 months, experiencing the loss of substantial revenues, but the administration and teachers were able to provide students with weekly lesson packets, ensuring that they did not lose that time in their education.

[217] Inventory in a December 9, 2002 letter. Private collection of Betsy Alexander.

Indeed, Annice Carter left behind little of material worth, but what she left behind of her Christian service was priceless. As far as possible, she had kept on doing what needed to be done.

CHAPTER 13
Reflections on Annice Carter's life

DONN HUTCHISON

When I think of Annice Carter, I think of the wonderful group of Quaker women who dedicated part of their lives to the education of Palestinian women. There was Alice Jones, who taught my mother-in-law and her sisters; there were Mildred White, Lois Snyder, and Anna Langston, who each taught my late wife and her sisters; and of course there was Annice Carter.

The only thing I remember that changed in Annice was the color of her hair. The style never changed. In pictures I have seen of Annice when she first came to Ramallah, it was the same hairstyle; when I came to know her, though, her hair was white; her skirts, as in that long-ago photo, were well below her knees; she wore sensible shoes and never any make-up.

I suppose she would have fit the proverbial stereotype of a spinster. She was strait-laced, principled, and unwaveringly honest; she voiced her opinion, and you always seemed to instinctively know where you stood in her estimation. Annice was also brusquely kind.

My father-in-law, like his father-in-law before him, was at one time the clerk of Ramallah Friends Meeting. He was clerk during part of Annice's service in Ramallah. I have seen her confront him after worship or a business meeting over something he had said. I can still see her, after all these years, standing before him (she was taller than he was) and pursing her lips as she smoothed an imagined wrinkle on his suit jacket, saying, "Now, Jirius, you *know that isn't true.*" There were very few people who would directly challenge him.

Annice and my late mother-in-law Ellen had a jovial relationship. I think that Ellen was never easily intimidated, and that she admired Annice for confronting Jirius. Perhaps, though Ellen was Ramallah born and bred, and Annice was a farm girl from Indiana, they were kindred spirits.

I believe that Annice, like a number of the Quaker missionaries who ended up in Ramallah, was certainly dedicated to service, but I think she might also have been escaping from the boredom of the ordinary. She, as they, wanted the *thrill* of an adventure in an exotic foreign land away from the humdrum of family, coworkers, and friends (though I suppose one might question the word "thrill" in reference to Annice!).

She related once that in her first years at the Friends School, on a visit to a small village on the outskirts of Ramallah, the *muktar* (head man) took a shine to her. He even proposed that she become one of his wives, as he had just built a new house! Annice just smiled, so she said, and politely refused. She ended the story by telling me, "He must have been crazy."

Annice and I were an unlikely duo. She was a woman close to retirement when I first met her; I had just graduated from college, young and naïve. The only thing we had in common was that at the time we both were employed by the Richmond Mission Board.

One encounter with her was when I went to the Girls School to see Sina Mansur. There was to be a combined choir of Friends students—boys and girls—to sing at the graduation ceremony. Sina directed the choir, and I was to accompany it. Annice was aware that I was coming. I arrived at the Girls School during recess. She met me at the side gate, and linking her arm with mine, escorted me through the throng of girls. When I had had my meeting with Sina, Annice was ready to escort me back to the gate. I felt a bit like the wolf among the lambs, or that that was how Annice viewed the situation.

She had been brought out of retirement after the Six-Day War in 1967 to give guidance and moral support to Peggy Paull, who had been appointed as the new principal of the Girls School. With Israel's military occupation of Ramallah and the West Bank, everything was different. She and Annice were to live in the Main Building with a handful of boarding girls who were in the graduating class. The Richmond Board thought that for an initial period of time I should also live at the School (well, not actually in the Main building but in a small, rented cottage that was adjacent to the School). They apparently thought that having a resident nerd was somehow going to protect the two women and handful of girls.

At the time, my bet was on Annice. I would have taken even odds that she would be a formidable opponent to any who would invade the School's sanctity. That proved to be true. One evening an Israeli jeep screeched through the gate, and the soldiers started firing their guns into the tree tops, a show of force meant to intimidate the recently occupied. Annice went out on the upstairs veranda in a flaming red robe (though she thought I had embroidered that detail to make the encounter more dramatic) and asked what they wanted. When they declared that they were firing their guns into the trees, she told them, "I know that! Now stop it! You're scaring my girls." She told them to turn around and leave, adding, "And close the gate after you!"

And they did. When I asked her later how she had summoned the courage to confront heavily armed soldiers, she said that she did what she had to do—but her knees were knocking under her bathrobe.

At times it was difficult to actually know what was sinful in the eyes of the American missionaries. As I said, I lived in a separate cottage, and there was a stone wall around three-quarters of it. One Sunday, when there were obviously no students in school, I did a hand wash and hung it on the line. I don't remember why Annice came into my yard, but she did. She saw the clothes pegged to the line, gently dancing in the wind. She pursed her lips, frowned and stared at me: "You do know it is Sunday, don't you? One's wash is never displayed on Sunday." I must confess I was new to Quakerism, and being a former Methodist had never heard that prohibition.

There was an occasion when Peggy Paull and Annice were going to Jerusalem. They wanted someone to chaperone the small group of girls, one of whom, Fatima, was blind. I offered to stay with the girls. Again, those pursed lips and disapproving stare: "You do know that Fatima is blind?" (I can only speculate what Annice thought that Fatima and I might engage in.)

Briefly, and naturally, there was a period of anti-Americanism over America's backing of the Israeli occupation. One afternoon Annice and I were walking down the main street on the way back to the Girls School. Again, she had her arm linked in mine as though this gave an impression of appropriateness. A young man came around the corner of a side street and threw acid at us. Most of it splashed into the street, but a little of it peppered holes in the wool skirt Annice was wearing. "Well, can you believe that," she muttered, "very poor aim." She then muttered under her breath the Arabic word for jackass!

When Annice left, I was sad to see her go. We had become good friends.

A few years later, I visited Annice where she was working as the director of the Quaker retirement apartments in Plainfield, Indiana. I had grown a goatee and asked Annice what she thought about it. Again those pursed lips and stare: "If you are fool enough to grow that thing, I am not fool enough to comment." (Ya gotta love her!)

Annice was not [then] the same Annice I had known. I think she missed Ramallah. I think she was winding down. Her vision was failing, and much of the old spirit was gone. I hugged her while saying good-bye, and surprisingly she hugged me back. It was the last time I saw her.

One of the early missionaries, and one or two newer missionaries as well, thought they were coming to enlighten the natives. They thought that the locals had to change in order to advance. Annice was certainly not one of them! I think she was genuinely interested in sharing her beliefs but wasn't interested in forcing those beliefs on anyone. I never got the sense that she felt that was part of her mission. (My mother-in-law used to have very strong opinions of two early missionaries who had the attitude that they were superior and that the locals must listen to them. There were two in particular, well-meaning I am sure, who she felt destroyed the lives of my father-in-law and of her sister, Najla, through their interference in things in which they had no business meddling.)

I think most who were associated with the Friends blessed the service of Alice Jones, Mildred White, Lois Snyder, Anna Langston, and, of course, Annice Carter.

Annice made the curtains and matching bedspreads for the guestroom at FGS from Damascus silk. Eventually that guestroom became the teacher's room. The curtains were relegated to the attic and ended up in the home of Roger and Laura Heacock. When they left Ramallah, they gave me those curtains. I cut them up and made pillows out of them for my guestroom. So Annice's sewing lives on. I feel privileged to have known her.

Donn Hutchison continues to live in Ramallah after nearly a half century of teaching at the Friends Girls and Friends Boys Schools, beginning in 1965. In retirement he has written a series of novels about the Palestinian experience; several devotional books; a biography of his father-in-law, Jirius Mansur, *A Stone House with Windows*; and a memoir, *The Male Mom*.

SALIBAH HANHAN

I remember Annice Carter as an imposing figure, tall, straight as a rod. She was never mean, but she wanted you to know she was around and didn't want any shenanigans. We certainly knew when she was present!

One memory stands out especially. The girls from FGS were scheduled to come to the Boys School for a performance, and we boys were very excited to see them. We lined the wall next to the auditorium awaiting their arrival. But when we saw Annice accompanying them as they entered the gate of the School, we all took off! I still remember it clearly more than 60 years later!

I miss those days. With everything that was happening in Palestine, the Friends School was like an oasis.

Salibah Hanhan and his family fled the coastal Palestinian city of Lod during the 1948 war that led to the establishment of the modern state of Israel. Settling in Ramallah as a refugee, Salibah attended the Friends Boys School from 1952 to 1959. After attending the American University of Beirut from 1959 to 1963, he taught chemistry and math at the Friends School for four years. Emigrating to the U.S. in the early 1980s, he opened The Jerusalem Market, a grocery and deli in Greensboro, North Carolina. After this, add: He passed away at 83 on August 2, 2023, in Greensboro, North Carolina.

HUDA QUBEIN KRASKE

I entered the Friends Girls School in 1952 in the fifth grade and graduated in 1962. Miss Carter provided the scholarship that enabled me to attend, and she paid special attention to me. She had taught my mother earlier and was trying to compensate for my lack of a normal family life. Quakers back in the U.S. sent relief packages and some were handed to me by Miss Carter. I was absolutely overwhelmed and grateful to have nice blouses, dresses, nightgowns, and coats. . . .

Sunday at the boarding school was the day we listened to the radio and got to know the latest hits in the U.S. . . . On Sunday evenings, some of us would assemble in the music room to listen to classical music, and when I heard Bach, Chopin, Mozart, and Beethoven, I was filled with a joy I had never experienced before. Miss Carter noticed my intense pleasure at hearing the music and paid for a year of piano lessons.

Sensing our longing for male company, Miss Carter started a program whereby students from the FGS and FBS met once a month to play games. She accompanied us and directed the games. One of the games I remember is musical chairs.

In the spring of 1960, when I was about to graduate from FGS, the principal of the School called me into her office. This was not Miss Carter, but her replacement. She said that I could not graduate unless I paid some unfulfilled fee of about $30. Had Miss Carter been there, she would never have imposed such a harsh burden on me....An uncle gave me the money, and I graduated as valedictorian of my class.

Huda Qubein grew up in Amman, Jordan, before attending the Friends Girls School. Following graduation, she attended American University in Washington, D.C., and went to work for the World Bank. Her reflections on Annice are excerpted from her memoir, *One of Us, One of Them* (self-published, 2014).

FAROUK SHAMI

I saw Annice Carter many times with my father talking to her, but personally I always said "hello," not more.

Farouk Shami attended the Friends Boys School in the 1950s and emigrated to the U.S., where he developed a line of hair-care products, founded the Houston-based Farouk Systems, and ran for Governor of Texas in 2009.

MAXINE KAUFMAN-LACUSTA

I remember Annice Carter from our 1979 FUM trip to Ramallah as a very strong, "in-charge" woman. She certainly knew her way around Ramallah and introduced us all to a wonderful restaurant, Na'oum's, where we had a memorable meal of *musakhan*. I also remember shopping with her at the produce market for fresh figs and other goodies.

On the other hand, I believe she was one of the group members who sometimes contended with me when I raised issues from my own Jewish background and questioned, "Why can't the Jews forgive the Nazis?" and insisted that we should. (By the way, my response hasn't changed: basically, that it's not my/our place to forgive what was done to others.) But I also recall her face among the first to greet me and offer water at the summit of Masada after my ill-advised noontime solo trek up the Snake Path.

Maxine Kaufman-Lacusta participated in the FUM-sponsored trip in 1979 to the Ramallah Friends School. Max, Jane, and Annice Carter were the co-leaders. Maxine identifies as Jewish and Quaker, and is active in Friends General Conference. She shares that the '79 trip was life-changing for her.

A RANDOM PERSON MET ON THE STREETS OF RAMALLAH

During the service-learning trip that Max and Jane Carter led to Ramallah in 2018, one of the participants was chatting with an elderly woman and her grandchildren as they walked down the street. Curious about what the American was doing in Ramallah, the grandmother learned that he was part of a group volunteering at the Friends School. She excitedly said that she had graduated from the Friends School, and the group member told her that the co-leader of the group had taught at the Friends School many years before. She asked about the name, and when she heard "Carter," she became even more excited and said, "My principal when I was a student was Miss Annice Carter, and I loved her! I became a principal myself and modeled my work after hers!"

DAN CARTER

I never felt particularly intimidated by her, but I certainly understand how others would. I'm fortunate not to have been on the receiving end of her reproaches, perhaps because I didn't grow chin feathers. I was always glad when she was returning from the mission field.

I felt I let her down once. It was in the mid or late '50s and the yearly meeting was having a speech contest for youth. She encouraged me to enter the contest and undertook to coach me. We had a few practice sessions and, with her help, I felt confident going into the evening of the contest. My speech was about a topic I liked, baseball. We contestants were cooling our heels out under the trees on the yearly meeting lawn, waiting our turns and making small talk. We were kind of amused when one of the contestants quipped, "Know how to sabotage a speaker? Sit in the back row sucking on a lemon!" We all had a chuckle. My turn came to stand on that big, wide stage with all those people in the audience. I proceeded with my speech as Aunt Annice had coached me, and was doing well until, maybe three-quarters of the way through, a thought of that lemon crossed my mind and, sure enough, my voice cracked and it was a struggle from then to the end. After such a promising beginning, I had a strong sense of having let her down after all her efforts.

I did receive a mild criticism from her once. It was during the time that I served as the yearly meeting presiding clerk, I think probably my first year. We had made it through a day or two of business without much difficulty. At the noon break she approached me and said, "You haven't called for disapproval yet." Of course that tipped me off about where she stood on that age-old debate. I made it through the rest of my years as clerk without further ado from her, and I was always glad to see her in nearly every session, sitting attentively near the front of the room.

Daniel Wayne Carter is a grand-nephew of Annice Carter's, the grandson of her brother Walter. A member of Annice's home meeting of Russiaville Friends, he is a retired high school teacher and former clerk of Western Yearly Meeting.

MAX L. CARTER

My first memory of Aunt Annice was seeing her standing erect behind the chair in which her aged mother, Milley Johnson Carter, was sitting, a blanket over her lap. It was in the house Annice's father had built on the farm in Russiaville, Indiana, when they moved from the "home place" just outside of town. Annice had returned from her assignment in Ramallah in 1941 to care for her ailing father, who died two years later. Annice remained stateside to assist her mother. Two years after her mother's death in 1955, Annice returned to Ramallah.

I don't recall seeing Annice much after that, for many years. She was in Palestine or Kenya until I went off to college. There would be the occasional sighting at a summer Carter reunion, but most of what I gathered about Annice during those years was through letters she sent home, which my grandfather Carter would read to us at family gatherings. It was only later that I heard Annice relate two stories that offer an insight into her political beliefs about Palestine and Israel, and her own navigation of being an "eligible" Western woman in Palestine:

Annice was very sympathetic to the Palestinian plight and the loss of their lands in the '48 war and the occupation of the West Bank and Gaza in the '67 war. When confronted—as she often was—by those who claimed

Charles and Milley in 1922 in front of the Russiaville homeplace.

that God had promised the land to the Jews, she snapped back, "It came with conditions!" What she meant by that were the dictates laid out in the Book of Deuteronomy.

She even was less sympathetic to the marriage offers she often received while traveling about—and had her own "conditions." Annice developed a standard response. When a man approached her with a proposal, she would say, "I'll consider it with these demands: I will have my own room with two windows; I will do no housework or cooking; I will have my own source of income; I will not be told what I can buy or where I can go; and there will be no other wives." That always worked in maintaining her unmarried status.

Annice also had a standard response to the shop owners who wanted to haggle over prices, which was standard operating procedure then. Perhaps owing to the heritage of Quakers having introduced the "single price" system in their English businesses, Annice would ask the shopkeeper what their best price was, and if it was too expensive, she would walk out of the shop—typically with the merchant following her in the beginning of the haggling process. She would tell the person that she had asked for the best price, and she wouldn't do business with someone who was dishonest. It wasn't long before shop owners in Ramallah knew to give her their best price immediately when she arrived!

I had gathered an impression of Annice as no-nonsense, and that impression was borne out in 1970 when, for my alternative service as a conscientious objector to war, I accepted an assignment to teach at the Friends Boys School in Ramallah. I had chosen that position in part because I had heard of Ramallah so often through Annice's letters home. I also wanted to make use of my undergraduate degree in education. Annice came to the Indianapolis airport to see me off, and I thought she might be touched that her grand-nephew was following in her footsteps. No such luck.

As I prepared to board the plane, she said to me, "Max! The Carters have a good name in Ramallah. Don't ruin it!" I'm sure she thought at the time she was being funny, but it didn't strike me that way in the moment! Then she told me something else: "Max, if you stay two years in Ramallah, you will always go back." She certainly nailed that one!

But to her credit, she had also advised me to wear sturdy shoes in Ramallah, and I took the pair that I had purchased the previous year for hiking in Germany. She was as right about the need for such footwear in rocky Palestine as she was in her assessment of the likelihood of my getting hooked on the region.

I don't remember any interaction with Annice during the time I was in Ramallah, but I certainly heard Annice stories there. When I returned home after my two years at the Boys School, the first I recall seeing her was when her United Society of Friends Women circle in Plainfield invited me to share about my experience. I chose to cover the political as well as the religious and educational aspects of my time in Palestine. Doing so in the presence of Annice was intimidating. Afterwards, however, she told me I had done a good job. Whew!

Annice was not as pleased, however, with the beard I had grown during my time in Ramallah. Each time she saw me, she gruffly asked why I had that "shrubbery" on my chin. When I reminded her that both of her grandfathers, Levi Carter and Fleming Johnson, sported beards, she equally gruffly replied, "That was THEN!"

I took another encounter with far less grace—although it was through correspondence. In 1974, having learned somehow that I was engaged to be married to Jane, she wrote me a letter registering her strong disapproval.

I'll leave it to Jane to say how Annice described her, but her description incensed me. For the first time in my life, I confronted her in the letter I sent back, and I was not overly kind in my wording. I essentially told her to bug off; it wasn't any of her business.

I never heard back from her. When I saw her at reunions, there was not a word spoken about it.

And then in 1979 I was asked to lead a work trip to Ramallah sponsored by Friends United Meeting. Harold Smuck, the Wider Ministries Secretary of FUM, recruited Annice to go along to do the cooking for the group—and probably to make sure that her young nephew didn't make a mess of things! She was an absolute godsend on the trip.

She not only knew her way around a kitchen, she knew her way around Ramallah! She got the makings for our meals at all her familiar shops, and she fed us well. She knew the language and the shop owners well enough that she could tell the butcher what cut of meat she wanted from the carcass hanging in the window—and when he got to that one later in the day, to set it aside for her. She also introduced us to her favorite souvenir shops in Jerusalem and Bethlehem. She was indispensable. And she didn't try to run the show herself; somehow she trusted me to lead the group's program.

The most unforgettable part of the trip regarding Annice, though, was when most of us got sick from food poisoning. I had taken the group to a hole-in-the-wall place in Jerusalem, and we probably had a bad salad. I became good friends with the toilet in our apartment, and Jane was so sick she was afraid she'd die—and then so sick she was afraid she wouldn't die! Again, I'll let Jane share the details, but Annice made chicken and noodles with homemade noodles she had brought from home, and she nursed Jane and the rest of us back from the brink of the grave. She was so sweet to Jane that all was forgiven from that letter of five years before.

That was to be the last time Annice would see her beloved Palestine. And I didn't see her much after that, either. She was in retirement in Plainfield, and I was working at Earlham College in Richmond. Again, it was mostly at the summer Carter reunion when I would see her. Meetings became even more rare when I moved with the family to Philadelphia in 1982.

I was shocked to learn of her death in 1988. She had seemed to me to be indestructible. I hadn't seen her in her final years while we were away, so she remained in my mind the ramrod straight, indomitable force who could "shoo" a jeep full of soldiers out of the Girls School courtyard or intimidate a nephew into not bringing disrepute to the Carters' good name.

Only later did I hear the many stories of the heart of gold she carried under that gruff, nephew-eating exterior. I am delighted to have known her—and to know more about her through the revelations in this book.

Max L. Carter taught at the Friends Boys School in Ramallah from 1970 to 1972 and has made more than 37 return trips, most with academic programs and with service-learning groups. He has written about his early experience in Palestine in his book, *Palestine and Israel: A Personal Encounter* (Barclay Press, 2020). Annice Carter was the sister of Max's paternal grandfather, Walter Carter.

JANE CARTER

My first impression of Aunt Annice was not a positive one. Before she had even met me, she wrote a forceful letter to Max telling him that he "shouldn't marry that hussy, Janey Deichler!" A number of emotions came to the surface, including astonishment, anger, and hurt to name a few. The emotion of fear was added to this list as many people told me their experiences with Annice.

The summer of 1979, Friends United Meeting arranged a workcamp trip to the Ramallah Friends School, to be led by Annice and Max. We took our two young daughters (10 months and 3 ½ years) with us. Annice was in charge of the kitchen and cooking, and each of us was assigned days/meals to work. Her one absolute rule was that there were to be no children in the kitchen! It was a difficult thing to try to explain to two children who were used to being in the kitchen, and sometimes even helping in the kitchen, that they were not allowed even when their Mommy was in there! And since ours were the only children attending the work camp, once again it felt very personal.

On the other hand, watching Annice in action in Ramallah was impressive. Not only did people know her, but they clearly respected and loved her! It became clear that she had quietly helped many young girls during her tenure there.

I, however, didn't personally experience that side of her until I became dreadfully ill after Max took us all to a dive of a falafel stand in Jerusalem!

Two of us suffered terribly as a result of that meal, and I was down and out for a few days.

As my tummy and intestines were finally empty and settling, Annice came upstairs and sat on the side of my bed, offering me a cup of hot mint tea. As she sat with me she told me that she had been afraid that they might have lost me. (My response was that there were many moments in the past few days when I would have willingly gone.) She was comforting and kind, and I was grateful for the care. Finally I saw her soft side.

The first night that the other invalid and I made it downstairs to supper, Annice pulled out the packages of homemade noodles she had brought from home and made us chicken and noodles with mashed potatoes. What a thoughtful gesture! We were both quite moved by her thoughtfulness in providing us with a mild, familiar meal for our first one after being so sick.

I don't think I ever completely lost the feeling of being a bit in awe of Annice. I was always a little off-balance in her presence. You never knew what would set her off, but you always knew what she was thinking about the topic at hand! My mental image of Annice has always been a strong, sturdy, nine-foot-tall woman, with one eye in the middle of her ample forehead!

But her strength and commitment to her "girls" remains her legacy, and I'm glad I got to know her.

Jane Carter is an Earlham College graduate with a master's degree in math education. In addition to serving in ministry at West Richmond Friends and New Garden Friends Meetings, she served for 21 years on the teaching and administrative staff of New Garden Friends School. With Max, she has led two dozen service-learning trips to Ramallah.

C. WAYNE CARTER

My first memory of my Aunt Annice was when I was a pre-teen and in the Youth Temperance Crusade (YTC), a program of the Women's Christian Temperance Union (WCTU). The YTC had "readings," which were speech competitions, and I practiced mine with Annice. She drilled me in elocution, pronunciation, and delivery.

I vividly remember her going with us on a Holy Land trip I led in the 1970s. She had promised, "I won't be any trouble," and she wasn't! But she was for one of our tour guides. I'll never forget how she sat on the bus with our Israeli guide and lectured him on historical sites and events, turning him every which way but loose. Before he knew it, she had cleverly given him a lecture on how Israel had given the Palestinians a raw deal! Another favorite memory from the trip was of how on my wife Betsy's and my May 4 wedding anniversary she had the bus driver stop in front of a bakery. She hopped off and came back with a cake. She had purchased a celebratory cake that was decorated for the Jewish holiday of Purim! At the Friends Girls School in Ramallah, she showed me a cistern she had built which she laughingly said was nicknamed "Carter's Folly."

Like others, I had my "Annice took me by the lapels and lectured me" moment. I was the program director for FUM's Triennial in 1972, and we had decided to hold it for the first time outside Richmond, Indiana, at the Baptist conference facility in Green Lake, Wisconsin. After the session at the previous Triennial where the decision was made, Annice took me by the lapels and said, "Now you know, Wayne, this will mean that I and others will not be able to attend!" Annice meant that she would not be able to afford the extra expense of residency at a conference in Wisconsin.

Annice had strong convictions, but she didn't impose them on others. The Friends Church in Russiaville that she grew up in was deeply influenced by Wesleyan Holiness theology, and some of the preachers there were firebrands. I remember one, John Retherford, who turned so red in the face and emotional when he preached that I feared he'd have a heart attack! But Annice was a moderate. I think her experience in a broader world influenced her that way. She never shared with me what her religious beliefs were or why she went into missionary work, but I'm convinced that she felt the Lord was leading her there.

C. Wayne Carter is a retired Friends minister and administrator, having served Quaker meetings and organizations in Indiana and North Carolina, including Carmel Friends and First Friends Richmond in Indiana and Winston-Salem Friends in North Carolina. He was on the staff of Five Years Meeting (now Friends United Meeting) and was the interim Superintendent of Western Yearly Meeting. Annice was his father's youngest sister.

MARY FRANCES TAYLOR

My first memory of Aunt Annice was of going to the Kokomo, Indiana, train station with my parents to meet her when she returned from Ramallah. I was probably only three years old. All I can recall, though, is that I was fascinated by how big the steam locomotive's driver wheels were—and that Annice said she was served octopus while she was on the ocean liner, and she didn't like it!

Annice would make me dresses when I was a little girl, and they were so pretty and so well made. She could lay out the fabric and cut the patterns wonderfully. I remember a blue and white plaid with a white bodice and one that was a yellow polka dot. I also remember her saying that her students in Russiaville could never keep a needle, but her girls in Ramallah kept one all year. I also liked to wear pretty shoes—and high heels when I could. Annice advocated "sensible shoes" and told me that later on I would regret wearing my fancy shoes.

When I graduated from high school in Russiaville, Annice was still at home living with her widowed mother, Milley. She had a job in the welfare office in the courthouse in Kokomo, and I took a clerical job in an agricultural office in the same building. She was careful to warn me about a custodian who worked there, but I always found him very courteous and kind to me.

We often rode to work together, and sometimes she would make a stop at the home of one of her welfare clients. I recall one time we stopped in Gateway Gardens, and she said it was a joy to visit the mother and children who lived there; her husband was in jail, but she kept an immaculate house. I also remember that when Annice had to appear in court on a welfare case, she would always affirm rather than swear an oath.

During our rides to work, Annice would often share interesting observations. One that has stuck with me was a comment she made about the new trend of drive-in movie theaters. "I think they may solve the racial issue," she said. "It may be resolved in the back seats of cars!"

I grew up in the same Russiaville Friends Church that Annice did, and it was much the same as it had been in her youth. Worship services could be emotional. I remember a time when my great-aunt Martha got happy in the Spirit and started waving her white handkerchief! We had spring and fall revivals, and the preachers at Russiaville were revivalistic. One of them I recall was John Retherford. Another was Bill Wagner, who thought that Annice should be more evangelistic in her missionary work than she was.

Other memories I have are that my grandmother Milley had two sisters who thought Annice was Milley's "spoiled brat." Once when Annice visited our house, the dog crawled up in her lap, and she wanted nothing to do with it! When our son Bill was two years old, we went to visit Annice at Milley's, and Bill tickled Annice's knee. I was mortified, but she didn't mind.

[Bill walked in during the interview and shared this memory: "When I was much younger, I was the chair of the Western Yearly Meeting budget committee, and there was a decision we had made that didn't meet Annice's approval. When she saw me, she hooked her finger around my tie and a button on my shirt and didn't let go until she had shared her concern!"]

I don't recall Annice sharing much about her views about politics or the situation in the Middle East, but one time I overheard a conversation between her and my brother-in-law. He had told her, "Annice, you know that the Jews are God's chosen people, don't you?" Annice simply responded, "Well, if you believe that, then why don't you become one?"

Mary Frances Taylor is a retired Western School Corporation bookkeeper and lives on her family's farm near Russiaville. She is the daughter of Annice's older brother, Oakley Carter.

PHILLIP D. CARTER

Annice was my grandfather's "little sister." My grandfather, Oakley J. Carter, was the fourth of five siblings. Annice was five years younger. My grandfather would occasionally make comments about Annice, and the fact that she may have been slightly spoiled, which is easy to imagine by her being the baby of the family. Despite this, I always felt like Grandpa had great respect for Annice and the things she did.

Whenever Annice came back to Indiana from the mission fields, she always made it back to Russiaville to visit and was usually present at the Russiaville Friends Meeting on Sunday morning. Aunt Annice always had input during "quiet time." She had her views, and they were well ingrained. Nobody was going to change them. There is a story in Oakley's family about the time she got into a discussion with one of my uncles about the Jews in Israel. My uncle, being a staunch Baptist, had a few different views from Annice, the Quaker missionary from Ramallah. Annice, being Annice, made sure that she got my uncle straightened out in no uncertain terms. I do not think that my uncle ever brought up the Middle East with her again.

My great-grandfather Charles, Oakley's and Annice's father, began farming with very little. However, through hard work and perseverance he managed to obtain many acres of farm land. Most of the ground he owned was in Howard County, Indiana, near Russiaville. Charles lived on the western outskirts of Russiaville on a farm that is still in possession of the Carter family. I never knew how, when, or why, but he obtained 80 acres of farmland west of Russiaville in Clinton County. Before his passing, Charles gave each of his five children a farm. Annice inherited that Clinton County farm.

My father Merle, Oakley's oldest son, was discharged from the army in 1945 and decided to farm. The inheriting of the farm and my father's discharge coincided with each other, and my father took over the management of Annice's 80 acres. This is the farm that my brother, sister, and I grew up on. A house was built on the farm in 1947, and my parents used the farm as the base for my father's farming operation. This operation included growing crops, milking dairy cows, and raising pigs and chickens. Over time the existing barn was updated and more buildings were added. My father never owned the farm, but my brother came into possession of it in 1979 upon the untimely death of my father at age 57. It is still in the family today.

Aunt Annice had an agreement with my father which I was not aware of until after his passing. Since Annice was usually in the mission field, she was not involved in the operation of the farm. My father managed and was in complete control of it. In return for living on the farm, my father gave her a percentage of the income from the crops. We also stored many of her belongings in the basement and attic of the house, since, technically, it was her house. She never reclaimed most of these items. To this day I have a glass-fronted cabinet in my home that belonged to her.

Although she did not have anything to say about the farm operation, one particular incident in the late 1960s stands out. When the power company was going to run a high-tension power line across the middle of the farm, my father notified her. Her reply was typical of Aunt Annice: "We're going to fight this, right?" My dad just smiled and replied, "I don't think so."

One other remembrance of Aunt Annice: she always called me Steve, my brother's name. At first, I found this slightly irritating, but I came to expect it. I don't remember ever trying to correct her.

To me, Aunt Annice is the prime example of a stern Quaker woman, very strong in her beliefs. No one was going to change her or her beliefs. Everyone should be so lucky as to have a role model like her.

Phillip D. Carter is one of Annice Carter's grand-nephews. A member of Russiaville Friends Meeting, he is a retired vocational agriculture teacher in Clinton County, Indiana.

PEGGY ANN HOLLINGSWORTH

One of my earliest memories of the United Society of Friends Women (USFW) comes from the mid-1950s when as a child I became aware that someone I knew personally in my own church in Russiaville, Indiana, was working on the details of printing a national magazine called the *Friends' Missionary Advocate*. I remember visiting in the farm home on the edge of town where she resided with her widowed mother and seeing the papers spread around which would become the pictures and the words arriving at the post office every month. I wondered about the various intriguing mementoes displayed here and there from her travels and years of teaching in the faraway Holy Land. And to think that she was publishing material for others to read which highlighted what Quakers were doing around the globe!

That person was, of course, Annice Carter, who served as the *Advocate* editor from 1952 to 1957. As time passed, Annice continued her focus on work that benefited Christ's kingdom, at home and abroad. En route, she served USFWI in many ways—as secretary of Young Women's Work, 1943-1948 (during which time she was responsible for including young men and changing the name to Young People's Work); Christian Service secretary, 1968-1974; and president of Western Yearly Meeting USFW in the 1970s. After her missionary service, she served in ministry as the first director of the Western Yearly Meeting Friends Apartment Homes retirement facility in Plainfield, Indiana. During those years, Annice was a "fixture" in the sessions of WYM in the nearby meetinghouse, attending to various duties, usually in relation to either USFW or the Board on Christian Outreach. She was always a force to be reckoned with, no matter what the task at hand, and everyone knew it!

Annice maintained her membership with Friends at her birth monthly meeting, Russiaville, no matter where she wandered. She claimed that was the "anchor" of her faith. Given all of the ministries she had throughout her life, her gifts were never "recorded" formally. In her times, this formal recognition was mainly reserved for pastoral ministers, and her service did not conform to that model.

Other random memories include the children's picture book, *People of the Promise*, which Annice gave to me in the spring of 1951 upon her return from the USFW Conference in Marshalltown, Iowa. She inscribed it, "For being a good little girl and letting your mother go to Iowa." As a preschooler and only child (at the time), I had stayed in Indiana with Father while Mother and her parents traveled. This gift, from an adult other than family, impressed me!

The carved olive wood manger scene which Annice provided to our meeting holds many memories for everyone who grew up at Russiaville. It was AMAZING that we had our very own connection to Bethlehem and the Christmas story, thanks to someone we knew personally and who knew the places Jesus knew so well. When I was privileged to visit Ramallah in 2005, I was honored to be able to see the places where both Jesus and Annice had lived and worked, centuries apart.

When Annice's mother Milley died, Mina Emily (Miller) Seidler of New London gave a fitting memorial book to our church library, picturing (in black and white) many scenes of the Holy Land. What a legacy that Mina Emily had preserved her correspondence with Annice so that now we can gain more insight into the work and service of Friends.

Peggy Ann Hollingsworth is a lifelong member of Russiaville Friends Meeting who served as the historian for the United Society of Friends Women International from 1974 to 2010. A retired high school librarian, Peggy has traveled widely among Friends and has attended a variety of Quaker gatherings since her infancy.

PHILIP GULLEY

Annice was the first person to encourage me to consider the Quaker ministry. She would invite me to her apartment to eat and the food was always burnt. Black peas. But she would make me eat them anyway. And when I grew a beard, she didn't talk to me for a month, until I reminded her that Jesus probably had a beard. Gosh, I miss her.

Philip Gulley is a Friends minister, theologian, and author. His novels and essays reflect the humor and depth of small-town and rural Indiana.

SAYYID SYEED

In a presentation at Guilford College in Greensboro, North Carolina, where his daughter Najeeba was a student from 1991 to 1995, Sayyid Syeed shared how the Islamic Society of North America (ISNA) had been formed as an amalgamation of several American Islamic organizations and planned a national office in Plainfield, Indiana. There had been some opposition to ISNA's building their new center there, but Annice Carter was a significant supporter of the project, helping allay people's fears about a Muslim society coming to town. In 1983, the new building was completed, and ISNA has experienced a peaceful existence in Plainfield.

Dr. Sayyid M. Syeed is the national director for the Office for Interfaith and Community Alliances for the Islamic Society of North America

JEAN ZARU

My mother, who was a student at the Girls School, respected Annice very much. She often repeated what Annice said as if it were gospel truth!

Annice was straightforward and direct with her opinions. People knew she wouldn't change her opinion. That was an important quality in this culture, especially in the leadership position she was in at the School.

At the time Annice was here, we had a tradition of meeting in each other's homes for mid-week worship, and the host would prepare a meal. When my mother was hosting once, she made two cakes: one for the worshipers, and one for some family members who might drop by but feel uncomfortable joining the group. Annice criticized my mother for being too excessive with two cakes, not understanding the circumstances.

When Annice returned to Ramallah after the '67 occupation, she was excited about the birth of our third child, Walid. She brought him diapers as a gift—a real luxury, as ours were very inadequate. My mother, who took care of Walid often, was very grateful for them!

Annice and my husband, who was principal of the Boys School after the occupation, worked together well, but he was the go-between with the Israeli military authorities and the Schools. Annice was busy assisting the new principal at the Girls School, Peggy Paull, and was not involved as he was with the Israelis.

Jean Zaru is an internationally well-known Palestinian and former clerk of Ramallah Friends Meeting. She has served on boards of the World Council of Churches and Sabeel, the Palestinian Liberation Theology Center. She is the author of Occupied with Nonviolence, a collection of essays reflecting on her work for peace, justice, and equality.

SARABETH MARCINKO

As a child, I only had brief encounters with my Grandma Achsa Carter Chapman's younger sister, Annice, mainly when we visited our great-grandmother, her mother. Our family lived in Bloomingdale, about 80 miles from Russiaville. Annice returned to Ramallah in 1957 when I was only nine, and I knew her as the revered missionary aunt who sent us mother-of-pearl necklaces, olive wood-covered New Testaments, and wooden camels.

My grandmother died in 1958 while Annice was still in Ramallah. In 1960 my grandfather, Leland Chapman, remarried to a close friend of Annice's, Helen Woodard Chapman. Helen and Annice had both served on the United Society of Friends Women (USFW) Executive Committee and worked together in Western Yearly Meeting and Western YM USFW. Helen was one of the "gals" to whom Annice wrote, and Annice's colleague Lois Snyder was from Georgetown (Illinois) Friends Meeting, where Helen belonged before her marriage to Grandpa. Helen and Grandpa even took a trip to the Holy Land (and Egypt) in 1964 while Annice and Lois were there. A letter from Annice to her brother Oakley and his family, dated June 21, described their visit and shows some of Aunt Annice's bluntness and dry wit:

> We [Annice and Lois] went to see Helen and Leland last night at the Dead Sea Hotel. We could not see how we could take time so did not plan to go. I was busy with this and that and did not get any correcting [of exam papers] done until afternoon and was disturbed various times during the afternoon. I finished a set of papers about 5:50 and decided that I wanted to go to [the] Dead Sea. I yelled up the stairs to Lois and then had another teacher call a taxi, changed my dress, grabbed a purse and off we went. It was very hot down there and we found them resting but they soon came to the lounge to see us. My! They are tanned and we thought they looked quite tired. They were to get up at 3:00 this AM, have breakfast at 3:30 and leave at 4:00 for Petra. They were to have a hard day. When we advised Helen to ride in through the Siq [a dim, narrow gorge that is the main entrance to the ancient Nabataean city of Petra in southern Jordan]

she immediately asked if we expected her to ride a horse. I immediately suggested that she take a donkey. She said she had ridden a camel at the pyramids so I suppose a donkey was too much of a come-down. I thought that if she rode in and out that she might be able to do the two climbs. They are enjoying the trip but do feel it is strenuous. It will be much better now for a few days as they will be in Jerusalem where it is not so hot and will not start so early. Lois will go to the hotel for them tomorrow and bring them out [to the school] for Commencement. They go on with the tour and then come back to us via Cyprus and Beirut and reach here on June 30. They will stay for a week or more before going home.

Annice and Helen were the same age (62), and I think Annice thought she was in better physical shape than Helen. She made carbon copies of many of her letters and would personalize them by writing different things on the back. She sent the same letter as above to her friend Mina Emily and added these even blunter comments about the visit with my grandparents (I don't think Helen would have been amused):

It was fun to see Helen last night. She was hot and without girdle and about as untidy as I've seen her. She has gained more weight I think . . . Maybe she won't like our Arabic food [and will eat less] when she comes to stay here. They are seeing lots of interesting things but seem to have some trouble taking everything in. They have a small group and the other couple come from near Shelbyville [Indiana], he is an engineer and is Madeline's [my mother's] age [41], so they think they are having some trouble keeping up.

My more personal and more numerous memories of Aunt Annice are closely tied to the time after she left her work in Ramallah and was living at Friends Apartment Homes in Plainfield, first as the resident manager and then just as a resident. I would visit with her, often with "Grandmother" Helen and my mother, at her apartment, and see her at Western Yearly Meeting activities, Western YM USFW events, Carter family reunions, and even during her visits to our Chapman family gatherings. I remember her still being very blunt and forthright in saying what she thought.

Perhaps my best memory is being able to take Annice and Helen to what would be their last USFW Triennial Conference in Wilmington, Ohio, in 1986. In a June 16 letter (that was probably copied and sent to others as well) to her niece Miriam Cosand Ward (daughter of her sister Nora), Annice wrote about the plans to go:

Sarabeth has offered that necessary arm to me if I will go to Wilmington to the USFW Triennial and I plan to go. That will be the last of June and first of July. It will be nice to attend one more Triennial and see the women. It is a good place to see old friends and make new ones. I am glad Sarabeth wants to go. She said that Helen also planned to go with her. I do not know what will work out as Leland is not well and Helen cannot care for him so he is in a nursing home in Rockville. Leland seems a bit better and it is reported that he walked a little one day. It is a situation that bothers the Chapman family. It is sure nice when everybody can stay well. [Brother] Oakley is still in a nursing home in Kokomo. They report that the other day he had packed a new clock, his Bible, and other important things, inside his shirt in preparation for going home. So it seems that the people in nursing homes prefer to be at home.

My grandfather did come home, as they found a local woman who came and helped care for him during the day, and my mother's sister, Aunt Milley, came from southern Indiana to stay while we went to the Triennial. I drove the three of us and another woman from our Bloomingdale USFW group to Wilmington, where Annice, Helen, and I stayed in a dorm room for three. I remember them, especially Helen, sometimes dozing off during business sessions. Perhaps the highlight for Annice was a personal visit with Nancy Nye, also a past principal of the Ramallah Friends Girls School, and her husband Mubarak Awad, a noted Palestinian peace worker. I was thrilled to be included and hear the conversation. It was the last USFW Triennial for both of them, as Helen died in the fall of 1987 and Annice in the spring of 1988. I do feel as if I have followed in their footsteps. I have served on the USFWI Executive Committee since 2004, first as Secretary for Children and Youth Missionary Education and then as editor of *The Advocate* since 2010. I wonder what Aunt Annice would think of the way I lay out the magazine and send it to the printer now. No letters, just emails, from secretaries with their articles. And then using a computer program to put the information together. I'm glad to be doing only six issues a year instead of the eleven she did.

Although she never married or had children, I think her letters show that family was very important to her. By sharing the family news she received from different sources and family lines, she acted as "glue" to keep the growing Carter family connected. Even in what was probably her last letter (dated April 4, 1988), she was sharing new baby news and telling of holiday celebrations she had attended at homes of her nieces or nephews. She was a good example to all of them of a life given in service to Christ and to others.

Sarabeth Craycraft Marcinko is a retired English teacher and school library media specialist. She grew up in and is still an active member of Bloomingdale (Indiana) Friends Church. In addition to her work with USFW from the local to the international level and editing *The Advocate*, she is the Presiding Clerk of Western Yearly Meeting and volunteers with several community organizations. Her grandmother Achsa Chapman was one of Annice's two older sisters.

BETSY ALEXANDER

Annice was a young teenager in 1916 when my mother, Miriam, was born to Annice's eldest sister, Nora. Naturally, Annice was called on to help take care of the little girl, and this was the start of her lifelong role caring for, and caring about, her 21 nieces and nephews and their children and grandchildren. She had a prodigious capacity for knowing who was who in every generation. She kept track of babies born and could tell you their names—and there were a lot of them! Whenever she was home from abroad, Annice was sure to appear at the annual reunion of Charles and Milley Carter's descendants. I remember hearing it announced one year that there were over 500 members of this family group. I'm guessing that Annice knew who every one of them was.

My earliest awareness of Aunt Annice came from the closely typed blue tissue paper airletters sent from Ramallah, and later from Kenya, that circulated through the family. Since my mother had settled on the East Coast, my brother and I saw Annice only occasionally, when she happened to be home during our annual summer visits to our grandparents—and usually only during the family reunions. We didn't have to spend a lot of time around her, though, to understand that she was, in essence, in charge of all us younger ones. There was no misbehaving around Aunt Annice!

In the early 1980s Aunt Annice came to visit me and my young family in northern New England, where we were living in a Buddhist-oriented residential meditation community. Annice, traveling with her friend Mina Emily Seidler, revealed no surprise or discomfort with this arrangement, but settled in for the couple of days of their visit and immediately made herself useful, asking for any sewing or other chores that needed to be done. I was pregnant again, and hadn't had time to assemble a new dress I had cut out. Annice sat right down at my sewing machine and produced the finished dress within a couple of hours.

Although I seldom saw her in person, there was no doubt in my mind that Annice was a pillar of the family. I've been grateful, in the course of the research for this book, to learn more about her life, rounding out my understanding. I wish she were here beside me now. I think we would have been very good friends.

Betsy Alexander, who grew up in Moorestown Friends Meeting in New Jersey, settled in New Hampshire to raise her family. She is retired from a 40-year career in academic administration at Dartmouth College, and now divides her time between independent editing projects, nonprofit board service, and singing. Her grandmother Nora Cosand was Annice's sister.

CONCLUSION

Are there lessons to be learned from Annice Carter's life? She would probably give one of her familiar disapproving glances and a "tsk, tsk" at the notion. She did not think of her life as anything special. She was simply doing what she believed her Christian calling and Quaker commitments required. Perhaps that is all that we need to learn. But there is so much more.

Annice's life of service offers a view into Quaker work in the world and changing ideas about missions, education, cross-cultural interaction, religion, important political issues, and human relationships. Her direct involvement in so many of these areas offers important insights. Of perhaps even more importance is the opportunity to experience through her life the forces that shape a person into an important contributor to society.

Religiously, Annice was clearly imbued with the biblical Christianity of her upbringing. When a fellow missionary in Kenya expressed his opinion that they should avoid expressing themselves in "absolute truths," Annice responded that the teachings of Jesus were absolute truth. Yet nowhere in her letters is there any indication of a desire to "save souls" or convert the non-Christian students of the schools in Palestine and Kenya to Christianity. A product of revivalism, she expressed a disdain for the emotionalism of the revivals being held in Kenya, even refusing to attend a Billy Graham Crusade in Nairobi and expressing a disinterest in many of the local revivals led by students at the Friends Bible Institute. When new staff arrived at the Kaimosi Mission, she expressed concern that she had heard they were "anti-modern" in religion.

For Annice, religion was not worn on the sleeve but displayed in the actions of daily life, and those actions were closely related to the "holiness code" with which she was raised: "Sabbath-keeping," honesty, hard work, worship attendance, thrift, care for others, modesty, and abstemiousness. In one of her first letters to the FUM Central Office after returning to Ramallah in '67, she reported that she had never been more disheartened about the Girls and Boys School than she was then. But this discouragement wasn't about the very trying times under military occupation. Annice was upset that one of the new teachers was wearing a mini-skirt, the principal of the Boys School was serving alcohol in his home, and staff were doing laundry on Sundays.

The purpose of Friends education, she believed, was to teach Christianity by example.

Politically, Annice was aware of the circumstances around her, but her focus always remained on the well-being of the work Friends were doing. She knew of the unrest around her in Palestine during her service, but that was often described as "elsewhere" in the earlier years. When she returned after Israel's occupation of the West Bank, including Ramallah, she urged the School staff to cooperate with the "victors" rather than join in strikes and demonstrations against the occupation.

Yet after she wrote her return address in the first letter in '67 as "Ramallah, Israel," all subsequent letters had "Ramallah, via Israel." In a lengthy letter to friends, family, and the FUM Central Office, she laid out her understanding of the history of the 20th-century events leading to the creation of the modern state of Israel, the Palestinian refugee crisis, and the June War. Her understanding was not sympathetic to Israel. When she would be confronted back in the U.S. about her sympathy for the Palestinians and told that "God gave the land to the Jews," Annice would inevitably respond, "It came with conditions that have not been met!"

In Kenya, Annice was well aware of the growing cry for independence from British rule, but felt Kenyans weren't ready for independence. She was critical of American staff at the Mission in Kaimosi who arranged to visit with anti-colonial activist Jomo Kenyatta in 1961 ahead of the national elections.

Culturally, Annice appreciated what Palestine and Africa had to offer. She traveled widely to take in the historical, religious, and natural offerings. But even after her many years of service in Palestine, she knew only a minimal amount of Arabic, and little about Islam. When Jordan insisted, during her tenure as principal in the '60s, that Muslim students be taught Islam at the School, she adamantly opposed it, even arguing against it with the Ministry of Education in Amman. She wrote back to the FUM Office that the Friends Schools should close rather than teach Islam.

When Islam was finally taught to the Muslim students, she dropped in on one of the classes and found that the students' recitation of the Qur'an reminded her of the old Quaker "sing-song" in prayer and ministry that she remembered from her grandparents' generation. After confessing only a few years before that she didn't know what the Eid ul-Mi'raj holiday was about, when it occurred in the fall of '67, she described it as "like the Christian Ascension Day"—a somewhat accurate description of Prophet Mohammed's ascension into the heavens to commune with the prophets and Allah.

Back in Plainfield in retirement, she supported the building of a national Islamic Center on the outskirts of the city when others opposed it, which endeared her to the president of the National Muslim Students Association.

In Kenya, Annice expressed her sense not only that Kenyans weren't ready for independence but that Kenyan students were also not ready for "integration" with European students in their schools. Her belief was that they were too far behind educationally, but acknowledged that some Quakers in the U.S. would not support the Friends Africa Mission so long as classes weren't integrated.

At the same time, Annice worked hard to raise the funds for a Kenyan student to attend Berea College in Kentucky, and relished her time teaching rural Kenyan women the mysteries of sewing—including humorously describing instruction in the French seam and bra-making. She strongly supported inter-racial harmony.

Raised staunchly Republican (her brother Walter stated that one couldn't be a good Quaker and a good Democrat at the same time!) and adamantly opposed to debt, she worked many years for the county welfare office. But she was critical even of the hand-outs to Palestinian refugees by UNRWA, believing the practice made them too dependent on the aid.

Although some family members were very suspicious of the UN, she mourned Secretary-General Dag Hammarskjöld's death in a plane crash in Africa while she was in Kaimosi, and worried about its impact on the UN.

How do we understand the "different Annices"? Perhaps she stated it best in various letters, where she described herself as "born decades too soon" when admitting to being something of a prude. Yet even with her foibles, and knowing what we know about Annice's upbringing, her more progressive understandings about "missionary" endeavor and encountering "the other" were well ahead of what might be expected.

Leaving home at a young age, perhaps to escape the restrictions and limitations of her family and background, she was inevitably exposed to a wider world culturally, religiously, politically, and personally. Her world had expanded far beyond the narrow confines of her farming and religious community, yet she always bore their imprint.

She developed a self-confidence that enabled her to stand up to soldiers, government officials, and the challenges of her work. In the Quaker world she was not intimidated by the Friends she inevitably encountered while in her service: Douglas Steere, Ernestine and Clyde Milner, Ranjit Chetsingh, Landrum Bolling, D. Elton Trueblood, and the administrative leaders of FYM, FWCC, and the schools where she worked.

But Annice also developed a keen self-awareness, and knew her limitations: of diplomacy, of "being up with the times," and even of energy. And her letters display a keen sense of humor that contrasted with her stern, "puritanical" reputation. Seeing photos sent to her in Ramallah of brother Oakley and wife Delta, obviously "portly," she commented, "I'm afraid they aren't getting enough to eat." She enjoyed a good steak—and, especially in Palestine, a good ham.

A product of her times who developed in meaningful ways beyond those times, she is both a cautionary tale and an inspiration. Being both, she is even more worthy of understanding. But perhaps the best lesson her life offers is that which early Friend George Fox urged on Quakers: "Let your life preach."

Annice could preach; she had a strong set of beliefs and often let people know about them. In the end, though, it was her life that spoke far more.

APPENDICES

A. *Devotionals found in Annice's handwriting in her personal Bible, now in the possession of her 2x grand-niece Laurel Whisler. These are shared as written.*

1.

Mark 1:40–45

Jeanette Lockerbie, *Salt in My Kitchen*

> Jesus put forth his hand and touched him.

> Asked to define the difference between "pity" and "compassion," a woman answered, "Pity feels bad for someone in trouble or need; "compassion" goes a-visitin', taking along a pot o' soup or a fresh baked cake."

> Compassion leads to personal involvement in another's problems. Jesus is our supreme example. He "touched a leper."

> A mother heard 5-year old Janey as she said her bed-time prayers, and then Janey said, "Mommie, I would like a Jesus with a face. I talk to Him, but I can't see Him. I can't hear Him if He talks to me."

> Then Janey's mother recalled something her pastor had said when Janey was presented for public dedication, "You will be the only "Jesus," the only "God" this child will know for many a day."

> To be the image of Jesus to a child whom we are eager to interest in a loving Saviour: What a solemn responsibility!

> To stand in the place of Christ in the eyes of one who will form his opinion of Christ by the image that we professed Christians project.

> A responsibility? Yes! And a privilege.

2.
To Renew a Right Spirit
USFW Theme 1969–70
Renewal — Western Yearly Meeting — 1969
I Seek Renewal, Howard Thurman

> There is a spirit of mind without which it is impossible to discern truth. It is this spirit that recognizes or senses the false, the dishonest, the bogus thing. It is this attitude that determines the use to which facts are put. This spirit of mind is the factor upon which the integrity of performance rests.
>
> Constantly, I must see the renewal of the spirit of my mind, lest I become insensitive, dulled, unresponsive to the creative movement of the spirit of God with which life is instinct.
>
> Here, I seek the renewal of the spirit of my mind that I may be a living, vital instrument in His hands this day!
>
> We are Christian women—are we committed to Christ?
>
> We see visions of many tasks that need to be done. Tasks that Christ would have done. But it is the visions we obey that transform our lives.
>
> "O thou, who art love, keep alive in our hearts that adventurous spirit which makes men enjoy the risks of selflessness, until thy will is accomplished and we be found worthy of those courageous souls who in every age have ventured all in obedience to thy call. O lord, give us courage, Amen"

3.
Take Courage
Acts 4:32–37

> Barnabas—one who encourages

John 15:10–12 and 16–17

> See how these Christians love one another

The Rich young man came to Jesus—What can I do to inherit eternal life? Sell all and give to the poor. The young man lacked courage to surrender all to Christ.

The hope of the world is in minorities. Quality not quantity. The Kingdom of Heaven is like leaven hid in three measures of meal. The call Jesus gave was—"Follow me!"

Minority movement with nothing to lose but everything to gain with a man who pledged his very life. Are we as leaven or a part of the three measures of meal?

Christians have stopped infanticide. It took years for Christians to outlaw slavery. It is taking years to make men see that war is wrong.

All over the world kings oppress their subjects. The great exercise power over the weak. But it is not as among Christians! "For in the Kingdom of Heaven, who wishes to be great must serve, and he who strives to hold high place must be a servant...."

This takes courage—It goes against the common idea of today. Risks and penalties today—Equality of races!

Pacifist position against war!

What has made progress possible? Isolated men and women—not content with slow, upward climb, but have risen on wings as eagles, who have been before their time. That takes courage.

B. *In May 1935 Annice applied for a "long-term" assignment to Ramallah through the American Friends Board of Missions. She was required to answer a long list of questions to assure that she was fit to represent Friends in missionary work. Following are some of the questions and Annice's responses:*

1. What does Jesus Christ mean to you personally?

    Answer: "Jesus is our Redeemer. He is an example sent by God to teach us how to live lives of love and service."

3. If you have a preference as to country, what are its religions and their elements of strength and weakness?

Answer: "Mohammedanism—faith in God, devotion to belief and the same for Judaism and Christianity. Weaknesses—lack of love for fellow man. Lack of principles to guide in living. Lack of individualism."

4. As a Christian missionary, what would be your attitude toward other religions?

Answer: "I think one should be tolerant and understanding, not condemning but showing the good in Christianity."

5. What have you in your Christian experience to share with non-Christians?

Answer: "A love for and desire to be of service to our fellow men instilled through a love of God our common Father."

6. What is your attitude toward the statement that the supreme and controlling aim of foreign missions is to make Jesus Christ known to all men as their Saviour and Lord?

Answer: "And in addition teach Christian principles of living and instill in them a concern for others." [Annice's subsequent answers and example throughout her life indicate that her lack of a response to the original question was intentional.]

7. What is the best method of making Jesus Christ known?

Answer: "By living according to his example as nearly as possible and teaching his way of life."

8. What is your attitude toward the view that missionaries frankly and without apology should seek to persuade men to become disciples of Jesus?

Answer: "If Christianity needs apologies it is not worth passing on."

9. If you have a country preference, what are some of its cultural values you think the missionary should help conserve?

Answer: "Many of the handicrafts of the Arabs and some of their social customs."

10. What does the Bible mean to you?

Answer: "Thy word is a lamp unto my feet and a light unto my path."

11. What does the Church mean to you?

Answer: "An organization of Christian people for the purpose of furthering God's kingdom on earth and to spread His gospel."

12. What is your approach to other religions?

> *Answer:* "With friendliness and attempting to understand viewpoints."

18. What is our mission in a country where the prevailing religion is Roman Catholic or Greek Catholic?

> *Answer:* "To uphold Christian principles and standards of living and to make them appreciative of the deeper meanings."

20. What significant social contacts have you had with people of other races?

> *Answer:* "Worked with Arabs, Armenians, Greek, and Jews in Ramallah."

22. What is your opinion with regard to the relative superiority of particular races?

> *Answer:* "I do not feel that any race is superior."

23. What is your attitude toward the American Negro?

> *Answer:* "He has been mistreated by whites. He deserves to live in a Christian country."

24. If in a colonial country, what should be the attitude toward the Government?

> *Answer:* "Cooperate as much as possible. Not, however, 'Government right or wrong'."

25. What should be the attitude toward the nationalistic aspirations of the people?

> *Answer:* "The Arabs wish to have a free and independent country. Missions should teach loyalty and responsibility and understanding."

28. How does your loyalty to your own country affect your international ideals?

> *Answer:* "I trust I can see the faults in my own country's dealing enough to be internationally concerned."

31. What leads you to believe you can adapt to new and strange conditions in a foreign country?

> *Answer:* "I feel I did it with a certain degree of success during my previous stay in Ramallah."

C. *Annice contributed more than 170 articles to the United Society of Friends Women's publication,* Friends Missionary Advocate *(now* The Advocate*), during her 17 years of service on the Executive Committee. Following are samples and excerpts from columns and editorials that may give added insight into her spiritual principles and ideas of Christian Service.*

1.

Description of Visit to Shepherds Fields on Christmas Eve—
Young People's Department
Annice Carter, Secretary
From *Friends Missionary Advocate*, January 1944

As we come to another Christmas season when thousands of Christians the world over will be celebrating in some way the birth of the Prince of Peace, in this time of War and Destruction, it seems helpful to describe for our young people an inspirational out-of-doors service of worship held each year at Bethlehem to commemorate the birth of Jesus. In Palestine only about one-sixth of the population are Christian [the percentage is much smaller now] and of those a very small percentage are Protestant. Most of the Christmas ceremonies are High Mass Services, therefore, the simple outdoor service sponsored by the Y.M.C.A. of Jerusalem and held on Shepherds Fields near Bethlehem is very much appreciated by the Protestant group. At sunset time a shepherd's feast is served at the site of an old cave to those who wish to taste the historic fare of the shepherd folk. Each guest is given a piece of whole wheat bread, baked in a flat loaf on small heated stones in an oven, and a piece of meat, highly seasoned lamb roasted on hot coals in an oven hollowed out in the ground. With bread in one hand and meat in the other, the guests stand around in small groups discussing the simple, but delicious, food and the age-old methods of preparation. Oranges are then passed to serve as a quencher of thirst and also to cool the heat of the highly seasoned meat.

After the supper is finished the people walk a short distance over to a knoll called "Boaz Heights" where preparation has been made for a large bonfire. For most of us it is impossible to imagine the effect made by a lovely bonfire in a country where fuel is so scarce. Standing there around the fire, looking across to the lights of Bethlehem nestled near the top of one of the mountain crests, the group listens to the reading of the Christmas Story, interspersed with the singing of appropriate Christmas Carols. Leaders of the Protestant Churches, either visitors or residents of Palestine, take part in this service by giving short talks or prayers. Each year on Christmas Eve, my friends and yours, both Americans and Arabs, gather there on Boaz Heights, in the shelter of Bethlehem to listen again to the oft told story of the birth of the Prince of Peace. This service is never broadcast, as is the High Mass at midnight, because the indescribable inspiration comes from being present in Shepherds Field, looking toward Bethlehem, the scene of the event that has had such influence upon the world throughout the intervening years. May we, as young people, on this, another anniversary, amidst war, hatred, and misunderstandings, pledge ourselves to greater effort in bringing about peace, love, and understanding, which is the kingdom of God on earth.

"And the peace of God, which passeth all understanding, shall keep your hearts and minds through Christ Jesus." — Philippians 4:7

2.

Stewardship
Young People's Department
Annice Carter, Secretary
From *Friends Missionary Advocate*, September 1944

The Christian church throughout the past has stressed stewardship mainly in terms of money. Now we have reached a time when our work is not held in check by lack of money alone, but also, from the lack of workers. Therefore, we must lay emphasis upon the importance of giving a proportionate share of our time, as well as our money and talent, unto the Lord.

"It is required of Stewards, nothing more, nothing less, that a man be found faithful to the whole task...."

It has been said that stewardship is "religion in practice." Each Christian steward may be thought of as a foreman in the great business enterprise of the kingdom; responsible to God, the Owner, for conducting the affairs of his own life. God has placed the Christian in charge. God has made him accountable for that part of His plan. He may work out in his life the purpose of God or he may make wreck and ruin of it. He may effect the greatest possible efficiency in his plant, eliminating waste and weakness, or he may have little concern for the profits of the Owner.

When we practice stewardship we find that it must necessarily be "partnership with Christ." It is impossible to be a good steward unless we become partners with him. In a true partnership the partners pool their resources. Both give their resources of personality, energy, time, money, influence, and effort. Such a partnership is a joyous relationship, but a costly one. Too often youth is unwilling to pool his resources, but attempts to share the resources of God without full surrender of his own. Luke 14:33 tells us this cannot work out. "In all thy ways acknowledge Him"— that is stewardship—"and he will direct thy paths."

Stewardship of our time! Often it is much easier to tithe our money than it is our time. We desire to use our time as we choose. The best solution for that problem is to dedicate ourselves so completely to God that we will CHOOSE to spend our time for Him.

If you should start a "ten per cent club" in your community, a club of people giving ten per cent of their time and effort to making the world better, would you be nominated for membership? If we give one-tenth of our money only, the gift is bare, we must clothe it with Love and Service which demands our time.

How different would your community be if each church member gave one-tenth of his time toward building a happier and better world? Would your community be a better place in which to live if that were done?

Stewardship demands Development. Jesus said, "I am come that they might have life and that they might have it more abundantly." He wants us to be at our best—physically, mentally, socially, spiritually. To be at our best we must do our best. Every steward is asked to give an account of his stewardship. If you had talents which you did not develop or use, can you be called a "good and faithful steward"? You have twenty-four hours--the same as everybody else--to be used for rest, for making a living, and for building a better world. If you are asked to account for your time and you have used it all for yourself--resting and making a living--you have not lived the abundant life Jesus made possible.

Any occupation to which God calls a young person—homemaker, clerk, stenographer, teacher, farmer, missionary—is a sacred calling and a stewardship. "Whatsoever ye do, do all to the glory of God."

"...Be the best of whatever you are."

Stewardship in the Life of Youth by Robert Donald Williamson and Helen Kingsbury Wallace was used as a basis for these remarks on stewardship.

3.

Indians Are People, Too—Study Book by Ruth Muskrat Bronson
Young People's Department
Annice Carter, Secretary
From *Friends Missionary Advocate*, January 1945

As I have been reading our study book and various other books about the Indians, I have been amazed at the extent of the injustice committed against the Indian by white men. Of course, we all know, in a more or less vague way, that the white man has taken the Indian land by fair means and foul, that the Indian was exploited in trade, and that he was forced to migrate long distances and confine himself within definite boundaries on reservations. This was a hardship for the Indian after being accustomed to roaming over great areas to hunt.

But we have consoled ourselves with the thought of our benevolent government caring for the Indians by granting land holdings, providing schools and hospitals, issuing allotments of food and clothing where necessary, and by paying an adequate monthly allowance according to treaty agreements.

However, these consolations are either completely untrue or have been inadequate for the needs of the Indian people. Instead, we find many Indian communities facing want and destitution. [Several statistics on the number of Indians, where they live, etc. are cited.] ...

An Indian described his feeling for America thus: "There are many distinctions I could claim for my people, but I am satisfied with one of them—the fact that America began with us. We are the possessors of a wonderful and beautiful legacy. We are of this continent as are the mountains and the hills; the buffalo and the beavers."

"Indian Americans only want and need the same things that people of other races do. They want the right to work. They want equality of opportunity. They want political and social freedom. They have never asked to be relieved of responsibility, nor are they asking for that now. They want the chance to carry their own burdens and to make their own mistakes. If equal opportunity is denied them, they do not suffer alone.

"Indian welfare and happiness, Indian needs and perils, are interdependent with your life and mine—for *Indians Are People, Too.*"

I have just picked up from my table the book "Will a Man Rob God?" With our shortcomings in relation to the Indian American from fresh in my mind, the thought came to me that we rob God in many ways. If we had fulfilled our obligations in sharing our opportunities as Christians, we might have encouraged the development of Christian workers from all races who could have helped greatly in carrying on God's work. By our selfishness and superiority toward the Indian, have we robbed God of great Indian leaders?

How democratic is the Christian church concerning Negroes, Indians, Migrant workers and Sharecroppers in our country?

4.
Brotherhood
Young People's Department
Annice Carter, Secretary
From *Friends Missionary Advocate*, February 1945

"Have we not all one father? Hath not one God created us? Why do we deal treacherously every man against his brother, by profaning the covenant of our father?" Malachi 2:10

"If we are to build a New World of lasting peace we must build it upon Christian fundamentals. There is no other way. *Only a world based on human brotherhood can endure.*"

If we believe the above quotation and count it fundamentally true, then what is wrong with our living? Can we have human brotherhood and continue to discriminate against Negroes, Japanese, members of other social groups, etc., whom we repeatedly exclude from our cliques?

This subject of Human Brotherhood has been much on my mind during recent years. In Mark 12:30, 31 we find the first and second commandments. "And the second is like, namely this, Thou shalt love thy neighbor as thyself. There is none other commandment greater than these." And we as Christians say the Golden Text of the Bible is Matthew 7:12, that it is one of the most important principles of Christianity. If that be true, how can we endorse some of our laws, permit certain business monopolies and cartels, and back our country in our present conflict?

In Thessalonians 4:9 we are told, "But as touching brotherly love ye need not that I write unto you: for ye yourselves are taught of God to love one another." In I John 4:1 we read, "And this commandment have we from him, That he who loveth God love his brother also." It would seem, that with teachings like these, we, as Christians, should be showing to our fellowmen a love that could come only from our love for God. . . .

It seems that Christians today have confused the values on life's commodities. We have placed the highest values on material things rather than spiritual things. So long as Christians continue to do this the world will remain in chaos.

I heard a sermon last night on the subject "The Greatest Sin" and I was not surprised when it was given the name of "selfishness." It was stated that every other sin has selfishness at its base. It is that same selfishness that keeps us from building the principle of true brotherhood among all peoples. . . .

If we are truly Christian, believing all peoples are sons of God, can we take active part in anything connected with the present war?

Can we be comfortable and happy knowing that thousands of children are homeless, cold and starving in war torn countries?

"Therefore all things whatsoever ye would that men should do to you, do ye even so to them: for this is the law and the prophets." Matthew 7:12

5.
The Enlarging Circle—Friends Missions and Peace
Adult Missionary Education
Annice Carter, Secretary
From *Friends Missionary Advocate*, November 1951

In thinking of our Peace lesson for this month let us consider the Peace work of our Friends missions. Of course, our missionaries are not essentially peace workers, but one cannot be a Christian Evangel without promoting peace. In talking with a friend the other day I asked, "What can one say about peace on our mission fields in this day and age?" She quickly replied, "Just say there is very little of it." But is there *very little* peace in our mission areas when we compare with other areas!

Our missionaries have tried to so live and work that people would know them as brothers. If we look into the history of our various mission fields we find that in times of conflict and danger, that people have trusted our missionaries and have depended upon them for care and protection. Friends have a reputation for being just and fair, giving help to those in need regardless of the cause for need. Friends have tried to have a sympathetic understanding of man's problems and to aid individuals to help themselves attain a degree of independence rather than accept dependence by continuing to depend upon others for their needs.

We have heard various missionaries tell of personal experiences where people from the area, either Friends or non-Friends, have come for counsel in settling a dispute, determining an equitable price or making a fair division. I have known men, both Muslim and Christian, in the area around Ramallah, when dispute arose over boundaries or division of crops, agree to walk together the many miles to Ramallah to seek Nameh Shahla's counsel in reaching an agreement. Nameh Shahla, our Friends Bible Woman, has so learned the Christian way of life that her own people have confidence in her and are willing to accept her counsel because they know her to be understanding of their problems and fair in her decisions. Many of our missionaries on all of our fields have gained the same respect and admiration. They have been peacemakers in the area of personal living.

During the past three and one-half years, when Arab Christian refugees have depended upon Christian Arab villages in Moslem territory to give refuge and care, the thousands of refugees in Ramallah have looked to Friends for physical help and courage and spiritual strength. The need has been so great that Friends were unable to meet them alone. The emergency needs of fellow Christians, regardless of denomination, has challenged the Christian Missions to cooperate to meet those needs. Church World Service joined forces to meet the emergency. One of our representatives, A. Willard Jones, was chosen to head up the work and supervise the distribution of material help. This choice was made partly because of his location in Ramallah, but more because he was a Christian that all groups could trust to be fair and equitable in the distribution of material help.

We have had so few Americans in our Ramallah mission to do those cooperative tasks that naturally fall to missionaries thus causing the few to be overloaded. We are glad that additional people are now on that field because tensions are so great and there is ample opportunity for peace making. . . . It is important that they be trained evangel's of peace in order to make a greater contribution toward real Christian living.

Of course we realize that all of opportunities for peacemaking are not in far away places. The representatives we send to mission areas cannot do our own peace work. Friends are faced with various areas of great need. We, the members of the United Society, have obligation to meet the financial needs of our society, those needs presented by our Christian Service Secretary and many others. Our Peace Secretary gives suggestions of various things we can and should do to promote peace in our own land. We support various Mission Boards which need increasing amounts of money to carry on the work started in our various fields. Friends are interested in a new central office building in Richmond so that the various departments can carry on their work more effectively and efficiently. Then there are local needs which must be met in order that each local meeting may grow. If we are to do satisfactory work in all of these areas we must have a high degree of cooperation among all our members. Understanding, a sense of fairness, and a zeal to reach a common goal are of upmost importance. There is no room for petty jealousies, local bickering and those things which hinder cooperation. There is a need for real Christian living in each of our local meetings and local communities. Those young workers we have sent to mission fields to represent us in Christian evangelism have the right to expect great things from our lives here at home.

Let us strive for a unity of spirit among our members so that we can live Christ-like lives and advance His work. Read Romans 12:9-18 for inspiration and guidance.

6.
Jig-saw Puzzle Pieces
Gleanings
Annice Carter, Editor
From *Friends Missionary Advocate*, February 1953

I like to work jig-saw puzzles. The one I am now putting together will be the picture of "Jesus Knocking at the Door" when completed. I have the border all together; that makes a boundary for the completed picture. I have also done the face of Christ. Those parts were easy because of their distinguishing shapes and colors. As I worked, it came to me that our lives are quite similar to a jig-saw puzzle. Those of us who profess to be Christian, quickly build around our lives a certain boundary for Christian living. Maybe we sometimes misplace a piece or two of that boundary which lets us get out-of-bounds sometimes. We also put in the parts of a picture of a Christian life that have distinctive colors or markings. But do we get our picture all completed in those areas where it is most difficult, the places where we have monotonous, solid color, such as sky or grass or trees?

Our special emphasis for this month is HUMAN RIGHTS. Certainly our attitude toward our fellowmen, and our consideration for them, is of importance in Christian living. In his letter to the Galatians, Paul listed the fruit of the spirit: "But the fruit of the spirit is love, joy, peace, long-suffering, gentleness, goodness, faith, meekness, temperance; against such there is no law." Galatians 5:22, 23 if we measure our attitudes toward others in the light of Paul's teaching, where do we stand in our treatment of those of other races, colors, and classes?

Many of the articles in the section OUTREACH in this issue mention our relationships with people of other races or colors. One mentions that "*some* of the churches" have accepted Negroes; another states that: "A segregated church is a betrayal of the Christ whom we serve." Certainly the *church* would not distinguish against any of God's children! Have we lost the pieces that fit into our jig-saw puzzle at that spot? Let us hunt them up and fit them in. . . .

7.
Do Something About It!
Gleanings
Annice Carter, Editor
From *Friends Missionary Advocate*, April 1953

A short time ago I was asked to speak at a Farmers Institute about Agricultural problems in Palestine. After pointing out some of the problems of agriculture, I branched out into other types of problems. For a closing thought I tried to give a vivid picture of the contrast between economic conditions of the average farm family in Indiana and that of the average farm family in the Jerusalem area. A few days later I received a letter from the chairman of the Farmers Institute committee enclosing a check with a request that I use the money in some way that would give most benefit to refugees in and around Ramallah. The letter contained the statement, "No use to get worked up about a condition if you are not willing to do something about it, is there?"

That bit of philosophy has forced my conscious attention many times since I received that letter. I have remembered times when I have been deeply disturbed by certain unfair practices that caused heartache or suffering; by destitute circumstances resulting from ignorance or neglect; by injustices that left discouragement and resentment in their wake. And what have I done! It is so easy to tell myself that one person can do nothing.

This month we are studying Africa. We have tried to present varied information about the continent in general, and some of the problems of various parts. We know that Africa has now reached a place in her development where she will make rapid progress in the next few decades.

Let us consider our mission work in Africa. Ground work has been prayerfully laid. Much progress has been made. Our mission work has grown rapidly with new doors of service opening each year. We have now reached a critical decision—To go on in service and growth requires additional financial support. To try to remain at the present level means slipping backward and loss of some of our educational opportunities. What should we do? What will we do?

Africa will continue to make progress. She has built up a great momentum that will carry her along. It is important that her growth have guidance and direction if she is to be a Christian power. If we, as Friends, could continue to grow in influence and leadership in Africa, we could play our part in giving Christian guidance. If we stop growing at this time, we fail our African Friends.

"No use to get worked up about a condition if you are not willing to do something about it, is there?"

Will you join me in doing something about it financially?

8.
Are You a Missionary?
Gleanings
Annice Carter, Editor
From *Friends Missionary Advocate*, June 1953

Charles Lampman, Administrative Secretary, Elect, of the American Friends Board of Missions, made the statement, in an address to the United Society of Friends Women of Western Yearly meeting, on April 28, that every Christian is in reality a missionary.

I began thinking of the popular idea of a "missionary," how we have come to think of missionaries as those people who go to distant places to carry the Gospel message and win men to Christ. I have been unable to find any Scripture reference that states that one is sent to *distant* places. Our most commonly used missionary quotation is Mark 16:15, "And he said unto them, go ye into all the world, and preach the gospel to the whole creation." I can't feel that Jesus made any distinction between the disciple who went far away and the one who stayed at home to preach. The command was to preach the gospel. Neither did he give instruction on how to preach, but the follower of Jesus is to preach in whatever way his talents lead.

As I searched for scripture about missionaries, I found the following:
"Follow me and I will make you fishers of men." — Matt. 4:19.
"And he came to the first and said, Son go work in my vineyard." — Matt. 21:28.
"And he said, Lord, what wilt thou have me to do?" — Acts 9:6.
"Serve the lord with gladness: come before his presence with singing." — Psalms 100:2

"For brethren, ye have been called unto liberty; only use not liberty for an occasion to the flesh, but by love serve one another." — Gal. 5:13.

"And when he had called the people unto him with his disciples also, he said unto them, whosoever will come after me, let him deny himself, and take up his cross and follow me. For whosoever will save his life shall lose it; but whosoever shall lose his life for my sake and the gospel's, the same shall save it." — Mark 8:34, 35.

"Now then we are ambassadors for Christ, as though God did beseech you by us: we pray you in Christ's stead, be ye reconciled to God." — II Cor. 5:20.

"Go ye therefore and teach all nations . . . to observe all things whatsoever I have commanded you: and lo, I am with you alway . . . — Matt. 28: 19, 20.

ARE YOU A DISCIPLE OF CHRIST? Then—*You are a missionary!*

9.
Spiritual Hitch-hikers
Gleanings
Annice Carter, Editor
From *Friends Missionary Advocate*, June 1954

One Sunday morning, several months ago, I had the radio turned on, without consciously listening to the sermon, when I caught the expression, "They remind me of spiritual hitch-hikers." Although I listened intently there was nothing further explained about spiritual hitch-hikers. I have frequently found myself mentally likening people to "spiritual hitch-hikers" and thinking about what it involved.

We think of a hitch-hiker as one who "hitches" a ride to avoid paying the expenses of a journey. The person "picking up the rider" has the car with gas in the tank and is "going that way anyhow." "It costs no more for one more to ride along." The man with the car has the responsibility of caring for the car, checking the air in tires, checking oil, and dozens of other similar items in addition to washing and cleaning the car. The hitch-hiker rides along.

Then what is a spiritual hitch-hiker? I presume there are many kinds. We all want churches in our communities and want those churches to make a good appearance and have high standing. Various service jobs are necessary if our churches measure up. Somebody must teach Sunday school classes, work with children and youth, mow the lawn, fire the furnace, order Sunday school supplies, sing in the choir, pay the preacher, take part in community work, meet on committees, keep accounts, set goals, see visions, and use head and hands for God's work.

There are always those who just "attend" the services, listen to the choir, take a small contribution to the church supper and a well filled plate "home to Henry who wasn't able to come out," "can't teach a Sunday school class," don't have time for committee work" and have "so little to spare" for paying the preacher. Anybody who expects to get more from the church than he gives to the church must come in the category of spiritual hitch-hikers.

Then there are those who consider it "respectable" to be seen in church circles on certain occasions. They do not have time to attend services regularly so that they become interested and take part in activities, but do go sometimes when there is nothing else to do or they are tired of other activities. Sometimes we get very close to "wrongdoing" and decide that we should appear in church circles to regain status. This must be one way of hitch-hiking spiritually. When one does not have God's spirit within, and wants to basking in the warmth of His spirit in others.

The greatest outreach of the church is through Christian Service. If our churches are to be strong enough to show God's love through service to all mankind, we must all join hands and "serve." We cannot let God's love shine afar if our feeble light is absorbed by spiritual hitch-hikers in our local meeting.

10.
Conference Hymn
From *Friends Missionary Advocate*, June 1954
Written by Annice Carter and Dorothy Stratton
Tune: Jesus Calls Us O'er the Tumult

Jesus calls us, upward, onward—
Let us work while it is day;
Tell the Gospel of the Savior

Leaving none to miss the way.

Jesus calls us, upward, onward—
Let us ever heed His call;
Life is only worth the effort
When we give to Him, our all.

Upward, onward, reaching ever
To be more like Him alway.
It matters not how small our talent,
But that we use it every day.

Jesus calls us to press onward
Greater heights to gain each day,
And to ever grow more like Him
As we walk His Upward Way.

11.
Visit to Indian Centers in Oklahoma
Gleanings
Annice Carter, Editor
From *Friends Missionary Advocate*, November 1955

For a number of years I have had a growing desire to visit our mission centers in Oklahoma. Last summer, I was able to get Margaret White and Helen Woodard to consent to go with me to make brief visits to each center. We were unfortunate in that our vacation time coincided with vacation plans of some of the missionaries, so that we did not get to visit with them personally. Because of our limited time, we were able to be in regular services of only two of the meetings. However, we had a most interesting trip, and we were able to get a better idea of the work being done in these centers. Now we wonder why we waited so long to make the visit, and why many more of us do not make plans to visit our nearer fields.

The history of Friends, and their activities in behalf of the Indian American, is outstanding among religious groups. The disturbing element is that we have not done enough in the cause of justice for the Indian. Driving across the eastern part of central Oklahoma in July, when it was extremely hot and dry, we could not feel proud of the fact that various tribes of Indians, formerly from eastern central states, had been forced to move from their original homes into this less desirable hunting and farming area. They became the "displaced persons" of America. Many times during that drive, Mildred White would exclaim, "Weren't we generous to give Oklahoma to the Indians!" Now, I would not give the impression that there are no desirable areas in Oklahoma, but I am saying that the areas given over for the Indian Reservations were not the best land for farming.

We are glad that Friends aided the Indians and showed ability to understand the injustices committed against them. As Friends appeared before government groups to plead for various Indian causes, the government was made aware of the success of Friends in dealing with Indians and asked Quaker leaders to act as agents in Indian territories. All of this led to the organization of the Associated Executive Committee of Friends on Indian Affairs in 1869, and it continues to administer the mission centers in Oklahoma. The American Friends Mission Board cooperates in this work by making a financial contribution toward the expense of the mission work.

The Associated Executive Committee began their work by opening schools and churches for Indians. The work grew and preparative meetings were started in many places. Gradually, the schools became government schools for Indian children, and many of the meetings have become independent members of Kansas Yearly Meeting. At the present time there are four missionary centers supervised by the Associated Executive Committee. They are: The Kickapoo center near McLoud, the Osage center at Hominy, the meeting at Wyandotte and Council House located in areas where several tribes are represented. (Wyandotte, Seneca, Quapaw, Modoc, and Ottawa)

At the present time, Armin and Mary Jane Saeger are supervising the work at McLoud. They were on vacation when we visited in July. We were interested to see the buildings and grounds and visit some of the members of the meeting. The Young Friends Work Campers moved in on Monday following our visit and the Kickapoo Meeting House has had a "face lifting" and other repairs. A brief visit was made at Hominy because we knew that Phillip and Susie Frazier were attending a conference of Indian workers at Estes Park, Colorado. More time was spent in the Wyandotte area where we attended regular services at Council House and Wyandotte. Mildred White spoke to these groups about Friends work in Ramallah[.] Ermin and Ruth Perisho of Wyandotte, and Lawrence and Lucille Pickard of Council House, have encouraged their members to keep informed about Friends Missionary endeavors and the meetings have made contributions to projects for Ramallah.

Friends can be proud of the work in Oklahoma. Many times it has been difficult and progress seemed slow, but a definite Christian witness is being made.

We are reminded of a quotation attributed to Henry Ford:

"Coming together is a beginning, Keeping together is progress, Working together is success."

Indian and white members of Friends Meetings are working together on the great Christian task of Kingdom Building. Indeed, it is a success!

12.
"Give Me" Attitude
Gleanings
Annice Carter, Editor
From *Friends Missionary Advocate*, January 1956

As material is being gathered for this issue of the ADVOCATE, we are in that confusing period just following Thanksgiving and entering into the Christmas season. I call it confusing because we can hardly give ourselves over to the idea of total thanksgiving while we are hearing announcements of Santa arriving on Friday; of the Christmas decorations being put up by street departments; and of the Christmas lights being turned on for the week-end following Thanksgiving.

Now, as you read this, both of these holidays have passed. Have we, as Christians, allowed ourselves to be pushed along with the hustle and bustle of a commercial holiday so that we have missed the blessing of taking time for thanksgiving, praise, giving, and sharing?

On the radio the other day a man was giving some statistics about the number of people who remember to give thanks for benefits received. He mentioned the one leper, out of the ten who were healed, who ran to Jesus and expressed joy at being healed. He cited the number of people who call upon God for help in guidance in the face of great trouble or emergency, and then forget about Him until another emergency comes. He then reported that over a certain number of years—I do not remember how many—when hundreds of thousands of letters have been sent to Santa Claus before Christmas by children throughout our nation, only one letter has been found in the mail following Christmas addressed to Santa Claus and expressing thanks for the gifts received. Then he asked the question, "What is the matter that we forget to say THANK YOU?" It seems so hard to remember to thank Him for those things that come to us daily and which we tend to take for granted.

Are we, Friends Women, allowing ourselves and our children to accept a "give me" attitude? Are we expecting that things shall always come our way? If that is so, it easily explains why we have difficulty raising the total budget for our mission programs. Why we find so many places to help in the extension of Christian Service, but our help is limited by the total amount that we give to be shared with others. The sharing of our material possessions is one evidence of our thankfulness for material gifts from God.

Since this is the month that we seek to know the truth about Cuba, we are all reading much about Cuba. If we have read the report from Cuba and the latest Board report, we are certainly encouraged. Cuba is the one Mission area that is making progress and growth without the aid of an American missionary. There has been no regular missionary in Cuba since the Hiltys left in 1948. Yet Juan Sierra, in his general report, has said, "I have been able to observe that our work in Cuba is growing and great possibilities of growth are opening before us."

Several months ago the Methodist Church had $1,048 that could be used for a chapel in Las Clabazas. The Methodists had no organized work there but the Quakers were holding Sunday school classes and a worship service for a small group of people. The Methodists offered to give the Quakers the available sum if they would build a chapel and develop a permanent church. The chapel was built and the church is growing. This is certainly an outstanding example of Christian cooperation. It speaks well for the Christian witness of our Cuban friends.

The November issue of QUAKER ACTION repeated the request of Cuban Friends for a Christian leader from the United States to give counsel and supervision in Friends work in Cuba. If Five Years Meeting Friends felt concern and appreciation for the work of the Friends in Cuba, we would certainly make it financially possible for them to have encouragement by sending a worker to them.

Knowledge develops Interest

Interest develops Concern

Concern brings Action

13.

The Task of Women

Gleanings

Annice Carter, Editor

From *Friends Missionary Advocate*, March 1956

One of the outstanding things about Jesus was the attitude he showed toward women in his day. The general belief was that they were definitely inferior to men and not capable of religious understanding. Jesus was as concerned about women as he was about men and touched and healed them whenever need arose. Jesus counted many women among his friends and followers, and he treated them with kindness and affection. We should be deeply thankful for this revolutionary attitude.

At the time of George Fox, little progress had been made in the status of women and it was quite generally believed that women had no souls. George Fox believed the Scripture "there is neither male nor female: for ye are all one in Christ Jesus." (Gal. 3:28). Many of his first followers were women and he accepted them as preachers. This attitude toward women was one of the causes of the unpopularity of the Quakers at that time. Many of the Quakers suffering persecution in the early days were women. The spiritual strength and courage of those early Quaker women was revolutionary and helped to bring about the acceptance of women as Christian leaders today.

The Task of Women

Throughout our Friends history, women have shown a pioneering spirit and have persisted in their efforts until the desired task was done. Much of the success of our missionary efforts during the years must be credited to the work and devotion of Quaker women.

Quaker women today must not lose that same pioneering spirit. There are many areas where pioneering in greater Christian living could be carried on if we proceeded with the same conviction, singleness of purpose, sincerity and perseverance of the early Quaker women. Evident success of our teaching of Christianity is found in the tide of revolution in the world today. The Christian ideas of love, freedom, self-respect, goodness, peace, joy, etc., have given people an idea of what life should be—and they don't find that kind of life, so they struggle to attain their material delusion of that better life. Better health, education, diet, medicine, cleanliness are good and worthy desires. But we have failed to provide the improved economic conditions which make those things possible.

Does it really disturb you to know that 3/4 of the people of the world have insufficient food?

Does the practice of segregation really bother you—or do you secretly think it is a comfortable practice?

Do you feel that as a Christian you have any responsibility to those hundreds of thousands of people forced from their homes because of fear, war or prejudice?

Pioneering with conviction and perseverance in Christian ways of changing the economic and social evils of this world would be revolutionary.

14.
Service Is Prayer in Action
Christian Service
Annice Carter, Secretary
From *Friends Missionary Advocate*, May 1969

"Habit is a cable. We weave a thread of it every day, and at last we cannot break it." — Horace Mann

What kind of habits are we weaving? Or, what kind of habits have we woven?

As youngsters we heard about eating habits, study habits, health habits, habits of fair play, and scores of others. When we think of happenings today and all the violent acts being committed in the world, we wonder where we have failed in forming good habits and in teaching good habits to our youth.

One area of our habits is especially in mind at the present time. How concerned are we about our own habits in demanding comfort, convenience, and possession, even to the exclusion of thinking of others? We are very thankful for the many people who are concerned about the health and needs of many underprivileged people. But it seems that not enough of us are enough concerned.

We hear and read about the thousands of innocent civilians who are deprived of homes and suffered serious injuries in the war all over the world. We read of the enforced destitution of countless thousands of refugees. . . . We see pictures of inadequate living conditions for helpless children. We see pictures of seriously injured civilians in war areas. We think of the destruction of public and personal property. Why do such things happen in a supposedly civilized world?

I am reminded of the theme used for World Day of Prayer, 1969—"Growing Together in Christ." There were some very pertinent statements in the prayer suggestions:

"We pray for wisdom in the use of knowledge and power given to us in the modern age. . . . Our health can be improved; our children can go to school; our national life can be developed through better roads, better housing conditions, and so many other blessings of the modern age. . . .

"Not all of our children enjoy these gifts. Millions of children have no school education, millions of people suffer from malnutrition, millions of sick have not the care that could be provided by modern medical knowledge and equipment.

"Let us affirm our desire to grow up—

"by increasing harmony among all peoples;

"in caring for the weak, the unprotected, the sick, the hungry;

"in love and respect for all persons.

"As we go out together, let us greet each other and share the joys and burdens of our hearts." — Excerpts from *World Day of Prayer Devotional Guide*.

The projects of USFW give opportunities to our 'neighbors.'

"Service to our fellowmen is prayer in action."

15.
From the Inside Out
Christian Service
Annice Carter, Secretary
From *Friends Missionary Advocate,* June 1970

"No person was ever honored for what he received. Honor is the reward for what he gave." — Sunshine Magazine

The story is told of the little boy, his eyes wide with wonder, who asked, "Why is it that when I open a marigold it dies, but if God does it, it becomes very beautiful?"

As the mother was fumbling and searching for an answer the little boy exclaimed, "I know, it's because God always works from the inside."

If Divine Love is in a man's heart his love too will open outward, showing beauty, like a flower, capable of producing fruit. God always works from within, with marigolds and with men.

In this present time we are hearing much about the need of love in this war-torn world. Did you ever wonder why we are so short of love, when we profess to be Christian, and so much of Jesus' teaching stressed love? John 13:34, 35 says, "A new commandment I give unto you: love one another. If you have love for one another, then all will know that you are my disciples." Have we failed to understand God's love and to have love in our hearts? We cannot show love if we do not have it in our hearts. It must come from the inside. And so, from lack of enough love we have children hungry, without education, sick in body and in soul. Thousands of adults and children are without homes and belongings because of the ravages of war in many areas of our world. We need some way to make our world better and help to meet the needs of our neighbors.

Francis Bacon, a British philosopher, said, "It is not what men eat but what they digest that makes them strong; not what we gain but what we save that makes us rich; not what we read, but what we remember that makes us learn; and not what we preach, but what we practice that makes us Christians."

It is the practice of the teachings of Jesus, in loving our fellowmen, that we really perform Christian Service. It is difficult to list all the things that come in Christian Service. The example that Jesus set was to meet the needs of the individual. It may be a friendly smile, an encouraging word, or a helping hand. If we have real love within it will respond to whatever they need.

"Your task—to build a better world,"
God said. I answered, "How?
The world is such a large place,
So complicated now;

And I so small and useless am,
There's nothing I can do."
But God in all his wisdom said,
"Just build a better you." — Dorothy Jones

16.
... *No Hands But Ours*
Christian Service
Annice Carter, Secretary
From *Friends Missionary Advocate*, November 1972

> *In every place where there are people, there are tasks to be accomplished by the use of dedicated Christian hands.*
> *I have two hands which I must use*
> *If I would like my Master be,*
> *To heal the sick and help the blind,*
> *To show my Savior to all mankind.*
> *I have two hands, O use them Lord,*
> *To help the blind man to see*
> *The hope of life eternal*
> *A better world yet to be.*
> *How can we fail if our hands are dedicated to God's use?*
> *— Amy Bolding, from* Please Give a Devotion

The above lines were copied from a devotional book several months ago because they especially appealed to me. I have frequently read the lines and feel that they are appropriate for all USFW women as we proceed into this year's study program on Faith and Justice. The use made of our hands is very indicative of our faith and dedication to the Master's work and of our interpretation of the idea of justice and right. Most often it is through our hands that we accomplish the things that represent our faith and give indication of our ideas of justice.

We recall the verse that says "Christ has no hands but our hands" to do His work. Hands are important and should be dedicated to His service.

It seems that I have many tasks that result in dirty hands. I do not like to wear gloves, so gardening and weed-pulling leave my hands dirty and stained. I have often made the remark that I'm so thankful that God gave us a covering that is washable. How inconvenient it would be if we could not wash our hands and make them clean. This remark startles some people because they have never thought about God's thoughtfulness for our good and convenience.

Let us be sure to keep our hands busy and useful in those things that help us deepen and cleanse our spiritual lives and show forth love and justice to our fellowmen and faith in our Lord and His work. As we keep our hands clean and sterile for the sake of physical health, we should also be sure that they do tasks that help both us and our neighbors attain spiritual health. This is Christian Service.

17.
"Compassion Goes a Visitin"
Christian Service
Annice Carter, Secretary
From *Friends Missionary Advocate*, July-August 1973

"But when he saw the multitude, he was moved with compassion on them, because they fainted and were scattered abroad, as sheep having no shepherd." — Matthew 9:36

Do you have real compassion? An article in Guideposts a few months ago suggested that compassion is the most healing of all human emotions, and it could transform the world if we would just let it. That is an idea about which we should think seriously.

The King James translation of the Bible uses the word "compassion" in many places while Good News uses the word pity. We think of these words as meaning about the same thing, but I like the story told of a discussion group where the leader asked for someone to explain the difference between "pity" and "compassion." An elderly, kindly, helpful woman gave this answer, "Pity feels bad for someone in trouble or need. Compassion goes a visitin' taking along a pot of soup or a fresh-baked cake."

Many of us Christian women feel pity for needy and distressed people of the world. We wish somebody would do something to help them overcome their deplorable conditions and to rise to a more healthful and comfortable life. But we tend to expect someone else to do the necessary something. If each of us would do our bit in sharing a "pot of soup or fresh-baked cake" we could certainly help in a few places at least. . . .

BIBLIOGRAPHY

Annice Carter Microfilm. Friends Collection and College Archives, Earlham College, MR-157.

Blueprints: Suggested Program Outlines. United Society of Friends Women. Collection of USFWI Program Editor.

Carter, Annice. Letters. Collection of Sarabeth Marcinko.

Carter, Annice. Letters. Collection of Betsy Alexander.

Carter, Max L. *Palestine and Israel: A Personal Encounter*. Newberg, Oregon: Barclay Press, 2020.

The Crescent Student Newspaper. Library Archives & Special Collections, George Fox University.

Dowty, Alan. *Israel/Palestine*. Malden, Massachusetts: Polity Press, 2008.

Edwards-Konic, Patricia. *Enduring Hope: The Impact of the Ramallah Friends Schools*. Richmond, Indiana: Friends United Press, 2008.

Friends Missionary Advocate. United Society of Friends Women.

Friends Missionary Advocate. United Society of Friends Women, 1938–1978. Collection of Sarabeth Marcinko.

Friends United Meeting Wider Ministries Records. Microfilm, Friends Collection and College Archives, Earlham College, Microfilm 157, No. 5.

Hutchison, Donn. *A Stone House with Windows*. Privately published by Donn Hutchison, 2021.

J. Floyd Moore Letters. Quaker Archives, Guilford College.

Jones, Christina. *Friends in Palestine*. Richmond, Indiana: Friends United Press, 1981.

Jones, Christina. *The Untempered Wind.* London: Longman Group, Ltd., 1975.

Jordan, Lois Harned. *Ramallah Teacher: The Life of Mildred White, Quaker Missionary.* Self-published, 1995.

Laura Davis Letters. Quaker Archives, Guilford College.

Leas, Judy. "Missionary Says Problems Outweighed by Rewards." *Kokomo Tribune.* June 26, 1963.

Letters and Papers of Levi Pennington. Library Archives & Special Collections, George Fox University.

McDowell, Nancy Parker. *Notes from Ramallah, 1939.* Richmond, Indiana: Friends United Press, 2003.

Painter, Levinus. *The Hill of Vision: The Story of the Quaker Movement in East Africa, 1902–1965.* Kaimosi, Kenya: East Africa Yearly Meeting of Friends, 1966.

Pendle Hill Records. Friends Historical Library, Swarthmore College.

Ruth Outland Letters. Quaker Archives, Guilford College.

Shaheen, Naseeb. *A Pictorial History of Ramallah.* Beirut: Arab Institute for Research and Publishing, 1992.

Shavit, Ari. *My Promised Land: The Triumph and Tragedy of Israel.* New York: Spiegel & Grau, 2013.

Ward, Miriam Cosand. *A Family History: A Long Time In the Making.* Self published, 2009.

Printed in the USA
CPSIA information can be obtained
at www.ICGtesting.com
JSHW082046041023
49550JS00001B/6

9 781956 149227